Frommer's

Yellowstone & Grand Teton National Parks

8th Edition

by Eric Peterson

WILEY

John Wiley & Sons, Inc.

Published by:
JOHN WILEY & SONS, INC.
111 River St.
Hoboken, NJ 07030-5774

ISBN 978-1-118-07473-2 (paper); ISBN 978-1-118-22256-0 (ebk);
ISBN 978-1-118-26141-5 (ebk); ISBN 978-1-118-23646-8 (ebk)

Editor: Andrea Kahn
Production Editor: Heather Wilcox
Cartographer: Guy Ruggiero
Photo Editor: Richard Fox

Production by Wiley Indianapolis Composition Services

Front cover photo: Lower Yellowstone Falls, Yellowstone National Park, Wyoming. © Rollie Rodriguez / Alamy Images

For information on our other products and services or to obtain technical support, please contact our Customer Care Department within the U.S. at 877/762-2974, outside the U.S. at 317/572-3993 or fax 317/572-4002.

Wiley also publishes its books in a variety of electronic formats. Some content that appears in print may not be available in electronic formats.

Manufactured in the United States of America

5   4   3   2   1

CONTENTS

List of Maps vii

1 INTRODUCING YELLOWSTONE & GRAND TETON NATIONAL PARKS 1

A Look at Yellowstone 2

A Look at Grand Teton 4

Making the Most of Your Trip 5

The Best of Yellowstone & Grand Teton 5

2 YELLOWSTONE & GRAND TETON NATIONAL PARKS IN DEPTH 13

Yellowstone & Grand Teton National Parks Today 13

Looking Back: Yellowstone & Grand Teton History 17

ROAD OPENINGS & CLOSINGS 19

DATELINE 20

When to Go 21

GENERAL RESOURCES FOR GREEN TRAVEL 25

Responsible Travel 25

Tours 26

3 EXPLORING YELLOWSTONE NATIONAL PARK 29

Essentials 30

The Highlights 35

If You Have Only 1 or 2 Days 37

Yellowstone: The Extended Tour 38

Self-Guided Driving Tours 65

Organized Tours 65

Ranger Programs 66

4 HIKES & OTHER OUTDOOR PURSUITS IN YELLOWSTONE NATIONAL PARK 68

Day Hikes 68

Exploring the Backcountry 77

WILDERNESS U: GUIDED BACKPACKING WITH THE YELLOWSTONE ASSOCIATION INSTITUTE 79

Other Activities 83

Winter Sports & Activities 87

WINTER ROAD CONDITIONS 88

5 EXPLORING GRAND TETON NATIONAL PARK 91

Essentials 91

The Highlights 95

If You Have Only 1 Day 97

Touring Grand Teton 99

Organized Tours & Ranger Programs 107

6 HIKES & OTHER OUTDOOR PURSUITS IN GRAND TETON NATIONAL PARK 109

Day Hikes 109

ESPECIALLY FOR KIDS 114

Exploring the Backcountry 117

Other Activities 120

Winter Sports & Activities 124

7 WHERE TO STAY & EAT IN THE PARKS 126

Where to Stay in Yellowstone National Park 127
WHAT YOU'LL REALLY PAY 128
Where to Camp in Yellowstone 133
Where to Camp near Yellowstone 135
Where to Eat in Yellowstone 136
Where to Stay in Grand Teton National Park 141
Where to Camp in Grand Teton 145
Where to Camp near Grand Teton 147
Where to Eat In Grand Teton 147

8 GATEWAYS TO YELLOWSTONE & GRAND TETON NATIONAL PARKS 151

West Yellowstone, Montana 151
Gardiner, Montana 157
Cooke City, Montana 160
Jackson, Wyoming 161
Cody, Wyoming 184

9 A YELLOWSTONE & GRAND TETON NATURE GUIDE 195

The Parks Today 196
Landscape & Geology 198
Plant Life in the Parks 202
Wildlife in the Parks 208
BLACK BEAR OR GRIZZLY BEAR? 210
WOLF OR COYOTE? 212
Birds in the Parks 215

10 PLANNING YOUR TRIP TO YELLOWSTONE & GRAND TETON NATIONAL PARKS 219

Getting There & Getting Around 219

Tips on Accommodations 223

Special Permits 223

Planning a Backcountry Trip 225

Recommended Reading 226

FAST FACTS: YELLOWSTONE & GRAND TETON NATIONAL PARKS 227

Index 240

Accommodations Index 249

Restaurant Index 249

LIST OF MAPS

The Yellowstone/Grand Teton
   Area   3

Yellowstone National Park   32

Mammoth Hot Springs   45

Canyon Village   51

Yellowstone Lake: Fishing Bridge
   to Bridge Bay   55

Yellowstone Lake: West Thumb
   to Grant Village   57

Old Faithful Area   61

Mammoth Area Trails   71

Grand Canyon Area Trails   73

Old Faithful Area Trails   77

Grand Teton National Park   92

Jackson Lake: Colter Bay
   Area   100

Jackson Lake: Signal Mountain
   Area   101

Jenny Lake Area & Trails   105

Jackson   169

ABOUT THE AUTHOR

A Denver-based freelance writer, **Eric Peterson** has contributed to numerous Frommer's guides covering the American West and has written *Frommer's Montana & Wyoming, Frommer's Utah,* and *Ramble: A Field Guide to the U.S.A.* (www.speckpress.com). Peterson also writes about travel and other topics for such publications as *ColoradoBiz, Delta Sky,* and the *New York Daily News*. In his free time, he's an avid camper and hiker, a lifelong Broncos fan, and a part-time rock star (at least in the eyes of his niece Olivia and nephews Mitch and Sam).

HOW TO CONTACT US

In researching this book, we discovered many wonderful places—hotels, restaurants, shops, and more. We're sure you'll find others. Please tell us about them, so we can share the information with your fellow travelers in upcoming editions. If you were disappointed with a recommendation, we'd love to know that, too. Please write to:

Frommer's Yellowstone & Grand Teton National Parks, 8th Edition
John Wiley & Sons, Inc. • 111 River St. • Hoboken, NJ 07030-5774

AN ADDITIONAL NOTE

Travel information can change quickly and unexpectedly, and we strongly advise you to confirm important details locally before traveling, including information on visas, health and safety, traffic and transport, accommodations, shopping, and eating out. We also encourage you to stay alert while traveling and to remain aware of your surroundings. Avoid civil disturbances, and keep a close eye on cameras, purses, wallets, and other valuables.

While we have endeavored to ensure that the information contained within this guide is accurate and up-to-date at the time of publication, we make no representations or warranties with respect to the accuracy or completeness of the contents of this work and specifically disclaim all warranties, including without limitation warranties of fitness for a particular purpose. We accept no responsibility or liability for any inaccuracy or errors or omissions, or for any inconvenience, loss, damage, costs, or expenses of any nature whatsoever incurred or suffered by anyone as a result of any advice or information contained in this guide.

The inclusion of a company, organization, or website in this guide as a service provider and/or potential source of further information does not mean that we endorse them or the information they provide. Be aware that information provided through some websites may be unreliable and can change without notice. Neither the publisher nor author shall be liable for any damages arising herefrom.

FROMMER'S STAR RATINGS, ICONS & ABBREVIATIONS

Every hotel, restaurant, and attraction listing in this guide has been ranked for quality, value, service, amenities, and special features using a **star-rating system.** In country, state, and regional guides, we also rate towns and regions to help you narrow down your choices and budget your time accordingly. Hotels and restaurants are rated on a scale of zero (recommended) to three stars (exceptional). Attractions, shopping, nightlife, towns, and regions are rated according to the following scale: zero stars (recommended), one star (highly recommended), two stars (very highly recommended), and three stars (must-see).

In addition to the star-rating system, we also use **seven feature icons** that point you to the great deals, in-the-know advice, and unique experiences that separate travelers from tourists. Throughout the book, look for:

special finds—those places only insiders know about

fun facts—details that make travelers more informed and their trips more fun

kids—best bets for kids and advice for the whole family

special moments—those experiences that memories are made of

overrated—places or experiences not worth your time or money

insider tips—great ways to save time and money

great values—where to get the best deals

The following abbreviations are used for credit cards:

AE	American Express	DISC Discover	V Visa
DC	Diners Club	MC MasterCard	

TRAVEL RESOURCES AT FROMMERS.COM

Frommer's travel resources don't end with this guide. Frommer's website, **www.frommers.com**, has travel information on more than 4,000 destinations. We update features regularly, giving you access to the most current trip-planning information and the best airfare, lodging, and car-rental bargains. You can also listen to podcasts, connect with other Frommers.com members through our active-reader forums, share your travel photos, read blogs from guidebook editors and fellow travelers, and much more.

INTRODUCING YELLOWSTONE & GRAND TETON NATIONAL PARKS

Long before you reach the entrance to Grand Teton National Park, your sights will be set on the towering spires of the Teton Range— those signature hornlike peaks made famous through countless photographs. From afar, Yellowstone is not as dramatic because much of the parkland comprises heavily forested mountains, burn areas, and arid, high-country plateaus. However, at a closer glance, Yellowstone's natural marvels are startling: hundreds of geysers, scores of inspiring waterfalls, and a gorge—carved by time and water—that rivals the Grand Canyon in Arizona. Both parks command the imagination and envelop the senses from the moment of arrival.

Creatures great and small thrive in Yellowstone and Grand Teton national parks. In the wilderness of Yellowstone's southern corners, grizzlies feed on cutthroat trout during their annual spawning run to the Yellowstone headwaters. In the soft blue depths of Octopus Pond, microbes of enormous scientific value are incubated and born; in the mountain ridges, gray wolves make their dens and mountain lions hunt bighorn sheep. Bald eagles and ospreys soar above the banks of the Snake River in Grand Teton, moose munch their way through meadows of native foliage, and elk and bison traverse the park on the same roads as visitors.

When John Colter, a scout for Lewis and Clark, first wandered this way in 1807, his descriptions of geysers, sulfurous hot pools, and towering waterfalls drew jeers and suspicion.

No one doubts him now, but these are still places you should see for yourself. The explorers of today come in minivans and on bicycles, aboard snowmobiles and Telemark skis, and in such numbers that the parks sometimes seem to groan under the strain.

In the early days of Yellowstone, first established as a national park in 1872, visitors were so sparse that their unregulated activities—catching 100 trout at a time, washing their underwear in the hot pools—left few noticeable scars. Now, with millions of people visiting the parks annually, the strain on everything from sewer systems to fish populations is immense. Yet while there are problems, these parks still radiate extraordinary beauty: the jagged Tetons, the glassy surface of Jenny Lake, the awe-inspiring Grand Canyon of the Yellowstone, the towering Obsidian Cliff, the steamy meandering of the Firehole River. Wildlife that most Americans see only in zoos wanders freely here, from the grizzly to the river otter, the trumpeter swan to the rufous hummingbird. Aspen groves, fields of lupine, the howls of coyotes and wolves— all these testify to the resilience and vitality of the Greater Yellowstone Ecosystem, which extends outside the borders of the park to Grand Teton and beyond.

This is not just a paradise for sightseers—it's a scientific preserve as well. The hot pools support a population of unique microbes known as thermophiles and extremophiles; studies of the elk herds and grizzly have yielded crucial information on habitat needs and animal behavior; and the rocks of Yellowstone are like the earth turned inside out, a treasure-trove for geologists.

Most visitors will see or know little of this. They park in a pullout on U.S. Hwy. 191/89/26 to pose in front of Grand Teton, or they sit on crowded benches to watch Old Faithful erupt. If you have more time, however, I suggest that you take little sections of these parks—just the Jenny Lake area in Grand Teton, say, or Yellowstone's northeast corner, the Lamar Valley—and savor them in all their fine detail, rather than embark on a madcap race to see every highlight.

Definitely get out of your car and away from the road, into the wild heart of the backcountry. These parks embody our country's beginnings: as a landscape of wilderness, of challenging and rugged extremes, and of extraordinary bounty and beauty. Use this guide as a set of footprints to help you find your way there.

A LOOK AT YELLOWSTONE

What other national park boasts an assortment of some 10,000 thermal features, including more than 300 geysers? Even when the rest of North America was still largely wilderness, Yellowstone was

The Yellowstone/Grand Teton Area

unique. Its collection of geothermal features is richer and more concentrated than any other in the world, with mud pots, geysers, and hot springs of all colors and sizes. Plus, there's a waterfall that's twice as tall as Niagara Falls and a canyon deep and colorful enough to be called "grand." Sure, other parks have great hiking trails and beautiful geologic formations—Grand Teton is pretty spectacular in its own right, as is Yosemite—but a sizable percentage of the geology in Yellowstone is reachable by visitors in average physical shape.

Ever focus your camera lens on an untamed grizzly bear, or a bald eagle? What about a wolf? Thousands of visitors have these experiences here every year. Protected from development by the national park and surrounding forests, Yellowstone is home to herds of bison and elk, packs of grizzly bears, flocks of trumpeter swans, schools of Yellowstone cutthroat trout, and subtler beauties such as wildflowers and hummingbirds.

And the park doesn't appeal solely to the visual senses; you'll smell it, too. By one biologist's estimate, Yellowstone has more than 1,100 species of native plants. When wildflowers cover the meadows in spring, their fragrances are overpowering. The mud pots and fumaroles have their own set of odors, although many are less pleasing than that of a wild lily.

Your ears will be filled with the sounds of geysers noisily spewing forth thousands of gallons of boiling water into the blue Wyoming sky. After sunset, coyotes break the silence of the night with their high-pitched yips.

You can spend weeks hiking Yellowstone's backcountry or fishing its streams, but the park's road system makes it easy to see its highlights from behind the windshield in a day or two. Roads lead past most of the key attractions and are filled with wildlife commuting from one grazing area to another, and many visitors to Yellowstone tour the park without hitting the trail. While there's no doubt that driving through the park yields vivid memories, those who don't leave their cars are shortchanging themselves.

Yellowstone closes in fall and then reopens as a winter destination come December, when cross-country skiing, snowshoeing, and snowmobiling are the prime pursuits. There's no cozier place than the lobby of the Old Faithful Snow Lodge, the only hotel in the park's interior that stays open during Yellowstone's long, cold, and snowy winter season. I highly recommend a visit when snow covers the ground. You often have the park to yourself, but dress appropriately (read: no less than three layers) and be ready to incur an extra expense in the form of snowcoach fare.

A LOOK AT GRAND TETON

Because the magnificent mountains of the Teton Range stand so tall, with the park curling snugly at their feet, visitors sometimes fail to appreciate the surrounding environment of rivers and high valley floor. The Tetons are a young range of old pre-Cambrian granite, abrupt and sharp-edged as they knife up from the Snake River valley along a 40-mile-long fault sculpted over the course of the last 13 million years, with help from geological upheaval, retreating glaciers, and erosion. The result is a masterpiece. Many visitors regard Grand Teton National Park—with its shimmering lakes, thickly carpeted forests, and towering peaks blanketed with snow throughout most of the year—as more dramatically and immediately scenic than its northern neighbor.

It's also a very accessible park. You can appreciate its breathtaking beauty on a quick drive-by, or take to the trails and waterways in search of backcountry lakes and waterfalls. The Tetons themselves are especially popular with mountain climbers, who scale them year-round.

There's a dynamic relationship between the Tetons and the valley below. The elk and other wildlife migrate from the high country down to the open grasslands to forage during the winter, when the snowmelt curls across the valley floor and west through a gap in the mountains, and the moraines and alluvial soils that slough off the mountains provide rich soil for the pastures below.

Visitors can float and fish the lively Snake River; visit the National Elk Refuge in the winter; hike in nearby ranges, such as the Wind River or the Gros Ventre; or play cowboy at one of the dude and guest ranches that dot the valley of Jackson Hole. Skiers and snowboarders have a blast on the slopes here, as well as at Grand Targhee on the other side of Teton Pass. And the chic town of Jackson, with its antler-arched square and its busy shops, offers everything from fly-fishing shops to classy art galleries to noisy two-step cowboy bars.

MAKING THE MOST OF YOUR TRIP

Yellowstone and Grand Teton are more than photo ops and zoos where the animals roam free. They aren't museums, either, where magnificent scenery is merely on display. Both parks, unlike a picture hanging lifelessly on the wall of a museum, are works in progress; they are living, breathing wilderness areas. Plant your feet in a comfortable pair of walking or hiking shoes, find a trail head, and set off into the woods with a sack lunch and a big bottle of water. Better yet, if you can afford the time, plan an excursion around Shoshone Lake or to the south end of Yellowstone Lake by boat to areas few visitors ever see. There are isolated spots in Grand Teton, too—even on the far shore of popular Jenny Lake— where, with a little hiking, you'll be rewarded by a pristine, forested glade with nothing to distract you but wild moose and an awe-inspiring mountaintop.

If you're more adventurous, take a white-water trip down Snake River Canyon, or let a guide take you up to Grand Teton's summit. In Yellowstone, sleep under the stars and listen to the wolves howl at Slough Creek Campground; or backpack for a week on the Thorofare Trail.

You'll never plumb the absolute depths of these parks—no one ever will. You could spend your whole life trying, though, and have a wonderful and illuminating time doing it.

THE best OF YELLOWSTONE & GRAND TETON

A "best of" list could never do justice to Yellowstone and Grand Teton national parks. These are just starting points, the best of the excellent accommodations and food the parks offer, as well as the unique sightseeing and recreational opportunities. Some involve backcountry expeditions; others can be enjoyed from behind a windshield. In the wildly diverse environments of these two parks, you can be as adventurous as you want—climbing peaks and spending the night deep in the wilderness, or simply enjoying the more civilized side of the parks at grand lodges and enchanting roadside overlooks.

The Best Views

You'll never get it all in a camera lens, but you'll undoubtedly try. Don't let your camera dominate your vacation; take a few shots, or shoot a short video, and then put the camera down so you can enjoy this place with all your senses.

o **Grand Canyon of the Yellowstone River** (Yellowstone): The waterfalls are spectacular, especially the 308-foot Lower Falls (twice the height of Niagara), and the steeply cut canyon walls are colorful and alive with life. Do the short, easy hikes to **Inspiration Point** or **Artist Point,** and you'll see the falls that stimulated Thomas Moran's creativity. If you're in reasonable shape, hike down the short but steep trail to the **Brink of the Upper Falls** or the 328-step steel staircase known as **Uncle Tom's Trail.** (Be careful of slick spots during the spring and following afternoon thundershowers.) See "Yellowstone: The Extended Tour," in chapter 3.

o **Lamar Valley** (Yellowstone): Bring your telephoto lens or binoculars to the northeast corner of the park, one of the best places to spot wildlife: **bison** and **elk** grazing along the Lamar River, **gray wolves** at Slough Creek and among the big ungulates, and the occasional **grizzly bear** on its never-ending quest for food. See "Yellowstone: The Extended Tour," in chapter 3.

o **Yellowstone Lake** (Yellowstone): Sunrise over Yellowstone Lake is stunningly beautiful (especially if there's fog on the lake), whether you watch it from the sunroom at the Lake Yellowstone Hotel or, better, from a campsite along the southern wilderness shore. For an equally spectacular sunset view, drive 10 miles east of the hotel to **Lake Butte Overlook.** See "Yellowstone: The Extended Tour," in chapter 3.

o **Cathedral Group** (Grand Teton): The three central mountains of the Teton Range rarely disappoint, except on the unusual occasion when weather gets in the way—clouds tend to accent rather than obscure their majesty. You'll need a wide-angle lens to get it all in from the valley floor (there are pullouts along the highway between Moran Junction and Jackson), but if you want a panoramic shot, drive east on U.S. Hwy. 26/287 toward Togwotee Pass. See "The Highlights," in chapter 5.

o **Elk** (Grand Teton): While visiting the Jackson/Grand Teton area during the winter, take the opportunity to ride a horse-drawn sleigh out among thousands of elk on the **National Elk Refuge.** You'll get close-up shots of some of the biggest antler racks in the world, and you'll often see coyotes and sometimes wolves. See "Jackson, Wyoming," in chapter 8.

The Best Thermal Displays

Yellowstone has more thermal features—geysers, mud pots, and steam vents—than the rest of the world combined. When you're angling for a good shot of a colorful pool or a belching mud pot, obey the signs; otherwise, you could find yourself (quite literally) on shaky ground.

o **Old Faithful Geyser** (Yellowstone): While not quite as faithful as it used to be the intervals average about 90 minutes but sometimes stretch as long as 120 minutes—it's still the most predictable geyser on the planet, blasting water 130 feet into the air more than 20 times a day. How could you skip this one? See "Yellowstone: The Extended Tour," in chapter 3.

o **West Thumb** (Yellowstone): This lakeside thermal area is a must-stop for its collection of gemlike hot pools and steaming vents, as well as Fishing Cone, where early visitors poached their catch—until they realized the scalding water had natural traces of arsenic. See "If You Have Only 1 or 2 Days," in chapter 3.

o **The Mammoth Hot Springs Terraces** (Yellowstone): Here you can observe Mother Nature going about the business of mixing and matching heat, water, limestone, and rock fractures to sculpt the landscape. This is one of the most colorful areas in the park; its tapestries of orange, pink, yellow, green, and brown, formed by masses of bacteria and algae, seem to change colors before your eyes. The mineral-rich hot waters that flow to the surface here do so at an unusually constant rate, roughly 750,000 gallons per day. See "Yellowstone: The Extended Tour," in chapter 3.

The Best Day Hikes

Just a few hundred yards off the road, things get a lot less crowded, and you'll have the views and the wildlife (almost) to yourself. The hikes described below are rated "easy," but you'll find more challenging options later in the book.

o **The Mount Washburn Trail** (Yellowstone): Starting at Dunraven Pass, south of Tower Junction, this walk to the fire lookout atop Mount Washburn offers unsurpassed views of both parks plus the opportunity to see mountain wildlife, such as bighorn sheep. See p. 72.

o **The Lonestar Geyser Trail** (Yellowstone): This gentle, 5-mile hike along the Firehole River presents several places to stop and take in the scenery, fish, and—at the endpoint—view this active, medium-size geyser of its name. It is also one of a few bicycle-friendly trails in Yellowstone, and in the winter, it's a popular cross-country skiing trail. See p. 76.

o **Cascade Canyon Trail** (Grand Teton): This hike can be short and sweet or long and rewarding. Make a day of it, or simply take a boat ride across the lake and hike to Hidden Falls, and you'll barely break a sweat. See p. 115.

o **Signal Mountain Summit Trail** (Grand Teton): The hike to the summit of Signal Mountain is rewarding for its solitude. While everyone else drives to the top, you'll have the same views and be closer to the greenery and wildlife. See p. 112.

The Best Backcountry Trails

o **Thorofare Trail** (Yellowstone): This hike will take you deeper into road-free wilderness than you can get anywhere else in the lower 48 states. You'll spend a few nights on the trail, climbing up to the park's southern border and beyond to the Yellowstone River's headwaters, a high valley bursting with wildlife. Early in the summer, if the snow has melted, the cutthroat spawning run attracts grizzlies and fishers. It's not for the faint of heart. See "Exploring the Backcountry," in chapter 4.

o **Shoshone Lake Loop** (Yellowstone): Circumnavigate the largest backcountry lake in the lower 48 and get a remote geyser basin all to yourself on this time-tested route near Old Faithful Geyser Basin. Some of the lakeside campsites are accessible only by canoes, which must be carried into the wilderness. See "Exploring the Backcountry," in chapter 4.

o **Cascade Canyon Loop** (Grand Teton): Perhaps the most popular trail in Grand Teton, the Cascade Canyon Loop, which starts on the west side of Jenny Lake, winds northwest 9.5 miles on the Cascade Canyon Trail to Lake Solitude and the Paintbrush Divide, then returns past Holly Lake on the 10-mile Paintbrush Canyon Trail. The payoff comes at the highest point, Paintbrush Divide, which offers marvelous views of Jackson Hole Valley and Leigh Lake. See "Exploring the Backcountry," in chapter 6.

The Best Campgrounds

If you stay in developed campgrounds in the parks, the outdoor life is pretty civilized. You'll have running water and, in most cases, flush toilets, plus there are opportunities to meet fellow campers.

- **Jenny Lake Campground** (Grand Teton): Situated near the edge of the lake from which it takes its name, Jenny Lake Campground is nestled among spruce and fir trees just a short walk away from the South Jenny Lake area. It's the perfect place to spend the night if you plan to hike around the lake to Hidden Falls or up Cascade Canyon the next day. The only caveat is that there are no site reservations, and sites are usually taken early in the morning. See p. 146.

- **Norris Campground** (Yellowstone): Although it's away from the hotels and services, the Norris Campground has excellent sites with a little elbowroom, as well as flush toilets and the Solfatara Trailhead. A small hillside amphitheater hosts campfire talks by rangers. The campground is across the street from the Norris Geyser Basin and within walking distance of the Museum of the National Park Ranger. See p. 135.

- **Slough Creek Campground** (Yellowstone): Another favorite is out in the Lamar Valley. The campground is smaller, but it's away from the crowds and close to fishing and wolf viewing. Because of the wildlife-watching and fishing opportunities here, it fills quite early. See p. 134.

The Best Places to Eat in the Parks

Don't expect five-star dining (with one exception) or a great variety, but the food is well prepared, the servers are cheerful, and the dining rooms are mostly big, convivial gathering places. All of these options are detailed in chapter 7.

- **The Old Faithful Inn** (Yellowstone; ✆ **866/439-7375**): Can't beat the ambience: a grand stone-and-timber lodge perched next to the most famous geyser in the world. The food's pretty good, too, but it can be inconsistent. See p. 140.

- **The Lake Yellowstone Hotel** (Yellowstone; ✆ **866/439-7375**): Enjoy a bit of Victorian-era hospitality (without dressing up) and the finest food in the Wyoming wilderness. There are views of the lake from the dining room and the comfortable lounge area off the lobby. See p. 139.

- **Jenny Lake Lodge Dining Room** (Grand Teton; ✆ **307/733-4647**): This is my favorite restaurant in any national park. Dine where presidents have dined on five-course meals featuring such delicacies as smoked sturgeon ravioli. Breakfast and dinner are included in the price of a room; nonguests can call for reservations, but it's not cheap. See p. 150.

- **Signal Mountain Lodge** (Grand Teton; ✆ **307/543-2831**): Both **Trapper Grill** and **Deadman's Bar** make good casual meals (including mountainous plates of nachos in the latter), with a view of Jackson Lake and the Tetons or, in the lounge, a view of one of the few televisions in the park. **Peaks** offers finer dining, with a largely organic menu. See p. 143.

The Best Places to Sleep in the Parks

My Yellowstone favorites are both grand hotels, but they're very different. In Grand Teton, I lean toward the rustic options. All of these are detailed in chapter 7.

○ **The Lake Yellowstone Hotel** (Yellowstone; ✆ 866/439-7375): Try this recipe for a great vacation: a quiet drink in the sunroom overlooking the lake, a friendly meal in the big dining room, a walk by the lake, and then a comfortable bed in one of the big wings. See p. 131.

○ **The Old Faithful Inn** (Yellowstone; ✆ 866/439-7375): As if the wonders outside aren't enough, this is the park's architectural high point: a cavernous lobby with an 85-foot-high ceiling and lodgepole balconies inside and out. Get a room in the old lodge, not the wings, even if the bathrooms are down the hall. See p. 132.

○ **Jenny Lake Lodge** (Grand Teton; ✆ 800/628-9988): Solitude, great food, and beautifully appointed cabins, all with only one downside: the high prices. See p. 144.

○ **Colter Bay Village** (Grand Teton; ✆ 800/628-9988 or 307/543-3100): Rough it in a roomy canvas tent with a stove and bunk beds and firewood delivered to your door (or flap). The rates are relatively inexpensive, and the fresh air is free. For a step up, try the rustic cabins. See p. 148.

The Best Places to Eat Outside the Parks

These restaurants serve food so good that you won't mind spending $15 to $30 for entrees. All of the establishments below are detailed in chapter 8.

○ **In Jackson, Wyoming: Rendezvous Bistro** (✆ 307/739-1100; p. 181) offers steak, seafood, and game dishes with creative twists, not to mention the perfect balance of chic and casual atmosphere. Mornings, though, you'll find me at **Nora's Fish Creek Inn** (✆ 307/733-8288; p. 182), in nearby Wilson, with a bottomless cup of coffee and a huge plate of huevos rancheros.

○ **In Cody, Wyoming: Cassie's Supper Club** (✆ 307/527-5500) is a brothel turned cowboy eatery, plating up some of the best steaks in the Rockies. After dinner, country bands hold court over the bustling dance floor. See p. 193.

o **In West Yellowstone, Montana:** Sydney's **Mountain Bistro** (© 406/646-7660) offers an intimate setting, an excellent wine list, and a menu that balances seafood and vegetarian fare with beef, poultry, and pork. Entrees such as sweet-chili salmon and a porterhouse pork chop with butternut squash make this my pick for a special meal at the west entrance to Yellowstone. See p. 157.

The Best Places to Sleep Outside the Parks

All of the following are detailed in chapter 7.

o **In Jackson, Wyoming:** The **Wort Hotel** (© 307/733-2190; p. 173) is a Jackson landmark with comfortable "New West" style rooms; it's also a good value for its downtown location. In nearby Wilson, I love the wooded whimsy of **A Teton Treehouse** (© 307/733-3233; p. 175), a B&B located 95 steps from the road up a forested hillside where flying squirrels glide in the canopy.

o **In Gardiner, Montana:** The **Absaroka Lodge** (© 406/848-7414) has modern rooms and decks overlooking the Yellowstone River, near the center of town. See p. 158.

o **In West Yellowstone, Montana:** Sleek and opulent, but definitively Western, the newly renovated lodge rooms and cabins at the **Bar N Ranch** (© 406/646-0300; p. 154) are the most distinctive lodgings in the chain-dominated town. **Moose Creek Cabins** (© 406/646-9546; p. 155) is a good value and one of the better maintained properties in town, with cabins (good for families) and cabin-style motel rooms with queen beds.

o **In Cody, Wyoming:** Centered on a serene and green courtyard, the new-and-improved **Chamberlin Inn** (© 888/587-0202; p. 190) features charming historic rooms and apartment units. Located on the west end of town, **The Cody** (© 307/587-5915; p. 191) has a colorful, thoroughly Western-chic design in both common areas and guest rooms.

The Best Things to See & Do Outside the Parks

Don't assume that a Yellowstone and Grand Teton vacation must be limited to within park boundaries. Here are a few area attractions worth checking out. See chapter 8 for more information.

o **In Cody, Wyoming:** The **Buffalo Bill Historical Center** (© 307/587-4771; p. 187) is the best museum in the region.

Another can't-miss is the **Cody Nite Rodeo** (© 800/207-0744;
p. 189), the only rodeo held every night throughout the summer.

o **In Jackson, Wyoming:** Glimpse some of the finest artistic inter-
pretations of the natural world at the fantastic **National
Museum of Wildlife Art** (© 307/733-5771; p. 170), which
houses 1,300 pieces within its red-sandstone walls. At the top of
the **Jackson Hole Aerial Tram** (© 307/739-2753; p. 170),
at Jackson Hole Mountain Resort, you can see the Tetons from
an elevation of more than 10,000 feet. During busy summer
days, the tram carries 45 passengers, packed in like the skiers
who take the lift in the winter.

o **In West Yellowstone, Montana:** For a look at Yellowstone's
cultural history, pay a visit to the **Yellowstone Historic Center** (© 406/646-1100) in the historic Union Pacific depot.
See p. 153.

The Best Scenic Drives

Roll down the windows, crank up your favorite music, and take
time to relax as you travel these byways.

o Every stretch along the figure eight of roads at the center of Yellowstone has some scenic allure, but my favorite is the part
along the western and northern shores of **Yellowstone Lake.**
There's less traffic than around Old Faithful or the Grand Canyon of the Yellowstone, and you're likely to see wildlife east of
Fishing Bridge, as well as steaming geothermal features near
West Thumb. The drive is best in the morning, when the sun
is rising over the steaming lake. See chapter 3.

o From the northeast entrance of Yellowstone, head across the
Beartooth Highway (U.S. Hwy. 212) to **Red Lodge, Montana;**
at Red Lodge, head southeast toward **Cody** (Mont. 308 to Wyo.
120), and then catch the **Chief Joseph Highway** (Wyo. 296) and
return to the park. Imagine this: dramatic mountain peaks, river
valleys, painted landscapes, and two Old West towns, all on this
155-mile drive. See chapter 3.

o A twisting, narrow road climbs **Signal Mountain** to a fine
360-degree view of the valley and surrounding peaks. On the
way up, you'll see wildflowers and birds; from the top, you can
study the moraines and potholes left by retreating glaciers. See
chapter 5.

YELLOWSTONE & GRAND TETON NATIONAL PARKS IN DEPTH

I n Yellowstone and Grand Teton national parks, spectacular scenery combines with a genuine frontier history to create what we consider the real American West. The land is uncluttered and the setting is one of rugged beauty: the remote wilderness of Yellowstone's Thorofare country, the soaring peaks of the Teton Range, and the geothermal activity sprouting from below the surface of the Earth.

There's a little more modern civilization here than there was in years gone by, but this is still one of the few places in the U.S. where there are vast tracts of untouched wilderness. Make sure to take the time to experience it without the noise of cellphones, cars, and other trappings of the 21st century: Your hiking boots and canteen may be the most important items in your luggage.

YELLOWSTONE & GRAND TETON NATIONAL PARKS TODAY

The struggle to balance recreation and preservation is as old as the parks themselves, and it's an issue that continually comes to a boil when long-standing park policies, such as those regarding the use of snowmobiles, are revisited with a critical eye. Suzanne Lewis, former superintendent of Yellowstone National Park, knows all too well that the mission of the U.S. National Park Service is a tricky balancing act.

"How do you get your hands around 2.2 million acres?" said Lewis in an interview with Frommer's. "You just can't put it in perspective until you come here. And you have almost three million visitors a year who come for this once-in-a-lifetime experience. The magnitude of people's expectations is enormous, and it takes a lot of management."

Bison, Bears & Wolves

In the frontier West—where bison seemed to be everywhere, grizzly bears were fearsome, and wolves regularly raided livestock—wildlife was treated as more of a nuisance than a national treasure. Eventually, the bison and grizzly populations around Yellowstone and Grand Teton were whittled down nearly to extinction, and ranchers and federal agents completely eradicated wolves by the 1930s.

It took some intensive management to bring grizzlies and bison back to reasonably healthy numbers in the area, and now the wolves, which were reintroduced from Canada in 1995, are reaping the benefits of the huge ungulate herds that have enjoyed a nearly predator-free environment for quite some time. But these high-profile species—called "charismatic megafauna" by biologists—are not out of the woods yet. Given the pressures of development around the parks, they might never be secure again.

There are now more than 3,500 bison in Yellowstone and Grand Teton, and, naturally, they pay no mind to the parks' invisible boundaries. In the winter, when the snow is deep, they leave the park to forage at lower elevations, sometimes in ranch pastures inhabited by domestic cattle. The ranchers fear that the bison will spread brucellosis, a virus that can be transmitted to cattle, causing infected cows to abort their unborn calves. There have been no documented cases of bison-cattle transmission, but because of the perceived threat to livestock, Montana officials allow bison to be shot once they wander outside the park. Animal-rights activists are outraged, and park and state officials continue to search for some middle ground.

Wolves are another sore point with area ranchers. The reintroduction has been astonishingly successful. Rapidly reproducing, feeding on abundant elk in Yellowstone's Lamar Valley, wolves now number several hundred in the Yellowstone area and over 1,000 in the Northern Rockies, and the packs have spread as far south as Grand Teton, where several have denned and produced pups. Although the Defenders of Wildlife have set up programs to compensate ranchers for livestock lost to wolves, the ranchers have gone to court seeking to have the wolves removed. The wolves have, indeed, been implicated in the deaths of sheep and cattle, and a federal judge in Wyoming ruled in 1998 that all reintroduced wolves should be removed. This decision was overturned in 2000, and the wolves are finally entrenched in Yellowstone for the long haul. In Yellowstone, the wolves' numbers soared to about 250 before plunging to about 125 due to a bout with distemper in 2008. In all of the Northern Rockies, there were about 1,500 wolves as of early 2012, about half of them in Idaho.

Grizzly bears once teetered on the brink of extinction in the parks, but they've made a slow comeback, reaching an estimated population of about 500 in the Yellowstone area. (It seems the wolves have helped, because their hunting results in many more carcasses to scavenge.) Because of this success, in March 2007 the U.S. Fish and Wildlife Service removed the grizzly from the threatened species list for the Yellowstone area, a decision that was subsequently reversed in 2010. Nonetheless, the grizzly habitat in the Greater Yellowstone Ecosystem keeps shrinking, as more and more development takes place around the plateau.

Grand Teton: A Multiple-Use Park

Grand Teton National Park is much more than just a preserve of mountains and lakes and wildlife. Its land is used for all sorts of things that most people don't expect of a national park. There's a big dam holding irrigation water for potato farmers in Idaho; a commercial climbing business that charges big bucks for escorting climbers up the peaks; and even a commercial airport and a country club.

Each year, one of these conflicting uses makes headlines. Lately, it's cattle, which graze in the fall only a short lope from a den of young wolves. What's the purpose of this park, critics ask—to feed a rancher's cattle or to protect wildlife?

As park spokesperson Jackie Skaggs points out, these are the sorts of public-lands conflicts that arise more often in modern times. With its pockets of private land, uses that predate the creation of the park, and heightened debate between park purists and multiple-use advocates, Grand Teton is a prime example of the difficulty of modern park management.

A Burning Issue

Yellowstone's park managers faced the ultimate test of their noninterference philosophy of fire management in 1988, when nearly one-third of Yellowstone was burned by a series of uncontrollable wildfires. These violent conflagrations scorched more than 700,000 acres, leaving behind dead wildlife, damaged buildings, injured firefighters, and ghostly forests of stripped, blackened tree trunks.

The debate over park and public-land fire policies still rages, although things have quieted down some. After years of suppressing every fire in the park, Yellowstone, in 1988, was operating under a new "let it burn" policy, based on scientific evidence that fires were regular occurrences before the settlement of the West and part of the natural cycle of a forest.

What you will see, as you travel Yellowstone today, is a park that may be healthier than it was before the 1988 fires. Saplings have sprouted from the long-dormant seeds of the lodgepole pine (fire stimulates the pine cones to release their seeds), and the old, tinder-dry forest undergrowth is being replaced with new, green shrubs, sometimes as thick as one million saplings per acre. Visitors who want to better understand the effects of the fires of 1988 should check out the exhibits at the Grant Village Visitor Center; the coverage there is the best in the park.

Snowmobiles: To Ban or Not to Ban?

Winter in Yellowstone is a time of silent wonder, with fauna descending from the high country in search of warmth and food. The only dissonance in this winter wilderness tableau is the roar of snowmobiles, which inhabit the park's snow-packed roads in ever-growing numbers. The noisy, pollution-heavy engines are not exactly ecologically friendly, but the gateway towns are staunch snowmobile proponents because the activity boosts their economies in the moribund winter.

Before President Clinton left office in 2001, he "ended" the ongoing controversy by establishing a ban on snowmobiles in Yellowstone,

America's National Parks: We're Ready for Our Close-Up!

Ken Burns and Dayton Duncan's six-part, 12-hour 2009 documentary series *The National Parks: America's Best Idea* tells the dramatic story of the origin of the national park system. Starting in the 1850s with the appreciation of the areas that became Yosemite and Yellowstone national parks, the series depicts the ongoing battle between the preservation of the parks and industrialization and commercialization of the land. You can watch scenes from the series at **www.pbs.org/nationalparks**, or purchase the DVDs, companion book, and soundtrack CD.

effective the winter of 2003–04. However, gateway communities and snowmobile manufacturers responded with lawsuits; and the Bush administration also voiced its opposition to a total ban, delighting the outfitters in West Yellowstone and Cody. In mid-2004, a judge overturned the ruling enforcing the ban.

In the winter of 2011–12, snowmobiles continued to ramble through Yellowstone and Grand Teton; all trips were guided by licensed outfitters with a daily quota of 318 machines, and the technology met best-available standards. Additionally, over-snow travel on the Continental Divide Snowmobile Trail has been discontinued in Grand Teton National Park and on the John D. Rockefeller, Jr. Memorial Parkway. If you're planning a trip, you can get up-to-date information on winter use policies at **www.nps.gov/yell**.

LOOKING BACK: YELLOWSTONE & GRAND TETON HISTORY
Yellowstone National Park

Before the arrival of European settlers, the only residents on the plateau were small bands of Shoshone Indians known as "Sheepeaters," who lived on the southern fringe. Three other Indian tribes came and went: the Crows (Apsáalooke), who were friendly to the settlers; the Blackfeet, who lived in the Missouri Valley drainage and were hostile to both whites and other Indians; and the Bannocks, who largely kept to themselves. The nomadic Bannocks traveled an east-west route in their search for bison: from Idaho past Mammoth Hot Springs to Tower Fall, and then across the

Lamar Valley to the Bighorn Valley, outside the park's current boundaries. Called the Bannock Trail, the route was so deeply furrowed that evidence of it still exists today on the Blacktail Plateau near the Tower Junction. (You'll see remnants of the trail if you take Blacktail Plateau Drive, described in chapter 3.)

The first white explorer to lay eyes on Yellowstone's geothermal wonders was probably John Colter, who broke away from the Lewis and Clark expedition in 1806 and spent 3 years wandering a surreal landscape of mud pots, mountains, and geysers. When he described his discovery on his return to St. Louis, no one believed him. Miners and fur trappers followed in his footsteps, reducing the plentiful beaver population of the region to almost zero, and occasionally making curious reports of a sulfurous world still sometimes called "Colter's Hell."

The first significant exploration of what would become the park took place in 1869, when a band of Montanans, led by David Folsom, completed a 36-day expedition. The group traveled up the Missouri River and into the heart of the park, where they discovered the falls of Yellowstone, mud pots, Yellowstone Lake, and the Fountain Geyser. Two years later, an expedition led by U.S. Geological Survey director Ferdinand V. Hayden brought back convincing evidence of Yellowstone's wonders, in the form of astonishing photographs by William Henry Jackson.

A debate began over the potential for commercial development and exploitation of the region, as crude health spas and thin-walled "hotels" went up near the hot springs. There are various claimants to the idea of a national park—members of the Folsom party later told an oft-disputed story about thinking it up around a campfire in the Upper Geyser Basin—but the idea gained steam as Yellowstone explorers hit the lecture circuit back East. In March 1872, President Ulysses S. Grant signed legislation declaring Yellowstone the nation's first national park.

The Department of the Interior got the job of managing the new park. There was no budget for it and no clear idea of how to take care of a wilderness preserve; many mistakes were made. Inept superintendents granted favorable leases to friends with commercial interests in the tourism industry. Poachers ran amok, and the wildlife population was decimated. A laundry business near Mammoth went so far as to clean linens in a hot pool.

By 1886, things were so bad that the U.S. Army took control of Yellowstone; iron-fisted management practices resulted in new order and protected the park from those intent upon exploiting it.

road OPENINGS & CLOSINGS

In Yellowstone Traveling Yellowstone's roads during spring months can be a roll of the dice because openings can be delayed for days (sometimes weeks) at a time, especially at higher altitudes. There is always some section of road in Yellowstone under construction (projects for Dunraven Pass and the stretch between Madison and Norris being the current hot spots)—so call ahead and get a road report (© **307/344-7381**). It's irritating, but don't take it out on the road workers; they often labor through the night to cause as little inconvenience as possible.

The only road open year-round in the area is the north entrance to **Mammoth Hot Springs.** From Mammoth, a winter access road to the northeast entrance and **Cooke City** is plowed throughout the winter. This service for Cooke City residents gives visitors a great opportunity to watch wildlife in winter in the Lamar Valley. Just be watchful of the weather; the road is often slick with ice.

Snowplowing begins in early March. In Yellowstone, the first roads open to motor vehicles (usually by the end of Apr) include **Mammoth-Norris, Norris-Canyon, Madison–Old Faithful,** and **West Yellowstone–Madison.** If the weather cooperates, the east and south entrances, as well as roads on the east and south sides of the park, will open early in May. Opening of the road from **Tower-Roosevelt** to **Canyon Junction,** however, might be delayed by late-season snowfall on Dunraven Pass.

The **Sunlight Basin Road** (which is also called the **Chief Joseph Highway**), connecting the entrances in Cooke City, Montana, and Cody, Wyoming, often opens by early May. The **Beartooth Highway,** between Cooke City and Red Lodge, Montana, is generally open by Memorial Day weekend.

Winter road closures typically begin in mid-October, when the Beartooth Highway closes. Depending upon weather, most other park roads remain open until the park season ends on the first Sunday in November.

In Grand Teton Because Grand Teton has fewer roads and they're at lower elevations, openings and closings are more predictable. **Teton Park Road** opens to conventional vehicles and RVs around May 1. The **Moose-Wilson Road** opens to vehicles about the same time. Roads close to vehicles on November 1, although they never close for nonmotorized use.

(However, the military did participate in the eradication of the plateau's wolf population.) By 1916, efforts to make the park more visitor-friendly had begun to show results: Construction of the first roads had been completed, guest housing was available in the area, and order had been restored. Stewardship of the park was then transferred to the newly created National Park Service, which remains in control to this day.

Grand Teton National Park

Unlike Yellowstone, Grand Teton can't boast of being the nation's first park and a model for parks the world over. This smaller, southern neighbor was created as the result of a much more convoluted process that spanned 50 years.

The first sign of human habitation in the Grand Teton region dates back 12,000 years. Among the tribes who hunted here in the warmer seasons were the Blackfeet, Crow, Gros Ventre, and Shoshone, who came over the mountains from the Great Basin to the west. Indians spent summers hunting and raising crops, before heading to warmer climes.

Trappers and explorers, who first arrived in the valley in the early 1800s, were equally distressed by the harsh winters and short growing seasons, which made Jackson Hole a marginal place for farming and ranching. Among these early visitors were artist Thomas Moran and photographer William Henry Jackson, whose images awoke the country to the Tetons' grandeur. Early homesteaders quickly realized that their best hope was to market the unspoiled beauty of the area, which they began doing in earnest as early as a century ago.

DATELINE

18,000 B.C. Earliest evidence of humans in Wyoming.

11,000 B.C. Earliest evidence of humans in Montana.

A.D. 1620s Arrival of the Plains Indians.

A.D. 1807 John Colter explores the Yellowstone area, going as far south as Jackson Hole.

1867 The Union Pacific Railroad enters Wyoming.

1869 A party led by David Folsom undertakes the first modern exploration of Yellowstone.

1871 The Hayden Expedition surveys Yellowstone.

1872 Yellowstone is established as the nation's first national park.

The danger of haphazard development soon became apparent. There was a dance hall at Jenny Lake, hot dog stands along the roads, and buildings going up on prime habitat. In the 1920s, after some discussion about how the Grand Teton area might be protected, Yellowstone park officials and conservationists went to Congress. Led by local dude ranchers and Yellowstone superintendent Horace Albright, the group was able to protect only the mountains and foothills, leaving out Jackson Lake and the valley; Wyoming's congressional delegation—and many locals—were vehemently opposed to enclosing the valley within park boundaries.

Then, in 1927, something called the Snake River Land Company started buying ranches and homesteads at the base of the Tetons. The company turned out to be a front for John D. Rockefeller, Jr., one of the richest men in the world, working in cahoots with the conservationists. He planned to give the land to the federal government and keep a few choice parcels for himself. But Congress wouldn't have it, and Rockefeller made noises about selling the land, about 35,000 acres, to the highest bidder. In the 1940s, President Franklin D. Roosevelt created the Jackson Hole National Monument out of Forest Service lands east of the Snake River. That paved the way for Rockefeller's donation, and in 1950, Grand Teton National Park was expanded to its present form.

WHEN TO GO

Summer, autumn, and winter are the best times to visit the Northern Rockies. The days are sunny, the nights are clear, and the humidity is low. A popular song once romanticized "Springtime in the Rockies," but that season lasts for about 2 days in early June.

1876 Warriors from the Sioux, Lakota, and Cheyenne tribes defeat General George A. Custer and his troops at the Battle of the Little Bighorn.

1877 Chief Joseph of the Nez Perce tribe surrenders to U.S. soldiers in the Bear Paw Mountains after a flight that took his tribe though Yellowstone.

1883 The Northern Pacific Railroad crosses Montana.

1886 The U.S. Army takes over management of Yellowstone.

1889 Montana, on November 8, becomes the 41st state in the Union.

1890 Wyoming becomes the nation's 44th state.

1916 The U.S. National Park Service takes over control of Yellowstone from the U.S. Army.

continues

The rest of the season formally known as spring is likely to be chilly and spitting snow or rain. Trails are still clogged with snow and mud.

Typically, from mid-June on, you can hike, fish, camp, and watch wildlife, and if you come before July 4 or after Labor Day, you won't have to share the view all that much. Wildflowers bloom at these elevations in early summer—beginning in May in the lower valleys and plains, while in the higher elevations they open up in July.

Autumn is not just the time when the aspens turn gold, it's also the time when gateway motel and restaurant rates are lower and the roads are less crowded. That allows you to pay more attention to the wildlife, which is busy fattening up for the winter.

Winter is a glorious season here, although not for everyone. It can be very cold, but the air is crystalline, the snow is powdery, and the skiing is fantastic. If you drive in the parks' vicinity in the winter, *always* carry winter clothing, sleeping bags, extra food, flashlights, and other safety gear. Every resident has a horror story about being caught unprepared in the weather.

The Climate

The region is characterized by long, cold winters and short, relatively mild summers. There is not a lot of moisture, winter or summer, and the air is dry, except for the brief wet season in March and April.

I've already warned you about the brief glimpse of spring in these parts. Cold and snow can linger into April and May—blizzards can even hit the area in mid-June—although temperatures

1929 Grand Teton National Park is established, consisting of only the main peaks of the Cathedral Range.	**1995** Gray wolves are reintroduced into Yellowstone National Park.
1950 National forest and private lands are added to Grand Teton National Park, forming the park that it is today.	**2007** The U.S. Forest Service removes the Greater Yellowstone grizzly bear population from the threatened species list.
1988 Five fires break out around Yellowstone, blackening approximately one-third of the park.	**2007–08** Due to brucellosis fears, over 1,500 Yellowstone bison are killed as they cross into Montana.

are generally warming. The average daytime readings are in the 40s or 50s (4°–15°C), gradually increasing into the 60s or 70s (16°–26°C) by early June. So, during **spring,** a warm jacket, rain gear, and water-resistant walking shoes could be welcome traveling companions.

The area is rarely balmy, but temperatures during the middle of the **summer** are typically 75° to 85°F (24°–29°C) in the lower elevations and are especially comfortable because of the lack of humidity. Remember, too, that the atmosphere is thin at this altitude, so sunscreen is a must. Nights, even during the warmest months, will be cool, with temperatures dropping into the 40s (4°–9°C), so you'll want to include a jacket in your wardrobe. Because summer thunderstorms are common, you'll probably be glad you've included a waterproof shell or umbrella.

As **fall** approaches, you'll want to have an additional layer of clothing because temperatures remain mild but begin to cool. The first heavy snows typically fall in the valley by November 1 (much earlier in the mountains) and continue through March or April. Aspen trees turn bright yellow; cottonwoods turn a deeper gold.

During **winter** months, you'll want long johns, heavy shirts, vests, coats, warm gloves, and thick socks. Temperatures hover in single digits (negative teens Celsius), and subzero overnight temperatures are common. Ultracold air can cause lots of health problems, so drink fluids, keep an extra layer of clothing handy, and don't overexert yourself.

For up-to-date weather information and road conditions, call ☎ **888/996-7623** (in state) or 511 (in-state mobile), or visit **www.wyoroad.info**.

2008 The gray wolf population in the Northern Rockies hits 1,600; the species is no longer listed as endangered.	**2011** The U.S. Congress returns gray wolf management to the states, effectively delisting the species again in Wyoming and Montana.
2009 Montana has its first legal wolf-hunting season since reintroduction in 1995.	**2011** A grizzly bear kills a visitor near the Grand Canyon of the Yellowstone, the first bear-related fatality in the park in over 20 years.
2010 A court ruling returns the grizzly bear to the threatened species list.	
2010 A court ruling returns the gray wolf to the endangered species list.	

Avoiding the Crowds

Between the Fourth of July and Labor Day, the Northern Rockies come to life. Flowers bloom, fish jump, bison calves frolic—and tourists tour. The park roads are crowded with trailers, with the well-known spots jammed with a significant portion of the millions who make their treks to Montana and Wyoming every year. Your best bet: Travel before June 15, if possible, or after Labor Day. If you can't arrange that, then visit the major attractions at off-peak hours when others are eating or sleeping, and you'll have the park more to yourself. Or, as I suggest over and over, abandon the pavement for the hiking trails.

Whenever you come, give these parks as much time as you can; you'll experience more at an unhurried pace.

Montana's Average Monthly Temperatures (High/Low)

	JAN	FEB	MAR	APR	MAY	JUNE	JULY	AUG	SEPT	OCT	NOV	DEC
BOZEMAN												
°F	28/3	34/9	39/15	54/28	65/37	72/44	83/48	82/47	71/39	59/30	43/18	34/10
°C	-2/-16	1/-13	4/-9	12/-2	18/3	22/7	28/9	28/8	22/4	15/-1	6/-7	1/-12
W. YELLOWSTONE												
°F	25/-1	31/2	39/7	49/19	59/27	68/33	79/38	77/35	67/28	53/21	37/9	27/1
°C	-4/-18	-1/-17	4/-14	9/-7	15/-3	20/1	26/3	25/2	19/-2	12/-6	3/-13	-3/-17

Wyoming's Average Monthly Temperatures (High/Low)

	JAN	FEB	MAR	APR	MAY	JUNE	JULY	AUG	SEPT	OCT	NOV	DEC
CODY												
°F	36/12	40/14	47/21	57/31	66/40	76/47	85/54	83/51	72/42	61/33	46/22	38/15
°C	2/-11	4/-10	8/-6	14/-1	19/4	24/8	29/12	28/11	22/6	16/1	8/-6	3/-9
JACKSON												
°F	27/4	32/7	40/15	52/24	63/31	72/37	82/41	80/39	71/31	58/24	40/16	29/7
°C	-3/-15	0/-14	5/-9	11/-4	17/-1	22/3	28/5	27/4	22/0	15/-5	4/-9	-2/-14
YELLOWSTONE												
°F	23/-1	28/0	35/5	43/16	52/25	61/33	72/39	71/3761/30	49/23	35/12	25/3	
°C	-5/-18	-2/-18	2/-15	6/-9	11/-4	16/1	22/4	22/3	16/-1	10/-5	1/-11	-4/-16

Holidays

Banks, government offices, post offices, and many stores, restaurants, and museums are closed on the following legal national holidays: January 1 (New Year's Day), the third Monday in January (Martin Luther King, Jr., Day), the third Monday in February (Presidents' Day), the last Monday in May (Memorial Day), July 4 (Independence Day), the first Monday in September (Labor Day), the second Monday in October (Columbus Day), November 11 (Veterans Day/Armistice Day), the fourth Thursday in November (Thanksgiving Day), and December 25 (Christmas Day). The Tuesday after the first Monday in November is Election Day, a

GENERAL RESOURCES FOR
green TRAVEL

In addition to the resources for Yellowstone and Grand Teton listed above, the following websites provide valuable wide-ranging information on sustainable travel. For a list of even more sustainable resources, as well as tips and explanations on how to travel greener, visit www.frommers.com/planning.

- **Responsible Travel** (www.responsibletravel.com) is a great source of sustainable travel ideas; the site is run by a spokesperson for ethical tourism in the travel industry.
- **Sustainable Travel International** (www.sustainabletravel international.org) promotes ethical tourism practices and manages a directory of sustainable properties and tour operators around the world.
- **Carbonfund.org** (www.carbonfund.org), **TerraPass** (www.terrapass.org), and **Cool Climate Network** (http://cool climate.berkeley.edu) provide info on "carbon offsetting," or offsetting the greenhouse gas emitted during flights.
- The **"Green" Hotels Association** (www.greenhotels.com) recommends green-rated member hotels around the world that fulfill the association's stringent environmental requirements. **Environmentally Friendly Hotels** (www.environmentallyfriendlyhotels.com) offers more green accommodation ratings.
- For information on animal-friendly issues, visit **Tread Lightly!** (www.treadlightly.org).

federal government holiday in presidential-election years (held every 4 years, and next in 2012). The park is always open on holidays, but visitor centers are often closed.

RESPONSIBLE TRAVEL

Heavy summer auto traffic and the annual impact of millions of human beings have raised questions about the sustainability of these national parks. But a visit to Yellowstone and Grand Teton can be a relatively green vacation. In Yellowstone, concessionaire **Xanterra Parks & Resorts** (© **866/439-7375** or 307/344-7311; www.yellowstonenationalparklodges.com) has implemented numerous environmental initiatives, launching a recycling program, sourcing seafood from sustainable fisheries, and encouraging guests to reuse towels, conserve heat, and otherwise be as sustainable as possible. The Old Faithful Snow Lodge, the newest lodging in the park, was built in part from reclaimed wood from the sawmill that cut the timber for the Old Faithful Inn, and the new gift shop at Mammoth has all sorts of green mementoes, as well as a kiosk for visitors to determine their personal carbon footprint and other interactive exhibits. Campgrounds have recycling bins near their entrances. In Grand Teton, the **Grand Teton Lodge Company** (✆ **800/628-9988** or 307/543-2811; www.gtlc.com) has also implemented very successful sustainability programs to lessen the human impact on the park. The company has purchased wind credits to offset its energy use and diverted 50 percent of its waste into reusing and recycling everything from aluminum cans to horse manure to food waste.

But perhaps the best way to look at sustainability is to go off the grid on an overnight backpacking trip. The website of the outdoor-ethics organization **Leave No Trace** (www.lnt.org) provides useful tips for backpackers on how to leave a campsite in the same condition—or better—than they found it. Backpacking is a refreshing counterpoint to modern life that will give perspective on the issues of sustainability and personal energy dependence. For more on backpacking, see "Special Permits," in chapter 10, and the sections on each park's backcountry, in chapters 4 and 6.

TOURS
Academic Trips

One of the best ways to turn a park vacation into an unforgettable experience is to join an educational program. There are no finals in these courses; they're just a relaxed, informative way to spend time outdoors.

The **Yellowstone Association Institute** ★★★, P.O. Box 117, Yellowstone National Park, WY 82190 (✆ **406/848-2400;** www.yellowstoneassociation.org/institute), operates at the historic Lamar Buffalo Ranch, in the northeast part of the park, and at other locations in the vicinity. It typically offers several hundred courses a year, covering everything from winter wildlife tracking to wilderness medicine to the history of fur trappers on the plateau. The courses, some of which are offered for college credit, run from 1 to 7 days, with forays into the field and lectures and demonstrations at the institute's cozy quarters. The classes are a study in camaraderie as well as natural history, with participants sharing meals and stories in the common kitchen. Prices are reasonable (around $125 a day for tuition), and some classes are specifically targeted to families and youngsters. To make the most of a class, you'll want to stay at the ranch itself, where simple, comfortable cabins are available for $30 a night per student. Customizable 1-day hiking and wildlife-watching **private tours** with an experienced naturalist run about $500 per day for groups of up to five people, including transportation. The institute has also teamed with Xanterra Parks & Resorts to offer 3- to 5-night **Lodging & Learning** packages, which include days spent exploring trails with guides coupled with nights at comfortable lodgings throughout the park. Rates are about $250 per person per day and include breakfast, a box lunch, and in-park transportation; contact **Xanterra Parks & Resorts** (© 866/439-7375; www.yellowstonenational parklodges.com).

The **Teton Science Schools ★★**, 700 Coyote Canyon Dr., Jackson, WY 83011 (© 307/733-1313; www.tetonscience.org), is a 30-year-old institution that offers summer and winter programs for students and adults. Classes review the ecology, geology, and wildlife of the park, and there are photography and tracking workshops as well. Classes cater to different age groups, and the emphasis is on experiential, hands-on learning. College credit is available.

The Teton Science Schools' **Wildlife Expeditions** (© 877/406-6626 or 307/733-1313) include trips in open-roof vans, on rafts, in sleighs, and by foot. These tours bring visitors closer to wildlife than they're likely to get on their own. Wildlife Expeditions offers trips ranging from a half-day sunset safari ($125) to week-long trips through the park, usually lodging in park hotels. Adult seminars usually run about $150 to $200 per day, but more inclusive ones cost upwards of $500 per day.

Adventure Trips & Guided Tours

For a detailed list of outfitters, guides, and equipment rental providers categorized by activity, see the "Other Activities" sections in chapters 4 and 6.

In addition, **AdventureBus,** 375 S. Main St., No. 240, Moab, UT 84532 (© 888/737-5263 or 909/633-7225; www.adventurebus.com), offers trips on its customized buses with an emphasis on outdoor adventures, including multisport and mountain biking tours in the Yellowstone and Grand Teton national parks. The rate is about $1,000 per person for a week-long trip. **Austin-Lehman Adventures,** P.O. Box 81025, Billings, MT 59108-1025 (© 800/575-1540; www.austinlehman.com), offers guided multiday mountain biking, hiking, and combination tours in and around Yellowstone and Grand Teton national parks. Six-night trips start around $2,300 per person. **Backroads,** 801 Cedar St., Berkeley, CA 94710-1800 (© 800/462-2848 or 510/527-1555; www.backroads.com), offers a variety of guided multiday road biking, mountain biking, and hiking in and around Yellowstone and Grand Teton national parks. The rate is about $2,000 per person (camping) to $3,000 per person (park lodgings) for 6 days. The **World Outdoors,** 2840 Wilderness Place, Ste. D, Boulder, CO 80301 (© **800/488-8483** or 303/413-0946; www.theworldoutdoors.com), offers a variety of trips, including multisport adventures that include hiking, mountain biking, rock climbing, and rafting in and around Yellowstone and Grand Teton national parks. Rates range from $1,700 to $2,700 per person for 6 days. **Escape Adventures,** 8221 W. Charleston St., No. 101, Las Vegas, NV 89117 (© **800/596-2953** or 702/596-2953; www.escapeadventures. com), offers 6-day guided road-biking tours of the parks. The rate is about $1,500 per person (camping) to $2,300 per person (park lodgings).

EXPLORING YELLOWSTONE NATIONAL PARK

You can scratch the surface in a day or two, or you can devote an entire summer to digging deeper. One trip, however long, never feels adequate, there's always a road not traveled and a trail not hiked. You can focus on the roadside highlights or venture deep into the backcountry. You can enjoy the old-style park hotels or pitch your own tent. You can learn about the geology and flora and fauna in visitor center exhibits or take a multiday class with expert naturalists.

There are 310 miles of paved roadways in Yellowstone, including a figure-eight loop at the center that takes you to some key attractions; you can cover this entire loop in 1 long day. This is a common strategy, but it doesn't do Yellowstone justice. Ultimately, those who embark on it are selling the park short.

I recommend you give yourself at least 3 days. Despite the crowds, you should check the famous sites because they're deserving of all the attention: **Old Faithful,** the **Grand Canyon of the Yellowstone, Fishing Bridge,** and **Mount Washburn.** If you're seeking knowledge, take a class at the **Yellowstone Association Institute,** or follow one of the rangers on a guided hike. If you want solitude, go early in the morning up one of the less-traveled trails, such as **Bunsen Peak** or **Mystic Falls,** or strap a pack to your back and go out on a multiday backpacking expedition: Less than 1 percent of park visitors spend the night in the backcountry.

You'll find more details in the chapters that follow on where to hike, fish, sleep, eat, and otherwise enjoy yourself in the park.

ESSENTIALS

ACCESS/ENTRY POINTS   Yellowstone has five entrances. The **north entrance,** near Mammoth Hot Springs, is located just south of Gardiner, Montana, and U.S. Hwy. 89. In the winter, this is the only access to Yellowstone by car.

The **west entrance,** just outside the town of West Yellowstone, Montana, on U.S. Hwy. 20, is the closest entry to Old Faithful. Inside the park, you can turn south to Old Faithful or north to the Norris Geyser Basin. This entrance is open to wheeled vehicles from April to November and to snowmobiles and snowcoaches from December to March.

About 64 miles north of Jackson, Wyoming, the **south entrance,** on U.S. Hwy. 89/191/287, brings visitors into Yellowstone from Grand Teton National Park. On the way to Yellowstone, drivers get some panoramic views of the Teton Range. Once in the park, the road winds along the Lewis River to the south end of Yellowstone Lake, at West Thumb and Grant Village. It's open to cars from May to November and to snowmobiles and snowcoaches from December to March.

The **east entrance,** on U.S. Hwy. 14/16/20, is 53 miles west of Cody, Wyoming, and is open to cars from May to September and to snowmobiles and snowcoaches from December to March. The drive up the Wapiti Valley and over Sylvan Pass is especially beautiful, when not marred by road-repair delays.

The **northeast entrance,** at Cooke City, Montana, is closest to the Tower-Roosevelt area, 29 miles to the west. This entrance is open to cars year-round, but from October 15, when the Beartooth Highway closes, until around Memorial Day, the only route to Cooke City is through Mammoth Hot Springs. When it's open, the drive from Red Lodge to the park is a grand climb among the clouds.

Regardless of which entrance you choose, you'll be given a good map and up-to-date information on facilities, services, programs, fishing, camping, and more.

VISITOR CENTERS   There are five major visitor and information centers in the park, and each has something different to offer.

The **Albright Visitor Center** (© **307/344-2263**), at Mammoth Hot Springs, is the largest and is open daily year-round (8am–7pm in summer; 9am–5pm in winter). It provides visitor information and publications about the park, has exhibits depicting park history from prehistory through the creation of the U.S. National Park Service, and houses displays on wildlife.

The **Canyon Visitor Education Center** (© 307/344-2550), in Canyon Village, offers books and an informative display about the park's geology, both focusing on the underlying volcanism. It's open 8am to 8pm daily in summer and staffed by friendly rangers used to dealing with crowds.

The brand-new, state-of-the-art **Old Faithful Visitor Education Center** (© 307/344-2751), opened in 2010, shows a film on Yellowstone's thermal features throughout the day and features exhibits focusing on the park's geysers and other thermal features. It also displays projected geyser-eruption times, making it a good first stop for those looking to see Old Faithful do its thing. It's open daily in summer from 8am to 8pm.

The **Fishing Bridge Visitor Center** (© 307/344-2450), near Fishing Bridge on the north shore of Yellowstone Lake, has an excellent display that focuses on the park's bird life. You can get information and publications here as well. It's open daily in summer from 8am to 7pm.

The **Grant Visitor Center** (© 307/344-2650) has information, publications, a video program, and a fascinating exhibit that examines the role of fire in Yellowstone. It's open daily in summer from 8am to 7pm.

Park literature and helpful staff are also found at several small information stations: the **Madison Information Station** (© 307/344-2876; summer daily 9am–6pm), home of the **Junior Ranger Station;** the **Museum of the National Park Ranger** (no phone; summer daily 9am–5pm) and the **Norris Geyser Basin Museum and Information Station** (© 307/344-2812; summer daily 9am–6pm), both at Norris; the **West Thumb Information Station** (© 307/344-2650; summer daily 9am–5pm); and the **West Yellowstone Visitor Information Center,** 100 Yellowstone Ave. (© 307/344-2876; summer daily 8am–8pm, limited hours the rest of the year). In Gardiner (but also within Yellowstone boundaries) is the **Yellowstone Heritage and Research Center** (© 307/344-2664), housing a library, archives, and other resources available to the public. It is open 9am to 4pm year-round, but is not equipped to handle standard visitor inquiries.

ENTRANCE FEES A 7 day pass costs $25 per automobile and covers both Yellowstone and Grand Teton national parks. A 7-day snowmobile or motorcycle pass costs $20, and someone who comes in on bicycle, skis, or foot will pay $12 for 7 days.

If you expect to visit the parks more than once in a year, buy an annual pass for $50. And if you visit parks and national monuments around the country, purchase an **Interagency Annual Pass** for $80 (good for 365 days from the date of purchase at nearly all

Yellowstone National Park

federal preserves). Anyone age 62 or older can get an **Interagency Senior Pass** for a one-time fee of $10, and people who are blind or who have permanent disabilities can obtain an **Interagency Access Pass,** which is free. All passes are available at any entrance to Yellowstone. While the Interagency Senior and Interagency Access passes must be obtained in person (to verify age or disability), Interagency Annual Passes are also available online at **http://store.usgs.gov/pass**.

CAMPING FEES Fees for camping in Yellowstone range from $12 to $20 per night, depending on the number of amenities the campground offers. The **Fishing Bridge RV Park** (p. 135) charges up to $37 per night and has full hookups; while other campgrounds in the park have sites suitable for RVs, this is the only one with hookups, and only RVs are allowed here. **Flagg Ranch,** just outside the south entrance, also has an RV camp with hookups; sites are $64 per night and tents are $35.

For more information on camping, see "Where to Camp in Yellowstone," in chapter 7. It is possible to make advance reservations at some campgrounds in both parks.

SPECIAL REGULATIONS & WARNINGS More detailed information about the following rules can be requested from the park rangers, at visitor centers throughout the park, or at **www.nps.gov/yell**.

o **Bicycles:** Bicycles are allowed on the park's roadways, but not on trails or boardwalks. There are some designated off-pavement bicycling areas; contact the park for more information. Helmets and bright clothing are recommended because of the narrow, winding nature of park roads and the presence of large recreational vehicles with poor visibility.

o **Camping:** A person may camp in the park for no more than 30 days in any given year, and no more than 14 days during the summer season (except at Fishing Bridge RV Park, where neither limit applies). Food, garbage, and food utensils must be stored in a vehicle or container made of solid material and suspended at least 10 feet above the ground when not in use.

o **Climbing:** Because of the loose, crumbly rock in Yellowstone, climbing is discouraged throughout the park and is prohibited in the Grand Canyon of the Yellowstone.

o **Defacing park features:** Picking wildflowers and collecting natural or archaeological objects is illegal. Only dead-and-down wood can be collected for backcountry campfires, and only when and where such fires are allowed.

o **Firearms:** As of February 2010, firearms are allowed in national parks. Those in possession of a firearm must have a legal license from their state of residence. Firearms are prohibited in marked facilities.

o **Littering:** Littering in the national parks is strictly prohibited—if you take it in, you have to take it out. Throwing coins or other objects into thermal features is illegal.

o **Motorcycles:** Motorcycles and motor scooters are allowed only on park roads. No off-road or trail riding is allowed. Operator licenses and license plates are required.

o **Pets:** Pets must always be leashed and are prohibited in the backcountry, on trails, on boardwalks, and in thermal areas. If you tie up a pet and leave it, you're breaking the law.

o **Smoking:** No smoking is allowed in thermal areas, visitor centers, ranger stations, or any other posted public areas.

o **Snowmobiling:** Yellowstone's latest winter use plan limits snowmobiles entering the park to 318 a day and requires a licensed guide for all trips.

o **Swimming:** Swimming or wading is prohibited in thermal features or in streams whose waters flow from thermal features in Yellowstone. (One exception is Boiling River near Mammoth, where visitors can take a warm soak between dawn and dusk, except during spring runoff.) Swimming in Yellowstone Lake is discouraged due to the cold water and unpredictable weather.

o **Wildlife:** It is unlawful to approach within 300 feet of a bear or within 75 feet of other wildlife. Feeding any wildlife is illegal. Wildlife calls, such as elk bugles or other artificial attractants, are forbidden.

THE HIGHLIGHTS

Yellowstone is a wonderland to which you can return again and again, sampling a different unique facet each time. All the sites mentioned here are easily accessible along the loop roads of the park. But the farther you get from the pavement, and the farther from July and August you schedule your visit, the more private your experience will be. Behind the wheel, expect to average about 30 mph during peak season.

The Upper Loop

MAMMOTH HOT SPRINGS   Here, 5 miles south of the park's north entrance at Gardiner, Montana, you'll find some of Yellowstone's spectacular thermal areas, including unique limestone terraces (the **Upper and Lower terraces ★★**, which are described in "Yellowstone: The Extended Tour," below). The Albright Visitor Center is here, with some interesting exhibits and a bookstore, as well as the Mammoth Hot Springs Hotel. Your best bet: Follow the interpretive trail through the Upper and Lower terraces.

NORRIS GEYSER BASIN ★★ South of Mammoth Hot Springs, you'll find several impressive **geysers** and geothermal areas of varying type and age, as well as two museums. Norris is conveniently close to the West Yellowstone entrance of the park. You can follow boardwalks north and south (the south has more activity, but the north takes you across the dramatic Porcelain Basin). Best bet: Tour both boardwalks.

CANYON VILLAGE AREA East of Norris, the **Grand Canyon of the Yellowstone River** ★★★ provides some of the park's best views. There are hikes of all lengths and for all abilities here. Canyon Village is one of the most developed sections of the park, with lots of facilities and lodging choices. The canyon might not be as big as the Grand Canyon in Arizona, but it's got its own dynamic beauty. Best bet: Hike one of the rim trails, and venture down Uncle Tom's Trail for a stunning view of Lower Falls.

TOWER-ROOSEVELT AREA The closest of the major park areas to the northeast entrance (just west of Cooke City, Montana), this is also one of the most easygoing areas of the park, away from the big crowds and a short drive from the **Lamar Valley** ★★★, dubbed "The Serengeti of North America" for its wildlife. The Roosevelt Lodge Cabins are a great budget lodging if you want to rough it without pitching a tent, and **Tower Fall** ★ provides a dramatic backdrop for photos. Your best bet: Scope Lamar Valley for wolves and bears; dusk and dawn are optimal times.

The Lower Loop

OLD FAITHFUL AREA Old Faithful ★★★ remains an enduring symbol of Yellowstone, and you'll find standing-room-only crowds at each eruption. The historic **Old Faithful Inn** (p. 132) is located here, and the new **Old Faithful Snow Lodge** (p. 133) is a worthy addition. The most convenient access is from West Yellowstone and the park's west entrance. Boardwalks crisscross the **Upper Geyser Basin,** offering views of numerous geysers other than Old Faithful. Your best bet: Climb to the top of **Observation Point** for a lesser-seen view of Old Faithful's classic burst.

LAKE VILLAGE AREA On the north shore of Yellowstone Lake, you'll find many fishing and boating opportunities, as well as fine dining and lodging choices. The regal **Lake Yellowstone Hotel** (p. 131) is one of the best in the park. This area is the closest to the park's east entrance in Cody, Wyoming (about 50 miles), and the beautiful **Hayden Valley** is nearby. You can rent a boat at Bay Bridge and try to catch one of those elusive lake trout, or take a scenic lake cruise. Best bet: Take a sunset tour from the hotel in one of Xanterra's classic 1930s touring buses.

GRANT VILLAGE/WEST THUMB AREAS   Grant Village is the southernmost of the park's developments, a nondescript collection of modern buildings on the south end of Yellowstone Lake. The **West Thumb Geyser Basin** and the Grant Village Visitor Center are nearby. West Thumb has a lakeside boardwalk that allows views of geysers on both sides of the water's edge. Your best bet: Take an afternoon stroll on the boardwalks and gander at some of the jewels of Yellowstone's geothermal wonders.

IF YOU HAVE ONLY 1 OR 2 DAYS

If you are pinched for time and have only 1 or 2 days to tour Yellowstone, here's an itinerary that highlights the best of the best. If you'll be spending the night, your best bets are Old Faithful Inn or Lake Yellowstone Hotel; if those are booked, try the new Old Faithful Snow Lodge, or get a campsite at Norris or Indian Creek. Other options along the itinerary route are given below.

The quickest route to the inner road loops of the park is along the west entrance road, so come in that way, stopping perhaps for a stroll along the banks of the **Madison River,** where you can see the forest recovering from the 1988 fires. You'll also spot wildlife: ducks and trumpeter swans on the river, and grazing elk and bison. Turn north at Madison Junction to **Norris Geyser Basin,** where there are two boardwalk tours; take the southern one if you're in a hurry.

You're now driving the **upper loop,** which goes north to **Mammoth Hot Springs,** east to **Tower-Roosevelt,** south to **Canyon Village,** and west again to Norris, finally returning to Madison Junction, a circuit of about 85 miles (or 3 hr. of driving minimum). If you go south, rather than west, at Canyon Village, you'll be on the southern loop, which will take you to **Fishing Bridge** and **Lake Village,** then by **West Thumb,** west over Craig Pass to **Old Faithful,** and back to the Madison Junction. The entire lower loop covers 96 miles (another 3 hr. in the car, at the very least).

Altogether, this 2-day circuit is called the **Grand Loop,** taking you through all the major areas of the park except the road between Norris and Canyon Village. You could do it in a day—it's less than 200 miles long—but you'd scare a lot of other travelers as you sped by.

THE UPPER LOOP   If you're pressed for time, the Norris Geyser Basin is a major concentration of **thermal attractions,** and also has a nice museum explaining the park's red-hot underpinnings.

Mammoth has one of the park's major attractions, the ever-growing **terraces** of Mammoth Hot Springs. In addition to the natural attraction, the **Albright Visitor Center** provides excellent historical background for everything you see in the park. There is a fine old hotel at Mammoth and lodging just outside the park in Gardiner, too, but I recommend that you continue farther around the loop on your first day.

From Mammoth, the route winds through forested areas that lead to the edge of the **Lamar Valley,** a deep, rounded path for the Lamar River that is a prime haven for wolves, bison, elk, and grizzly bears. Otherwise, you can continue south to Yellowstone's **Grand Canyon,** one of the most dramatic sights in the park.

THE LOWER LOOP This is the better way to go if you have only a day. You'll also see the two largest geyser areas in Yellowstone—**Norris,** to the north, and the park's signature attraction, **Old Faithful,** to the south. On the eastern side of this route, you'll find the **Grand Canyon of the Yellowstone** and **Hayden Valley,** where you'll often find a grazing herd of bison. Farther south, **Yellowstone Lake** offers fishing, boating, and places for picnicking on the shore.

YELLOWSTONE: THE EXTENDED TOUR

Stretching your visit to 4 or 5 days has several advantages. You'll have more time to visit the roadside highlights, plus you can hike a few of the trails and actually learn from the exhibits at the visitor centers instead of just blasting by them.

The **visitor centers** are a good source of information about the volcanic activity, the flora and fauna, and the history of the park; knowledgeable rangers are on hand who can answer your questions. There are 10 centers and information stations (see "Essentials," earlier in this chapter, for a complete list), but some might be closed if you visit the park during the off season. The **Albright Visitor Center** is open year-round, and the **Old Faithful Visitor Center** is open during summer months and from December to March. The others usually open concurrently with the lodging facilities in their area of the park. Ask the rangers about programs in their area, and check whether any geothermal features have undergone a change in their activity recently—geysers have been known to revive suddenly after years of placidity.

The roads in Yellowstone are organized into a series of interconnecting loops, which you can come into from any of the park's five entrances. To simplify things, I discuss attractions and activities going clockwise along each section of the **Grand Loop Road,** beginning at the **Madison Junction.** But you can enter the loop at any point and pick up this tour as long as you are traveling clockwise. I haven't suggested an optimum amount of time to spend on each leg of the loop because that depends on your particular interests. If you want to get away from the crowds, take time to get off the pavement and onto the trails.

West Yellowstone to Norris

Closest entrance: West Yellowstone (west entrance)

Distances: 14 miles from West Yellowstone to Madison; 14 miles from Madison to Norris

Because most visitors to Yellowstone enter at the **west entrance,** I'll use that as a jumping-off point to begin an extended tour of the park. As you travel the 14 miles from the gate to **Madison Junction,** you will find the **Two Ribbons Trail,** which offers an opportunity to walk through and inspect the effects of the 1988 fire. The trail head is 3 miles east of the West Yellowstone entrance at a well-marked turnout. Along this .8-mile loop trail, you'll see a mosaic of blackened, singed, and unburned timber—charred snags and green trees side by side among boulders shattered by the heat. A testament to the regenerative effects of fire, millions of bright green saplings have emerged from the soil that surrounds the scraggly, deformed branches and piles of rock.

Park maps don't identify all the observation points and side roads in the area, so now is the time to begin forming the habit of driving off the beaten path, even when you might not know where you're going. Keep a sharp eye peeled for the poorly marked **riverside turnout** on the Madison River side of the road; it's a paved road on the north side of the highway about 6 miles from the entrance. This back road takes you along a river, removed from most traffic, and has a number of turnouts perfectly situated to look for resident swans, enjoy a picnic, or test your fly-fishing ability.

As you continue toward Madison Junction, you'll see more vivid evidence of the 1988 fire and, odds are, a herd of bison that frequents the area during summer months. As frightening as the fire was, it had its advantages: There is evidence that the 1988 fire burned hotter here because the old lodgepole pines had been infected by beetles, decimating the trees long before the fires blazed. The good news is that the fire killed the beetles and remineralized the soil. When temperatures exceeded 500°F (260°C), pine seeds were released from fire-adapted pine cones, quickening the rebirth cycle. The shaglike carpet of tiny trees emerging from the soil is evidence that the forest is recovering quickly.

The .5-mile round-trip **Harlequin Lake Trail,** located 1½ miles west of the Madison campground on the West Entrance

Road, offers an excellent, easy opportunity to explore the area. It winds through the burned forest to a small lake populated by various types of waterfowl. Despite the lake's moniker, sightings of the rare harlequin ducks are uncommon.

An alternative hike, one of the best in the area, is up the **Purple Mountain Trail,** which begins ¼ mile north of the Madison Junction on the Norris Road. This hike requires more physical exertion because it winds 6 miles (round-trip) through a burned forest to the top of a large hill, with an elevation gain of about 1,500 feet.

Madison Junction is the confluence of the Gibbon and Firehole rivers, two famous trout streams that meet to form the Madison River, one of three that join to form the Missouri. The **Madison Campground,** one of the largest and most popular in the park, is situated at the junction, with hiking trails and sites in view of the river. If you're planning a stay here, it's wise to arrive early, or you might be disappointed.

This is where you enter the northern loop toward Norris Junction, along a winding 14-mile section of road that parallels the **Gibbon River.** The river was named for Gen. John Gibbon, who explored here in 1872 but whose main, dubious claims to fame were as the cavalry leader who buried Custer's army and who chased Chief Joseph and the Nez Perce Indians from the park as they attempted to escape to Canada.

At 84-foot **Gibbon Falls,** you'll see water bursting out of the edge of a caldera in a rocky canyon, the walls of which were hidden from view for several hundred years until being exposed by the fire of 1988. There's a delightful **picnic area** just below the falls on an open plateau overlooking the Gibbon River.

Before arriving at Norris Junction, you'll discover the **Artist Paint Pot Trail ★** in Gibbon Meadows, 4½ miles south of the Norris Junction, an interesting, worthwhile, and easy .5-mile stroll that winds through a lodgepole pine forest to a gurgling mud pot at the top of a hill, passing some small geysers, hot pools, and steam vents along the way.

Across the road from the trail head is **Elk Park,** where you have a good chance of seeing a large herd of the majestic ungulates.

Norris Geyser Basin

Closest entrances and distances: 28 miles from West Yellowstone (west) entrance; 26 miles from Gardiner (north) entrance

Perhaps more than any other area in Yellowstone, this basin is living testimony to the park's unique thermal activity. It is never the same, changing from year to year as thermal activity and the ravages of wind, rain, and snow create new and different ponds and landscapes. Trees fall, slides occur, and geysers erupt. The **Norris**

Watch Your Step!

In thermal areas, the ground might be only a thin crust above boiling hot springs, and there's no way to guess where a safe path is. New hazards can bubble up overnight, and pools are acidic enough to burn through boots; so stay in designated walking areas.

Geyser Basin ★★ was named for the second superintendent of the park, the outgoing Philetus Norris, whose name graces many park roads and attractions. It is also the location of one of the park's highest concentrations of thermal features, including the most active geysers, with underground water temperatures that reach 459°F (237°C).

There are two loop trails here, both fairly level with wheelchair access, to the Porcelain Basin and the Back Basin. If you complete both of them, you'll see most of the area's interesting thermal features. If you're pressed for time, however, take the shorter **Porcelain Basin Trail**, a .8-mile round-trip that can be completed in 45 minutes. Along this boardwalk are Black Growler Steam Vent, Ledge Geyser, and the descriptively named Whale's Mouth.

The 1.5-mile **Back Basin Loop** is easily negotiable in 1 hour and passes by **Steamboat Geyser,** which has been known to produce the world's highest and most memorable eruptions. However, these 400-foot waterspouts occur infrequently, so it will take some luck to see one—the geyser erupted about once a year during the 2000s, but blew its top only twice during the preceding 12 years and not at all between 1911 and 1961. In contrast, **Echinus Geyser,** farther down the trail, erupts several times a day.

Among the many highlights of the area is the **Norris Geyser Basin Museum** (✆ 307/344-2812), a beautiful single-story stone-and-log building, the stone archway of which leads to an overlook of the Porcelain Basin. The museum houses several excellent exhibits; with luck, you'll arrive in time for a ranger-led tour. In the past, ranger programs have been scheduled three times a day; ask at a visitor center for current schedules.

Also nearby is the **Museum of the National Park Ranger** (✆ 307/344-7353), which is little more than a room full of artifacts in a small building near the Norris Campground (see below).

Both museums open in mid- to late May, weather permitting, and are open until September; hours vary by season, but you can expect the museums to be open from 9 or 10am to 5pm during the busiest times (roughly Memorial Day to Labor Day, but weather is a factor).

The **Norris Campground,** which is just slightly north of Norris Junction, is another very popular campground, so plan an early arrival or be prepared to look for an alternative site, which isn't easy during the peak season.

Norris to Mammoth Hot Springs

Closest entrances: Norris is 28 miles from the West Yellowstone (west) entrance; Mammoth Hot Springs is 5 miles from the Gardiner (north) entrance

Distance: 21 miles from Norris to Mammoth Hot Springs

From Norris Geyser Basin, it's a 21-mile drive north to Mammoth Hot Springs, past the **Twin Lakes:** beautiful, watery jewels surrounded by trees. During the early months of the park year, the water is milky green because of the runoff of ice and snow. This is an excellent place to do some bird-watching.

The stretch of road between Norris Junction and Mammoth Hot Springs presents yet another excellent opportunity to see the effects of the 1988 fire. Try to use one of the turnouts to avoid blocking the road. The large meadow, on the west side of the highway, which begins 3 miles from Norris, is popular with moose, thanks to water from bogs, marshes, and a creek. As you travel alongside **Obsidian Creek,** you'll notice the smell of sulfur in the air, olfactory evidence of thermal vents.

On the east side of the road, 4 miles from Norris, is **Roaring Mountain,** a patch of ground totally devoid of brush and plant life, covered with trees and stumps from the fire. Its bareness is attributed to the fact that, as steam vents developed here, the ground became hot and acidic, bleaching and crumbling the rock and taking the undergrowth with it. Historians say that the noise from Roaring Mountain was once so loud that it could be heard several miles away; these days, the mountain is silent.

Just 2 miles up the road is the **Beaver Lake Picnic Area,** an excellent little spot for a snack. Keep an eye out for moose.

As you wend your way a half-mile to **Obsidian Cliff,** the terrain changes quickly and dramatically, and you'll find yourself driving through a narrow valley bisected by a beautiful green stream. Obsidian Cliff is where ancient peoples of North America gathered to collect obsidian, a hard black rock that was used to make weapons and tools.

If you didn't stop at Beaver Lake, consider taking time for a short (3-min.) detour on the road to **Sheepeater Cliffs** (unless you're driving an RV or pulling a trailer), which, like most park attractions, is in a well-marked area just off the pavement. Though close to the main road, this quiet, secluded spot sits on the banks of the Gardner River, beside a cliff of columnar basalt rock that was formed by cooling lava following a volcanic eruption. This area, once inhabited by the Sheepeater Indians, is now home to yellow-bellied marmots that live in the rocks, safe from flying predators and coyotes.

As you travel the final few miles to Mammoth Hot Springs, you'll be in an area with especially interesting geologic diversity. You'll see evidence of the fire, large springs and ponds, and enormous glaciated rock terraces and cliffs.

Exiting the valley, head north onto a high plateau, where you'll find **Swan Lake,** flanked by Little Quadrant Mountain and Antler Peak to the west, and Bunsen Peak to the north.

At the northernmost edge of the Yellowstone Plateau, you'll begin a descent through **Golden Gate.** This steep, narrow stretch of road was once a stagecoach route constructed of wooden planks anchored to the mountain near a massive rock called the **Pillar of Hercules,** the largest rock in a pile that sits next to the road.

Beyond Hercules are the **Hoodoos,** an ominous looking jumble of travertine boulders on the north side of the road, which have tumbled off the mountainside above to create a pile of unusual formations.

From the 45th parallel parking area on the North Entrance Road, north of Mammoth Hot Springs, a short hike leads to the **Boiling River ★★**. When water levels are safe following peak runoff, you can take a dip during daylight hours at the confluence of a hot spring and the Gardner River. The best time to soak is just before sunset, when your muscles are sore from hiking; you'll also see a dramatic demonstration by the hordes of bats in the area. As far as facilities go, there is only a restroom with pit toilets here.

Mammoth Hot Springs

Closest entrance and distance: 5 miles from the Gardiner (north) entrance

This area might offer the best argument for getting off the roads, out of your car, and into the environment. Although it's possible to see most of the wildlife and the major thermal areas from behind car windows, your experience of the park will be multiplied tenfold through the expenditure of a small amount of energy. Most people in average shape are capable of negotiating the trails here, a significant percentage of which are level or only moderately inclined boardwalks. Even the more challenging trails frequently have rest areas where you can catch your breath and, more importantly, absorb the magnificent views.

One of Yellowstone's most unique, beautiful, and fascinating areas is the **Upper and Lower terraces ★★**. Here you can best observe how the combination of heat, water, limestone, and rock fractures has sculpted the area. This is one of the most colorful parts of the park; its tapestries of orange, pink, yellow, green, and brown, formed by masses of bacteria and algae, seem to change colors before your eyes.

The mineral-rich hot waters that flow to the surface here do so at an unusually constant rate, roughly 750,000 gallons per day, depositing more than a ton of limestone every 24 hours. Contours are constantly changing in the hot springs as formations are shaped by large quantities of flowing water, the slope of the ground, and trees and rocks that determine the direction of the flow.

On the flip side of the equation, nature has a way of playing tricks on some of her creatures: **Poison Spring** is a sinkhole on the trail, so named because carbon dioxide collects there, often killing creatures that stop for a drink.

The **Lower Terrace Interpretive Trail** is one of the best ways to see this area. The trail starts at 6,280 feet and climbs another 300 feet along rather steep grades through a bare, rocky, thermal region to a flat alpine area and observation deck at the top. A park guide says that the 1.5-mile round-trip walk to the Upper Terrace and back normally takes 2 hours, but it can be done in less time.

Liberty Cap is a 37-foot-tall dome at the entrance to the interpretive trail. Once the site of a percolating hot spring, the domed cap deposit is the result of 2,500 years of continuous gushing. The Hayden Expedition named it as such because of its resemblance to hats worn by Colonial patriots during the French Revolution.

After passing **Palette Spring,** where bacteria create a collage of browns, greens, and oranges, you're on your way to **Cleopatra and Minerva terraces.** Minerva is a favorite of visitors because of its bright colors and travertine formations, the product of limestone deposits. In nature's way, these attractions occasionally become unruly and spray water and mineral deposits large enough to bury the boardwalk.

The hike up the last 150 feet to the Upper Terrace Loop Drive is slightly steeper, although there are benches at frequent intervals. From here you can see all the terraces and several springs— **Canary Spring** and **New Blue Spring** being the most distinctive—and the red-roof buildings of **Fort Yellowstone,** now the park headquarters, which was under command of the U.S. Army from 1886 to 1918 when the army controlled the park.

Near Fort Yellowstone is the large **Albright Visitor Center** (*C* 307/344-2263), which has more visitor information and publications than other centers, along with significant exhibits telling the story of the park from prehistory through the creation of the U.S. National Park Service. It's open daily from 8am to 7pm during peak season. Enclosed in floor-to-ceiling glass cases are uniforms, furniture, side arms, and memorabilia that reflect the park's varied human history. There are excellent photography exhibits, with

Mammoth Hot Springs

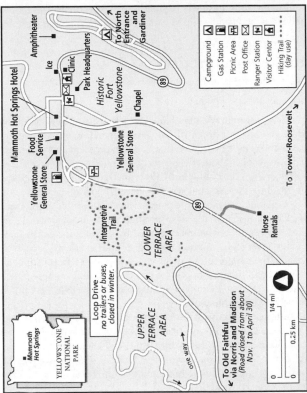

Amphitheater

Ice

Mammoth Hot Springs Hotel

Clinic

Park Headquarters

Food Service

Yellowstone General Store

To North Entrance and Gardiner

Historic Fort Yellowstone

Chapel

Yellowstone General Store

Campground
Gas Station
Picnic Area
Post Office
Ranger Station
Visitor Center
Hiking Trail (day use)

To Tower-Roosevelt

Interpretive Trail

Loop Drive - no trailers or buses, closed in winter.

LOWER TERRACE AREA

Horse Rentals

UPPER TERRACE AREA

one way

To Old Faithful via Norris and Madison (Road closed from about Nov. 1 to April 30)

Mammoth Hot Springs

YELLOWSTONE NATIONAL PARK

1/4 mi
0.25 km
0
0

most of the photographs taken by the first park photographer, William Henry Jackson. A second level is filled with displays of the wildlife that inhabits the park, including wolves, mountain lions, waterfowl, and other birds. Films on the park's origin and the art that it has inspired are shown throughout the day.

You can continue walking along **Upper Terrace Loop Drive,** which is also accessible by car. The Upper Terrace has its own unique attractions, including **New Highland Terrace,** which is a forest of tree skeletons engulfed by travertine, and **Angel Terrace,** known for its pure white formations.

Just steps from the lower terrace is the trail head for the **Beaver Ponds Loop Trail,** a 5-mile jaunt through fir and spruce, then sagebrush and aspen, along a trail that follows **Clematis Gulch.**

The ponds are about 2.5 miles from the trail head, after a moderate elevation gain, where the resident toothy engineers are most active early in the morning and at night. The area is also a hangout for elk and bears, and can be closed early in the summer season.

Mammoth Hot Springs to Tower Junction

Closest entrance: Mammoth is 5 miles from the Gardiner (north) entrance

Distance: 18 miles from Mammoth to Tower

Heading east from Mammoth on Tower Road, an 8-mile drive will bring you to the **Forces of the Northern Range Trail,** a flat, easy stroll along a boardwalk that offers an excellent opportunity to educate yourself about the effects of fire on the environment.

Two miles later is **Blacktail Plateau Drive,** a 7-mile, one-way dirt road that offers great wildlife-viewing opportunities and a bit more solitude. You'll be more or less following the route of the Bannock Trail, made by the long-vanished Indian inhabitants of the area. For centuries, the trail was used by Bannock Indians as they trekked from Idaho to bison-hunting grounds in eastern Montana; scars in the land made by their travois (luggage racks constructed of twin poles tied to a horse) are still evident along the trail. You'll emerge back onto Mammoth-Tower Road, about a mile west of the turnoff to the Petrified Tree.

Turn right onto this half-mile-long road to the **Petrified Tree,** the remains of a redwood that was burned by volcanic ash more than 50 million years ago, while it was still standing. If you have the time and energy, park your car at the base of the road after you turn off Mammoth-Tower Road and hike up, because the parking area is often congested.

Tower-Roosevelt

Closest entrances and distances: 23 miles from the Gardiner (north) entrance; 29 miles from the Cooke City (northeast) entrance

Just beyond the Petrified Tree, you'll come to **Tower-Roosevelt,** the most relaxed of the park's villages and a great place to take a break from the more crowded attractions. Even if you aren't going to stay, you might want to make a quick stop at the **Tower Soldier Station,** now the ranger residence at Tower Junction, one of three surviving outposts from the era of U.S. Cavalry management of the park. Also here is **Roosevelt Lodge,** a rustic building that commemorates President Theodore Roosevelt's camping excursion to this area of the park, in 1903. It now serves as a dining hall, bar, and registration area for visitors staying at nearby frontier cabins. You can get into the cowboy spirit by taking a guided trail ride, a stagecoach ride, or a wagon ride. A more adventurous alternative to the rather rustic dining-room atmosphere at Roosevelt Lodge is the lodge's Old West cookout, to which you will arrive by either horseback or wagon for a hearty meal (see "Where to Eat in Yellowstone," in chapter 7, for more details). There's a range of other services in this spot, including a Yellowstone Park General Store, if you need to buy provisions, and a gas station.

At **Specimen Ridge,** 2½ miles east of the Tower Junction on the Northeast Entrance Road, you'll find a ridge that entombs one of the world's most extensive fossil forests. Between 45 million and 50 million years ago, the mature forest that stood here was engulfed by deep volcanic ash some 27 times; subsequent erosion has exposed more than 100 different fossilized species in an area that spans 40 square miles.

A Detour: The Chief Joseph Highway

Closest entrance and distance: 29 miles to the Cooke City (northeast) entrance

Because all the major attractions in Yellowstone are located on the loop roads, some of the park's most beautiful and secluded areas go unnoticed by travelers. If you have an additional day or two, I suggest that you head for the eastern entrances on another loop tour. From Tower Junction, go east to Cooke City and then continue to Cody; or, from Fishing Bridge, head across Sylvan Pass to Cody. If you hurry, you can complete the trip in a day, although you'll miss the Cody rodeo.

From **Tower Junction,** you'll traverse the **Lamar Valley ★★★**, one of the prettiest and wildest areas of the park. This area was covered with a thick crust of ice during the last ice age, which began 25,000 years ago and ended 10,000 years later, leaving a valley shaped by melting glaciers that is dotted by glacial ponds and strewn with boulders dropped by moving ice. Before the ice came a volcanic eruption, 50 million years ago. Volcanic ash from the explosion engulfed the mature forest that once stood here, the results of which you can view at the Specimen Ridge wayside (see above). In addition to the region's natural beauty, it's the new home of packs of transplanted gray wolves and offers excellent fishing in the Lamar River and its numerous tributaries.

Cooke City might best be described as an outpost that provides essential services—including restaurants, motels, gas stations, and grocery stores—but it's a long way from being as developed as its sister gateway cities. See chapter 8, "Gateways to Yellowstone & Grand Teton National Parks," for more information about lodging and dining here.

Fourteen miles outside of Cooke City, take the **Chief Joseph Scenic Highway ★★** (Wyo. 296), which connects to Wyo. 120

into Cody. This highway, also called the Sunlight Basin Road, offers great opportunities for viewing wildlife.

Cody is the quintessential Western town. Folks are friendly, accommodations are well turned out and moderately priced, and there are enough tourist attractions—the nightly rodeo and the impressive Buffalo Bill Historical Center are the most famous—to make it worth the detour. See chapter 8 for more details.

From Cody, return to Yellowstone's east entrance on U.S. Hwy. 12/16/20. After you reenter the park, you'll cross 8,541-foot **Sylvan Pass** and travel through the Absaroka Range, estimated to be 50 million years old. Driving along the shores of Yellowstone Lake, you'll pass **Mary Bay,** yet another crater created by a volcanic explosion. You'll return to the main area of the park at **Fishing Bridge Junction,** where you can rejoin the Grand Loop Road and continue your tour.

From Tower Junction to the Grand Canyon of the Yellowstone

Closest entrances: 23 miles from the Gardiner (north) entrance; 29 miles from the Cooke City (northeast) entrance

Distance: 19 miles from Tower Junction to Canyon Village

A few minutes' drive from the Tower Junction area is the **Calcite Springs Overlook.** A short loop along a boardwalk leads to the overlook at the rim of the **Narrows,** the narrowest part of this northern section of the Grand Canyon. You can hear the river raging through the canyon 500 feet below and look across at the canyon walls comprising rock spires and bands of columnar basalt. Just downstream is the most prominent feature in this part of the canyon, **Bumpus Butte.** More noticeable than majestic, it is a box-shape outcropping between Rainy Lake and Calcite Springs.

A few steps from the general store, you'll find a trail to the 132-foot **Tower Fall** and an overlook that is typically crowded with sightseers. You'll have a more interesting and photogenic view if you continue past the overlook on the fairly steep path to the base of the falls where Tower Creek flows into the Yellowstone River.

Continuing south, you'll travel through the **Washburn Range,** an area in which the 1988 fires burned especially hot and fast. The terrain changes dramatically as the road climbs along some major hills toward **Mount Washburn.** The kinkiest section of this road is the aptly named **Mae West Curve.** Just before the curve, one stretch of this highway overlooks stands of aspen trees, a favorite summer haunt of the grizzly bear. Other sections are covered with sagebrush. During the fire, the sagebrush was incinerated, but roots were uninjured; so it now grows vigorously in soil that is fertilized by ash leached into the earth by snowmelt, another example of nature's artful ways.

There are trail heads for the **Mount Washburn Trail ★★★**, one of my favorites, on each side of the summit. One is at the end of Old Chittenden Road (the turnoff to this road from the Tower-Canyon Rd. is well marked); the other begins at Dunraven Pass, about a mile farther down the highway. Both hikes take 2 to 3 hours to complete, but because Old Chittenden has the larger parking lot, it might be more crowded; it's also more scenic (although steeper).

As you approach **Dunraven Pass** (8,859 ft.), keep your eyes peeled for the shy bighorn sheep; this is one of its prime habitats.

One mile farther south is the **Washburn Hot Springs Overlook,** which offers sweeping views of the canyon. On a clear day, you can see 50 to 100 miles south, beyond Yellowstone Lake. Get out of the car and take a look.

Canyon Village

Closest entrances and distances: 40 miles from West Yellowstone (west) entrance; 38 miles from Gardiner (north) entrance; 48 miles from the Cooke City (northeast) entrance; 43 miles from the east entrance

You're in for another eyeful when you reach the **Grand Canyon of the Yellowstone ★★★**, a vivid example of nature having unleashed its destructive power to create indescribable beauty.

The canyon has its geologic origins in the same volcanic eruptions that created Yellowstone Lake. As lava flows created lakes that overflowed their banks, walls of granitelike rock remained while softer minerals eroded. This process carved the canyon, which was subsequently blocked by glaciers. Eventually, when the ice melted, floods recarved each end of the canyon, deepening it and removing sand and gravel.

The result: a 24-mile crevasse that at some points is 1,200 feet deep and 4,000 feet wide, and two waterfalls, one of which is twice as high as Niagara Falls. Even the most reluctant hiker will be rewarded with sites as colorful as those seen in "the other canyon." Compared to the Grand Canyon of Arizona, Yellowstone's Grand Canyon is relatively narrow; it's equally impressive, though, because of the steepness of the cliffs, which descend hundreds of feet to the bottom of a gorge where the Yellowstone River flows. It's also equally colorful, with displays of white, orange, red, yellow, and gold. And you won't find thermal vents in Arizona, but you will find them here, a constant reminder of ongoing underground activity.

You should plan on encountering crowds when you reach **Canyon Village,** where you'll find many necessary services: a post office, a trio of restaurants, and two stores stocked with groceries, gear, and souvenirs. Accommodations are in cabins and a large campground. Concessionaires offer horseback trail rides from a nearby stable and other guided tours. See chapter 7 for more details about lodging and dining in the area.

The snazzy **Canyon Visitor Education Center** (© **307/344-2550**) is the place to go for books and excellent exhibits on the park's geology, with a focus on the underlying supervolcano and receding glaciers. It's also staffed with friendly rangers used to dealing with the crowds here.

An auto tour of the canyon follows **North Rim Drive,** a two-lane, one-way road that begins in Canyon Village, to your first stop, Inspiration Point. On the way, you'll pass a 500-ton **glacial boulder** that was deposited by melting ice more than 10,000 years ago. Geologists estimate that ice floes carried this chunk of rock 40 miles to its present location.

At **Inspiration Point,** a moderately strenuous descent down 57 steps takes you to an overlook with views of the Lower Falls and canyon. (At 8,000 ft., the hike will cause your pulse rate and blood pressure to rise, so it's wise to pause for a few extra minutes before making the return.) Evidence of recent earthquake activity is beneath the soles of your shoes. The viewing platform once extended 100 feet farther over the canyon; on June 30, 1975, it was shattered by an earthquake and tumbled into the canyon. You'll pass several other viewpoints along North Rim Drive before you reconnect with the main Canyon Village–Yellowstone Lake Road, which will take you down to South Rim Drive.

Along the way, you can also stop at **Grand View** overlook, where the river flows some 750 feet below the observation platform. During summer months, Grand View is an excellent spot from which to view ospreys, which normally nest in this area and can be seen riding the thermals. **Lookout Point** provides a better view of the Lower Falls; however, the observation deck is at the end of a steep, 150-foot trail. Hiking down is easy; the return trip is not recommended for those with heart or lung problems.

For the adventurous, an alternative to driving from one overlook to another is to negotiate the **North Rim Trail** ★★, which is 2.3 miles long, beginning at Inspiration Point. This trail ends at the Upper Falls parking area, where the Upper Falls Trail begins; it's another .8 miles to the bridge that connects the North and South rims. Unfortunately, the North Rim Trail is not a loop, so if you take the hike, you'll have to backtrack to get your car at Inspiration Point. The footpath brings you closer to what you want to see, and you won't be fighting for elbowroom like you will at the overlooks that are a stone's throw from the road.

Canvon Village

Whether you drive or walk, you should go down to the **Upper Falls View,** where a .3-mile trail leads down from the parking lot to the **Brink of the Upper Falls,** an overlook within splashing distance of the rushing river and the waterfall. At this point you won't just hear the power of the river; you'll feel it as it begins its course down the canyon.

The **South Rim Road ★** leads to several overlooks and better views of the Lower Falls. The most impressive vantage point is from the bottom of **Uncle Tom's Trail ★★**, a steep 500-foot steel trail to an unbeatable vantage point that begins at the first South Rim parking lot. The trail is named after Tom Richardson, an adventuresome turn-of-the-20th-century guide who led travelers to the base of the falls with ropes and ladders; these days, the trip is down 328 steps of a steel staircase attached to the canyon wall and paved inclines. The trail is rather steep but can be negotiated in about an hour, although it will be challenging for the neophyte hiker.

South Rim Road continues to a second, lower parking lot and a trail that leads to **Artist Point ★★**. The view here is astounding—one of my favorites in the park—and is best in the early morning.

It was at this point that Thomas Moran was inspired to create his famous painting of the falls, reproductions of which are seen in galleries and print shops throughout the world. This is one of the most photogenic (and most photographed) tableaux in the country—almost every visitor snaps a shot or two.

The **South Rim Trail** is an alternative to viewing the Lower Falls and the canyon from wooden observation decks. From the first South Rim parking lot, which is just beyond the South Rim Drive Bridge, follow trail markers to the partially paved trail and then trek 1.8 miles to Artist Point. (The trail follows the canyon for 3.3 miles beyond Artist Point, to **Point Sublime,** where you must double back along the same route.) You'll have several different views of the falls, and you can always hop off to access Uncle Tom's Trail, Artist Point, or **Lily Pad Lake.** Neither Point Sublime nor Lily Pad Lake is accessible by car.

Canyon Village to Fishing Bridge

Closest entrances: 27 miles to the east entrance; 43 miles to the south entrance

Distance: 16 miles from Canyon Village to Fishing Bridge

The road from Canyon Village winds through the **Hayden Valley,** which is a vast expanse of beautiful green meadows accented by brown cuts where the soil is eroded along the banks of the Yellowstone River. Imagine this: Ten thousand years before Ferdinand V. Hayden led the survey expedition of 1871, the entire Hayden Valley, except for the tallest peaks that surround it, was covered with a 4,000-foot-thick layer of ice. The valley is now a wide, sprawling area where bison play and trumpeter swans, white pelicans, and Canada geese float along the river. This is also a prime habitat for the grizzly, so during early-spring months, pay close attention to binocular-toting visitors grouped beside the road.

Nature is at her acidic best at the **Sulphur Caldron** and **Mud Volcano** areas, 12 miles south of the Canyon Junction, which were described by writer Edwin Stanley as "unsightly, unsavory, and villainous." You'll certainly want to explore this area; there's nothing quite like the sound of burping mud pots.

Vapors from Sulphur Caldron (on the east side of the road) rotted the overlook's foundation, and it collapsed in 1984. The acidity of the caldron is twice that of battery acid; if you stepped in one of these pools, your shoes would be reduced to ashes.

At **Dragon's Mouth Spring,** escaping steam and sulfurous gases propel turbid water from an underground cavern to the surface, where it colors the earth with shades of orange and green. The belching of steam from the cavern and the associated sound, which is caused by the splash of 180°F (82°C) water against the wall in a subterranean cavern, creates an aura of fantasy and medieval times; hence the name of the spring. Nearby **Mud Volcano** is a murky mud spring, the product of vigorous activity caused by escaping sulfurous gases and steam. The youngest feature in the area is **Black Dragon's Caldron,** which is often referred to as "the demon of the backwoods"—and rightly so. The caldron emerged from its subterranean birthplace for the first time in 1948, when it announced its presence by blowing a hole in the landscape, scattering mature trees hundreds of feet in all directions. Since then, continual seismic activity and intermittent earthquakes in the area have caused it to move several hundred feet south of its original position.

Le Hardy Rapids, a shaded area 2 miles farther south, is an ideal spot for a stroll along the river. In the early summer, this is a prime route for cutthroat trout on their way to spawn. It is also popular with the shy harlequin ducks and bald eagles. The scary side of the equation is that this innocent-looking stretch of water flows across a fault in the earth. Some geologists believe that this will be the spot where the next major eruption will occur and that it will be as large as, or larger than, the eruption that created the Yellowstone caldera 600,000 years ago. Their guess: The next explosion will likely occur in the next 100,000 years. In the short term, however, a sluggish lava flow is much more likely than a catastrophic eruption.

The road across the Yellowstone River at **Fishing Bridge** was once the only eastern exit in the park, the route leading over Sylvan Pass to Cody, Wyoming. The bridge, which was built in 1937, spans the Yellowstone River as it exits Yellowstone Lake and is another prime spawning area for native trout. As a consequence, it became so popular that as many as 50,000 fishermen would beat the water into froth every year. To protect the trout, fishing was banned in the 1960s, but the bridge remains a great vantage point from which to watch them as they head upstream. It's also an excellent spot for observing the white pelicans and Canada geese that inhabit the area.

The **Fishing Bridge Visitor Center** (☎ **307/344-2450**), which is open daily from 8am to 7pm, has an excellent wildlife display. The nearby Yellowstone Park General Store sells provisions as well as liquor. The **Fishing Bridge RV Park** (p. 135) is restricted to hard-sided vehicles only because this is a prime grizzly habitat. You'll find an excellent hiking trail, **Elephant Back Loop Trail ★**, leading off the short strip of highway between Fishing Village and the Lake Village area. The 2-mile loop leads to an overlook with panoramic views of Yellowstone Lake and its islands, the Absaroka Range, and Pelican Valley to the east. Instead of taking the entire loop around to the overlook, you can shorten the hike a half-mile by taking the left fork approximately 1 mile from the trail head and doubling back after you get to the overlook.

Yellowstone Lake Area

Closest entrances: Approximately 27 miles from Fishing Bridge to the east entrance; approximately 43 miles from Fishing Bridge to the south entrance

Distances: The lakefront from Fishing Bridge to the West Thumb Geyser Basin is 21 miles

As if the park didn't have enough record-setting attractions, at 7,773 feet, **Yellowstone Lake ★★** is North America's largest high-altitude lake. It is 20 miles long and 14 miles wide, contains 110 miles of shoreline, has depths ranging to 390 feet, and is *very* cold. Because the surface freezes by December, and remains crusted until late May, the temperature at the bottom stays at 39°F (4°C) year-round, and the surface temperature isn't a lot warmer. Considering its size relative to the entire volcanic caldera, the lake is considered by many to be just a puddle. At one point in its history, the entire area was filled with ice, most of which has since melted, so the lake relies on 124 tributaries, including the Yellowstone River, to maintain its present level.

The lake exhibits its multifaceted personality every day, which ranges on an emotional scale from a placid, mirrorlike surface to a seething tantrum of 3- to 4-foot waves. Boaters should be especially cautious because of the number of boat-related fatalities resulting from hypothermia. Compelling evidence of the ongoing changes occurring in the park as a consequence of subsurface thermal activity is the fact that the lake bottom is rising and tilting about 1 inch per year, a veritable sprinter's pace in geologic time. Trees on the south end of the lake drown as new beaches come into being on the north end, and existing beaches are expanding.

The fact that the lake has the largest population of native cutthroat trout in North America makes this an ideal fishing spot in summer. (See p. 85 for information on fishing regulations.) The lake is also an ornithologist's paradise; the skies are filled with ospreys, bald eagles, white pelicans, and cormorants. On the shore, moose and grizzly bears are especially prevalent during the trout runs in spring.

Lake Village, on the northwest shore of the lake, offers a wide range of amenities, the most prominent of which is the regal facade of the Victorian **Lake Yellowstone Hotel.** You'll find a fine-dining restaurant, as well as a little deli and an adjacent general store. Lodging is available in the hotel, its motel-style annex, and the surrounding yellow cabins, and at **Lake Lodge** in modestly priced, frontier-style cabins. See p. 130 for more details.

Yellowstone Lake: Fishing Bridge to Bridge Bay

Just south of Lake Village is the **Bridge Bay Marina,** the center of the park's water activities. Here you can arrange for guided fishing trips or small boat rentals, or learn more about the lake during an informative and entertaining 1-hour narrated boat tour. The views are magnificent, and the skipper shares fascinating facts about the area's history. The marina is usually open from mid-June to mid-September.

Campers will find a large campground here with sites for RVs and tents. Trees surround the campground area, which has been cleared, so campsites here have very little privacy.

Although the **Natural Bridge,** near Bridge Bay, is well marked on park maps, it's one of the park's best-kept secrets, and you might end up enjoying it by yourself. The mile-long path down to the bridge, a geologic masterpiece consisting of a massive rock arch, soaring 51 feet overhead and spanning Bridge Creek, is an excellent bike route.

Looking for a picnic area? Keep a sharp eye out for an inconspicuous paved road on the lake side of the highway, 13 miles west of Fishing Bridge, which leads down to a secluded spot near **Pumice Point.**

The **West Thumb** area, along the western shoreline, is the deepest part of Yellowstone Lake. Because of its suspiciously craterlike contours, many scientists speculate that this 4-mile-wide, 6-mile-long, water-filled crater came to be when a secondary caldera within the primary Yellowstone caldera burped ferociously some 125,000 years ago.

The **West Thumb Geyser Basin ★★** is notable for a unique series of geysers. Some are situated right on the shores, some overlook the lake, and some can be seen *beneath* the lake surface. Three of the shoreline geysers, the most famous of which is **Fishing Cone,** are occasionally marooned offshore when the lake level rises. (Fishing Cone was named for the park's early fishermen who used it as a combination casting spot/kitchen by swinging their catch from the lake into the geyser to cook it, hook still in mouth.) Fortunately, a half-mile of boardwalks crisscrosses the area, so it's easy to negotiate.

Near the center of an area that is totally surrounded by healthy trees is a tree graveyard. These pale, limbless trees were killed when thermal activity caused hot water to move toward them. When their roots absorbed the hot water, the trees were cooked from the inside out.

Details about the area, books, and maps are available at the **West Thumb Information Station,** housed in a log structure that functioned as the original West Thumb Ranger Station. The center is open daily 9am to 5pm from late May to September.

As you depart the West Thumb area, you are presented with two choices: either to head south, toward Grand Teton National Park, or to head west, across the **Continental Divide** at Craig Pass, en route to Old Faithful.

Grant Village to the South Entrance

Closest entrance and distance: 22 miles from Grant Village to the south entrance

Located on the southern shore of Yellowstone Lake, Grant Village offers dramatic views of summer squalls and one of Yellowstone's most inspiring sunrises. Perhaps the primary appeal of the village, the southernmost outpost in the park, is its location

Yellowstone Lake: West Thumb to Grant Village

Map legend:
- ▲ Campground
- Gas Station
- ⓘ Information
- ⊼ Picnic Area
- ⊠ Post Office
- Ranger Station
- Visitor Center

Map labels: Duck Lake; To Lake Village; WEST THUMB; Geyser Basin; To Old Faithful; S. Entrance Rd.; Yellowstone Lake; YELLOWSTONE NATIONAL PARK; area of detail; 191; GRANT VILLAGE; Amphitheater; Grant Village Dining Room; Showers/Laundry; Grant Village Lodging Complex; Yellowstone General Store; To South Entrance

Map scale: 0 — 1/2 mi; 0 — 0.5 km

as a jumping-off place for travelers leaving for Grand Teton National Park, or as a place for them to spend their first night in Yellowstone. Named for President Ulysses S. Grant, the village was completed in 1984. It's the newest of Yellowstone's villages and home to the park's most modern facilities.

The **Grant Visitor Center** (© **307/242-2650**) has information, publications, a slide program, and a fascinating exhibit examining the effects of fire in Yellowstone. A video about the fires of 1988 is shown daily.

The **Grant Village Dining Room** is a good restaurant with views of the lake. Reservations are recommended. Nearby is **Lake House,** which serves less-expensive pizza and pasta dinners in an informal dining room right on the shoreline. Guest accommodations are in a motel-style building. Other services include a general store that serves light meals and fast food, a modest gift shop, and a service station. For more details about dining and accommodations in the area, see chapter 7. Given the choice, I'd head north to a different destination or continue south to Grand Teton.

In contrast to this admittedly forgettable village is the beautiful 22-mile drive to **Grand Teton National Park** along high mountain passes and **Lewis Lake.** The lake, which is 108 feet deep, is the third largest in the park and is connected to Shoshone Lake by a narrow channel populated by German brown trout. After the lake loses its winter coat of ice, it is a popular spot for early-season anglers who are unable to fish streams that are clouded by the spring runoff.

Beyond the lake, the road follows the Lewis River through an alpine area and along the **Pitchstone Plateau,** a pile of lava more than 2,000 feet high and 20 miles wide that was created some 500,000 years ago. A high gorge overlooking the river provides views that are different from, but equally spectacular as, those in other sections of the park. At its highest point, the road winds across a plateau that is accented with forests of dead, limbless lodgepole pine—remnants of the 1988 fire.

West Thumb to Old Faithful

Closest entrance: 22 miles from West Thumb to the south entrance

Distance: 17 miles from West Thumb Geyser Basin to Old Faithful area

Craig Pass is an important geologic landmark because it is here, at the Continental Divide in the Yellowstone–Grand Teton area, that the headwaters of two major rivers are formed: one emptying into the Pacific Ocean, the other into the Gulf of Mexico. The Snake River winds from Grand Teton through Idaho to meet the Columbia River in Oregon and then drains into the Pacific Ocean at Astoria, Oregon. The Yellowstone River, which begins south of Yellowstone National Park, drains into the Missouri River, which drains into the Mississippi, which empties into the Gulf of Mexico.

An interesting phenomenon takes place on the Old Faithful route at **Isa Lake** atop Craig Pass. Unlike most lakes and streams, it has both eastern and western drainages and ends up in both the Pacific Ocean and the Gulf of Mexico. Amazingly, as a consequence of a gyroscopic maneuver, the outlet on the *east* curves *west* and drains to the Pacific, and the outlet on the *west* curves *east* and drains to the gulf.

Before you reach the Old Faithful geyser area, two additional detours are recommended. About 3 miles south of Old Faithful is an overlook at the spectacular **Kepler Cascades,** a 150-foot stair-step waterfall on the Firehole River. Near that parking lot is the trail head for the second detour, the 4.5-mile round-trip **Lonestar Geyser Trail ★★**. The geyser erupts every 3 hours, sending steaming water 30 to 50 feet from its 12-foot cone. The trail, which gently winds along the Firehole River through pastoral meadows and a forest, is a must-do; hiking, biking, and cross-country skiing are all popular. Even when others are on the trail, the area exudes a solitary air because it is possible to abandon the trail, follow the meandering stream, and find flat, open places to relax or picnic.

Old Faithful Area

Closest entrance and distances: 16 miles from Old Faithful geyser to Madison Junction, then another 14 miles to West Yellowstone (west) entrance

Despite the overwhelming sight of the geysers and steam vents that populate the Old Faithful area, I suggest that you resist the temptation to explore until you've stopped at the new-in-2010, $27 million **Old Faithful Visitor Education Center** (*C* 307/344-2751) with exhibits focused on the park's geothermal underbelly. You'll also want to check in here for the estimated times of geyser eruptions, and plan your schedule accordingly.

The Yellowstone Association's guides for **Old Faithful** and the **Fountain Paint Pots** include complete maps and explanations of the 150 geysers and many hot springs in the area, which happen to constitute a quarter of the world's total. Priced at 50¢, the guides are a bargain.

The number and variety of accommodations here are greater than at any other park center. The **Old Faithful Inn** is said to be the largest log structure in the world, consisting of seven stories underneath an 80-foot ceiling. The inn was finished in 1904 and is a National Historic Landmark. There are two other accommodations in this bustling center of activity: **Old Faithful Lodge** (p. 132), with rustic frontier cabins for rent, and **Old Faithful Snow Lodge** (p. 133), which was rebuilt in 1998 and has garnered awards for its rustic, environmentally friendly design.

Several dining choices are available, the nicest of which is the upscale dining room in the inn, where three meals are served daily; the requisite deli is situated off the lobby. Another good eatery is situated in Snow Lodge, as is a fast-food restaurant; a cafeteria with food to satisfy a variety of palates and an ice-cream stand are in the lodge, as is a large gift shop. Nearby are a gas station, an auto repair shop, a post office, a medical clinic, and a Yellowstone Park General Store, with various provisions and souvenirs. For more information about dining and lodging in the area, see chapter 7.

The Old Faithful area is generally divided into four sections: **Upper Geyser Basin,** which includes Geyser Hill; **Black Sand Basin; Biscuit Basin;** and **Midway Geyser Basin.** Paved trails and roads connect all of these areas. If time allows, go on a hike here; it's fairly level, and distances are relatively short. Between the

Old Faithful area and Madison Junction, you'll also find the justifiably famous **Lower Geyser Basin,** including Fountain Paint Pot and the trails surrounding it. You can see some of these geysers on Firehole Lake Drive.

Although **Old Faithful ★★★** is not the largest geyser in the park, and seems less inclined these days to be as faithful as it once was, its image has been on everything from postage stamps to whiskey bottles. It acquired its name when the Washburn Expedition of 1870 observed its predictable pattern of eruptions. Seismic activity has wrought changes in the geyser's habits, but it's still the most predictable geyser on the planet, erupting with an average interval of 92 minutes, although it can vary about 30 minutes in either direction. A typical eruption lasts 1½ to 5 minutes, during which roughly 4,000 to 8,000 gallons of water bursts skyward to heights up to 180 feet. For the best views and photo ops of the eruption in the boardwalk area, plan on arriving at least 15 minutes before the scheduled show, to ensure a front-row spot. Call *©* **307/344-2751** and press **"1"** for continually updated eruption forecasts.

An alternative to a seat on the crowded boardwalk is a stroll from the Old Faithful geyser up the **Observation Point Trail ★★** to an observation area that provides better views of the entire geyser basin. The path up to the observation point is approximately .5 mile, and the elevation gain is only 200 feet, so it's an easy 15-minute hike. The view of the eruption of the geyser is more spectacular from here, and the crowds are less obtrusive; watch out for bison and give them a wide berth.

From the vantage point of the Observation Point Trail, you'll have a different perspective of the entire **Upper Geyser Basin;** it's possible to see most of the major geysers as well as inaccessible steam vents in the middle of wooded areas. On clear, sunny days, sunbeams highlight the colors of the ponds and geysers in the valleys below. Interested in continuing your hike? From the top of the boardwalk, continue to the **Solitary Geyser** on a loop that leads back to the inn, adding only 1 mile to the trip on a mostly downhill trail.

Accessible by walkways from Old Faithful Village, the **Upper Geyser Basin Loop** is referred to as Geyser Hill on some maps. The 1.3-mile loop trail winds among several thermal attractions. **Anemone Geyser** might offer the best display of the various stages of a typical eruption as the pool fills and overflows, after which bubbles rising to the surface begin throwing water in 10-foot eruptions, a cycle that is repeated every 7 to 10 minutes.

Old Faithful Area

The **Lion Group** consists of four geysers that are interconnected beneath the surface. The eruptions of the **Lion Geyser,** the largest of the quartet, are usually preceded by gushes of steam and a deep roaring sound, from which it derives its name. **Doublet Pool** is especially popular with photographers who are attracted by a complex series of ledges and deep blue waters. Farther along the trail is **Giantess Geyser,** known for its violent eruptions, which cause the surrounding area to shake and quake as underground steam explodes before reaching the surface, where it can burst to heights of 200 feet. It erupts infrequently, at unscheduled intervals, so you should check with rangers to see if it's active.

Two other stars of the show in the Upper Geyser Basin are **Castle Geyser ★★** and **Grand Geyser ★★**. Castle Geyser, which has the largest cone of any geyser in the park, currently erupts for 20 minutes every 10 to 12 hours, after which a noisy steam phase could continue for half an hour. Grand Geyser, the tallest predictable geyser in the world, usually erupts every 7 to 15 hours, with powerful bursts producing streams of water that can reach 200 feet in height.

Impressions

We beheld one of the grandest displays of the kind we had ever beheld—a perfect geyser—an immediate volume of clear, hot water projected into the air one-hundred and fifty vertical feet, attended with dense volumes of steam rising upward for many hundred feet, and floating away in clouds. . . .
—Edwin Stanley, from *Rambles in Wonderland*, 1878

The **Riverside Geyser ★★** is situated on the bank of the Firehole River, near **Morning Glory Pool.** One of the most picturesque geysers in the park, its 75-foot column of water creates an arch over the river two to three times daily. **Morning Glory Pool** was named in the 1880s for its likeness to its namesake flower, but it has since lost some of its beauty. Vandals have tossed so much debris into its core over the years that it now suffers from poor circulation and reduced temperatures, which are causing unsightly brown and green bacteria to grow on its surface.

The **Black Sand Basin** is a cluster of especially colorful hot springs and geysers located 1 mile north of Old Faithful. It is interesting primarily because of its black sand, a derivative of obsidian. The colors of **Emerald Pool** algae—blues, greens, yellows, and oranges—are an excellent example of the effects of water temperature and sunlight on what are actually unexpected living organisms. **Biscuit Basin,** located 2 miles farther up the road, was named for biscuitlike deposits that surrounded colorful **Sapphire Pool** until a 1959 earthquake caused the pool to erupt, sending them skyward. Both the Black Sand Basin and the Biscuit Basin are easily viewed from flat boardwalks.

The **Midway Geyser Basin** extends for about 1 mile along the Firehole River. The major attractions here are the **Excelsior Geyser,** the third-largest geyser in the world and once the park's most powerful, and the well-known **Grand Prismatic Spring,** the largest hot spring in Yellowstone and the second largest in the world. A boardwalk leads to Excelsior, which, in the 1880s, erupted mightily, creating a 300-foot-wide crater in the process. Just beyond is Grand Prismatic Spring. Those colorful bands of yellow, red, and green are thermal algae.

Old Faithful to Madison Junction

Closest entrances: 30 miles from the Old Faithful area to the West Yellowstone (west) entrance; 39 miles to the south entrance

Distance: 16 miles from the Old Faithful area to Madison

Know Your Bacteria

Even the most casual visitor can do some scientific sleuthing at the **Fountain Paint Pots** ★, learning to identify water temperature by observing the colors in the pots. The colors result from different types of bacteria that survive at specific water temperatures. Some are yellow until temperatures reach 161°F (72°C), above which the yellow bacteria cannot live. As temperatures approach boiling—199°F (93°C) at this elevation—pinks begin to appear.

Believe it or not, there are other superb geysers and hot springs on **Firehole Lake Drive,** all viewable without leaving your vehicle. The turnoff for Firehole Lake Drive is about 8 miles north of the Old Faithful area. There are three geysers of particular interest on this road. The largest is **Great Fountain Geyser,** which erupts every 8 to 12 hours, typically spouting water some 100 feet into the air for periods of 45 to 60 minutes. Lucky visitors might even see the occasional "superburst" that reaches heights of 200 feet or more.

It is estimated that **White Dome Geyser** has been erupting for hundreds of years. Unfortunately, the age and height of this massive cone are not matched by spectacular eruptions. The vent on top of the cone has been nearly sealed with deposits of geyserite, so eruptions now reach only 30 feet. However, the sight of the cone itself is worth a trip down this road.

Farther on, **Pink Cone Geyser** couldn't be closer to the road, the builders of which cut into the geyser's mound during construction.

About a quarter-mile north of where Firehole Lake Drive rejoins the Grand Loop Road is the **Fountain Paint Pots** ★ area. This is a popular spot, so you might be forced to wait for a parking place. Although it's not large or spectacular, it's one of the most interesting areas in the park. All the various types of thermal activity are on display here, so as you stroll along the easy, .5-mile boardwalk, you'll be in an area that might have six geysers popping their lids at the same time. Though less impressive than other basins, these ponds, pots, and vents are among the most active in the park.

The first part of this natural exhibit offers an excellent example of how algae and bacteria are at work in these thermal areas. The centerpiece, literally, of this region is **Fountain Paint Pot,** which changes character as summer temperatures increase, causing once thin, watery mud to become very thick. The mud is composed of clay and particles of silica that are trapped in the paint pots. (If you see a bubble forming on the surface, be prepared for a burst that could throw mud over the guardrail.) **Leather Pool** has undergone a transformation since the 1959 Hebgen Lake earthquake. It was once a warm, 143°F (62°C) pool lined with leatherlike algae, but its temperature increased so dramatically after the quake that the algae were killed. **Red Spouter**'s temperament changes with the seasons as its water table changes. During summer months, when the water table is low, it is a fumarole; from late fall through the winter, it spouts red water and mud. The Fountain Paint Pots themselves are very colorful, with orange, yellow, blue, and green pots surrounded by bleached mud, gurgling like experiments in high school chemistry labs. All in all, it takes roughly 20 minutes to do the whole tour. Before departing, take a look across the large grassy area called **Fountain Flat.**

As you continue toward the Madison Junction, consider a detour along **Fountain Flat Drive,** a left turn about 2 miles beyond Fountain Paint Pot. This scenic paved road ends a quarter-mile north of Ojo Caliente, after which it is open only to hikers and bikers. One mile south of the Firehole River Bridge, you'll find the **Imperial Meadows Trailhead.** Park the car and head up the 3.8-mile trail to the 200-foot **Fairy Falls.** This trail gets less traffic than the popular Lonestar and Dunraven trails.

Although a detour along **Firehole Canyon Drive** will require backtracking when you're approaching Madison from the south, its great views of the canyon and **Firehole Falls** are worth the time you'll spend. The 2-mile, one-way road, which is a left turn off the Grand Loop Road just before you get to the Madison Junction, skirts 800-foot lava cliffs as it meanders along the canyon of the Firehole River in the shadow of National Park Mountain before rejoining the Grand Loop Road. The 1988 fire also scorched this area, so it offers excellent opportunities to see how quickly new growth is reconstituting the forest.

There are excellent views of the beautiful Firehole River as it rages through this narrow canyon, highlighted by a close-up of Firehole Falls. Be sure to bring a camera. Near the end of this 2-mile road is a popular **swimming hole** ★ complete with restrooms for changing. There are several places to soak weary feet during the hot days of July and August, and scuba enthusiasts have flocked to the spot to view river life and retrieve lost watches in a 45-foot-deep channel. For those without diving gear, bodysurfing the rapids is a popular endeavor.

SELF-GUIDED DRIVING TOURS

Depending on your driving skills and your tolerance for large numbers of cars, RVs, and auto-towed trailers, there is no substitute for a self-driven tour of the park. Although roads are narrow, there are hundreds of turnouts that afford opportunities to take in the views. On the downside, the roads twist, turn, and change elevation frequently, so freeway speeds are out of the question.

For $45 a day, gadget fiends can rent dashboard-mounted GPS units with prerecorded audio keyed to locations in both Yellowstone and Grand Teton from **GaperGuide,** 145 W. Gill Ave., Jackson, WY 83001 (© **307/733-4626;** www.gaperguide.com).

ORGANIZED TOURS

A number of tour companies offer bus and van tours of the park originating in gateway communities. **Yellowstone Alpen Guides** (© **800/858-3502;** www.yellowstoneguides.com) takes travelers around the park from West Yellowstone; rates run about $50 per person for a 4-hour tour. Salt Lake City based **AdventureBus** (© **888/737-5263;** www.adventurebus.com) takes groups to Yellowstone and Grand Teton between June and August; weeklong tours run about $1,000 per person. I also highly recommend **Escape Adventures** (© **800/596-2953;** www.escapeadventures. com), which offers supported 6-day road-biking tours of Yellowstone and Grand Teton for about $1,500 per person if you camp or $2,300 per person if you stay in the park's accommodations. If you are looking for specialized guided trips, such as photo safaris, contact the chamber of commerce in the gateway community where you want to begin.

Within the park, the hotel concessionaire, **Xanterra Parks & Resorts** (© **866/439-7375;** www.yellowstonenationalparklodges. com), has a variety of general and specialized tours. Five different motorcoach tours are available from all of Yellowstone's villages. For $66 ($33 for kids 3–11), you can explore the **Circle of Fire** (Old Faithful, Yellowstone Lake, the Hayden Valley); or you can do the **Yellowstone in a Day** tour. These are full-day tours, with stops at all the sights and informative talks by the guides. Eight restored **Old Yellow Buses** that roamed the Yellowstone roads in the first half of the 20th century are today back in service for

Xanterra. Tours in the buses range from 1 to 5 hours ($26–$85). Other specialty trips include custom van tours, photo safaris, wildlife trips up the Lamar Valley, and Yellowstone Lake sunset tours.

At Bridge Bay Marina, 1-hour **"scenicruises"** (© 877/439-7375) depart throughout the day from June to the end of September for a trip around the northern end of giant Yellowstone Lake. You view the Lake Yellowstone Hotel from the water and visit Stevenson Island while a guide fills you in on the history, geology, and biology. Fares are $15 for adults and $9 for children ages 2 to 11. Guided fishing trips on 22-foot and 34-foot cabin cruisers are also available at Bridge Bay ($160 and $200 for 2 hr., respectively), and you can rent smaller outboards and rowboats.

Buses are replaced in the winter by **snowcoach tours** (p. 89).

The **Yellowstone Association Institute ★★★** (© 406/848-2400; www.yellowstoneassociation.org/institute) offers a slew of guided classes, from daylong hikes to multiday backcountry adventures. Participants can bunk in cabins at the historic buffalo ranch in Lamar Valley or at the new-in-2010 Overlook Field Campus, featuring cabins with shared kitchens high on a bluff overlooking Gardiner, Montana. The institute has also teamed up with Xanterra Parks & Resorts to offer visitors **Lodging & Learning** packages, which are excellent options for those who want to delve into the park without too much of the traditional "roughing it." For more information, see "Academic Trips" (p. 26).

In September, the institute takes over **Roosevelt Lodge** with the **Roosevelt Rendezvous,** a series of 4-day educational experiences with a daily menu of different field trips led by park experts. There are also evening programs. Rates start at $729 per person, which includes tuition, a cabin, and three meals a day.

RANGER PROGRAMS

Yellowstone National Park continues to offer free **ranger-led educational programs** that will significantly enhance a visitor's understanding of the area's history, geology, and wildlife. Most programs run from early June to early September. Detailed information on locations and times is listed in the park newsletter distributed at the entrance gates; scheduling changes are made frequently, so consult this newsletter for the current calendar. You'll also run into ranger-naturalists roaming the geyser basins and the rim of the Grand Canyon in Yellowstone, and in areas where wildlife gather in both parks, leading informative walks and answering questions from inquisitive visitors.

Evening campfire programs are presented nightly in the summer at Mammoth, Norris, Madison, Bridge Bay, Grant, and Canyon. Many of these activities are accessible to those with disabilities. It's a good idea to bring a flashlight, warm clothing, and rain gear. Rangers also conduct hiking programs throughout the park, including half-day "Adventure Hikes" that are also free but require reservations that can be made at each visitor center.

Guided walks in the **Old Faithful** area can run as long as 1½ hours and usually focus on the geysers, their fragile plumbing, and their role in the Yellowstone ecosystem. There is an outdoor talk in the visitor center's amphitheater in the evening.

Beginning in June, daily hikes in the **Canyon** area skirt along the rim of the Grand Canyon; a ranger talk on the art inspired by the falls is held several times a day at the lower platform of Artist Point. An explanation of the origins of the hot pools and mud pots is conducted twice daily as part of a walk of the Lakeshore area of the **West Thumb Geyser Basin.** The **Lake Village/Fishing Bridge** agenda includes walking tours of the Mud Volcano area and the shores of Yellowstone Lake. There is an afternoon "Featured Creature" wildlife talk at the Fishing Bridge Visitor Center, and a discussion concerning the native cutthroat is held on the west end of the Fishing Bridge.

Mammoth Hot Springs is host to several interesting ranger-led programs, including talks on the park's natural and cultural wonders and a historical tour of the original site of Fort Yellowstone, established more than 100 years ago. There is also a guided tour of the hot springs terraces. The hottest, most dynamic, and oldest geyser basin in the park is at **Norris,** where a popular 1½-hour tour begins at the Norris museum on a daily basis during peak season.

HIKES & OTHER OUTDOOR PURSUITS IN YELLOWSTONE NATIONAL PARK

4

Those who complain that Yellowstone's three million annual visitors have compromised the park's wilderness should park their car and tackle a trail: There's still plenty of extremely wild country here, and only about 10% of visitors set foot in Yellowstone's backcountry.

There are short hikes on which you never lose sight of the road, moderate hikes requiring an afternoon to visit a spot of secluded beauty, and overnight trips on which you can hike for literally days without running into another human being.

In fact, there's so much to see and do here that it's easy to get overwhelmed. I've tried to make it easier by describing my favorite day hikes, backcountry experiences, and park activities.

DAY HIKES

Below is a small selection of good hikes, all of which can be completed in a day. The **Continental Divide Trail (CDT)** links many of these individual hikes together as part of a continuous trail from Mexico to Canada, roughly following the spine of the continent. The Yellowstone Backcountry Office maintains a guide to CDT trails. The **Howard Eaton Trail** system once went all through the park but was largely supplanted by the Grand Loop Road. Sections of the old trail are still maintained and are found in trail guides, although some of them closely parallel park roads.

Wherever you go, if you're planning to hike for more than 30 minutes, be sure to carry a supply of water and rain gear. Bear spray is also recommended; hiking alone is not.

West Yellowstone to Madison

Artist Paint Pot Trail ★ ☺ Free of heavy foot traffic, this interesting and easy .5-mile path winds through a lodgepole forest in Gibbon Meadows to the Amazonia Mud Pot atop a small hill. This thermal area contains some small geysers, hot pools, and steam vents, colored by hues of orange, bright red, and rust.

1.2 mile round-trip. Easy. Access: Trail head is 4½ miles south of Norris Junction in Gibbon Meadow.

Harlequin Lake Trail You'll get a good look at the interior of a burned forest en route to a small lake that is populated by various types of waterfowl, although few of the harlequin ducks that inspired its name remain. Short and level, this hike is a good choice for those who don't want to stray too far from the road. Be sure to bring insect repellent, though.

1 mile round-trip. Easy. Access: Trail head is 1½ miles west of the Madison Campground on West Entrance Rd.

Two Ribbons Trail This trail offers an opportunity to inspect the effects of the 1988 fire. Along the boardwalk, you'll see evidence not only of the blaze that ravaged the area but also of the beginning of a new cycle of life in the dense green shag of lodgepole saplings. You'll also see some of the calling cards of bison: wallows, or patches of rubbed-raw earth once used to scratch an itch.

1.5 miles round-trip. Easy. Access: Trail head is 5 miles east of the west entrance at an unmarked turnout on the north side of the road.

Norris Geyser Basin

Back Basin Loop ★★ This level boardwalk is easily negotiable in an hour and passes by **Steamboat Geyser,** known to produce some of the world's highest eruptions. How often? About once a decade, with an impressive spurt of activity since 2000: eight eruptions—and counting. Wait instead by **Echinus Geyser;** its colorful pool fills and erupts several times a day.

1.5 miles round-trip. Easy. Access: Trail head is located at Norris Geyser Basin.

Porcelain Basin Trail ★ You'll share this boardwalk with other folks, but it takes you across a broad, flat basin where steaming water makes colorful trails. You can complete the walk in less than an hour, but you'll probably stop to look closely at some of these geothermal features, a few of which periodically spit and rumble in small eruptions.

.5 mile round-trip. Easy. Access: Trail head is located at Norris Geyser Basin.

Mammoth Hot Springs Area

Beaver Ponds Loop Trail ★   Start at Clematis Gulch and make your way to a series of beaver ponds. Your best chance of seeing the big-tailed beasts is early morning or late afternoon, and you might spot a moose, pronghorn, or elk on the way. There are also some good views, including views of Mount Everts.

5 miles round-trip. Moderate. Access: Trail head is located at Mammoth Hot Springs Terrace.

Bunsen Peak Trail ★★ 🎒   This trail takes you up 1,300 feet in 2 miles to the 8,564-foot summit. Make the hike early, and you can watch the morning sun strike Electric Peak; then leave your thoughts in a rusted lockbox packed with the notes of thousands of past hikers. You can take an alternate route back down to the Osprey Falls Trail (see below).

4.2 miles round-trip. Moderate. Access: Trail head is across the road from the Glen Creek Trailhead, 5 miles south of Mammoth on Mammoth-Norris Rd.

Forces of the Northern Range Trail ☺   This fully accessible trail along a boardwalk presents an excellent opportunity to learn about the effects of fire on the environment. Signposts encourage kids to get down and dirty to examine the indications of the forest's rejuvenation.

.8 mile round-trip. Easy. Access: Trail head is on Tower Rd., about 6 miles east of Mammoth Hot Springs.

Lower Terrace Interpretive Trail ★★   This interpretive trail is one of the best ways to see Mammoth Hot Springs. The board-walk begins at 6,280 feet and climbs another 300 feet along marginally steep grades through a bare, rocky, thermal region to a flat alpine area and observation deck at the top; it's not a difficult climb in exchange for some splendid views. A park guide says the 1.5-mile round-trip walk to the Upper Terrace and back takes 2 hours, but it can be done in less.

1.5 miles round-trip. Easy. Access: Trail head is south of the village on the road to Norris.

Osprey Falls Trail ★★   The first 3.3 miles of this hike lead along an old, bike-friendly roadbed at the base of Bunsen Peak. From the Osprey Falls Trail turnoff, it's another 1.5 miles through

Mammoth Area Trails

a series of steep switchbacks in Sheepeater Canyon to a secluded waterfall on the Gardner River.

9.3 miles round-trip. Moderate. Access: Trail head is at Bunsen Peak Trailhead, 5 miles south of Mammoth Hot Springs on Mammoth-Norris Rd.

Sepulcher Mountain Trail ★★ The Glen Creek Trailhead presents hikers with several alternative paths through the Sepulcher Mountain area. During the early summer, this plateau is a beautiful, wide-open area that follows the base of Terrace Mountain. With huge expanses of sagebrush and pines interspersed with the brilliant yellows and blues of wildflowers, this is an excellent place to escape the crowds. You will also get a feel for the real park in this wilderness area without making much of a physical commitment. Because the trail is in the Gallatin Bear Management Area, you'll want to make noise or tie a bell to a shoe while hiking here.

Three miles from the trail head, you'll arrive at a fork in the trail. Now you have to make a choice: Continue another 2 miles up the steeper option to the mountain's summit, continue east on the Terrace Mountain loop of the **Snow Pass Trail,** or retrace your steps to the trail head. If you're continuing, I recommend the first option. It's a moderate hike that climbs 2,300 feet as the trail winds through a diverse selection of wildlife and scenery.

6–11 miles round-trip. Easy to moderate. Access: Glen Creek Trailhead, 5 miles south of Mammoth Hot Springs on Mammoth-Norris Rd.

Trout Lake Trail ★   A short, somewhat steep hike through spruce and fir, this trail's destination is the small Trout Lake, which is encircled by a footpath. The lake, nestled between dramatic cliffs and Druid and Baronette peaks, is a favorite fishing hole and one of the best places in the park to witness the fascinating cutthroat spawn. Because of the density of the fish, the lake once served as a major source of food for Cooke City and continues to attract otters, beavers, and bears.

1.3 miles round-trip. Easy. Access: 10 miles west of the northeast entrance, at the trail head 1 mile west of Pebble Creek campground.

Grand Canyon of the Yellowstone River Area

Clear Lake and Ribbon Lake Loop Trail ★   The hike to Clear Lake is 1.5 miles, a gradual climb across a high plateau, with Ribbon Lake less than 2 miles beyond it. Views of the plateau improve with each step until you find yourself surrounded by the mountains of the Canyon area. Clear Lake itself is intimately small and gives you the opportunity to see subsurface activity of the thermal areas below the lake. On a circumnavigation of the lake along a trail, you will see and smell vented gas making its way to the surface; in some spots, the lake looks like a small boiling pot. There is bear activity in this area early in the year, so check with rangers for current conditions before heading out.

6 miles round-trip. Moderate. Access: Wapiti Trailhead, across the street from the South Rim parking lot.

Howard Eaton Trail   Both the Clear Lake and Ribbon Lake trails give access to the Howard Eaton Trail, the means to a lengthy hike to Fishing Bridge and Yellowstone Lake. You'll see some riverside thermal features and waterfowl on the way, and pass a ford favored by bison crossing the Yellowstone River. There is bear activity in this area early in the year; check with rangers for current conditions before heading out.

Up to 12 miles one-way. Moderate. Access: Wapiti Trailhead, across the street from the South Rim parking lot.

Mount Washburn Trail ★★★   This is a relatively short hike to panoramic views, with wildflowers decorating the way and nonchalant bighorn sheep browsing nearby. You might also see marmots and red fox; for a few years, grizzly bears were regulars in a nearby

Storm Point Trail ★   The Storm Point Trail follows a level path that terminates at a point jutting into the lake, offering a rocky viewpoint of the lake, Stevenson Island, and the mountains beyond. (On a clear day, you'll see as far south as the Tetons.) It begins near Indian Pond, a favorite hangout for bison. During spring months, this is a popular spot with grizzlies, so the trail might be closed; however, even when it's open, check with rangers regarding bear activity.

2.3 miles round-trip. Easy. Access: Trail head is 3½ miles east of Fishing Bridge, directly across from the Pelican Valley Trailhead (on the lake side of the road).

Old Faithful Area

DeLacy Creek Trail ★★   This meanders through the forest alongside open meadows—great moose habitat—en route to Shoshone Lake, the largest backcountry lake in the lower 48. This trail represents the shortest route to the lakeshore.

6 miles round-trip. Easy. Access: Trail head is at Fountain Paint Pot parking lot.

Fairy Falls Trail ★   Though longer than the Mystic Falls Trail, the Fairy Falls Trail is popular because it leads to a taller waterfall, which drops 200 feet. The level hike begins either 1 mile south of Midway Geyser Basin at the Imperial Meadows Trailhead, or at a trail head 1 mile south of the Firehole River Bridge on Fountain Flat Drive. After following an old roadbed that winds through an area populated by elk along Fairy Creek, you'll pass the Imperial Geyser. From here, the trail joins Fairy Creek Trail and travels east to the base of the falls. (You can also access the falls via this trail, which is ultimately a shorter trip but less scenic.) The total gain in elevation is only 100 feet.

5-7 miles round-trip. Easy to moderate. Access: Trail heads are at Imperial Meadows in Biscuit Basin and at the end of Fountain Flat Dr.

Fountain Paint Pot Trail ★ ☺   This is a very accessible, popular area, so you might be forced to wait for a parking place. All types of thermal activity are on display, so as you stroll along the boardwalk, you'll be distracted at every turn by another bubbling pool or colorful mud pot.

.5 mile round-trip. Easy. Access: Trail head is at Fountain Paint Pot parking lot.

Geyser Hill Loop ★   One of the most interesting, and easiest, loops in the area, this trail winds among several thermal attractions. Anemone Geyser puts on a good display of the various stages of a typical eruption as the pool fills and overflows; the Lion Group consists of four geysers interconnected beneath the surface; Doublet Pool is popular with photographers who are attracted by a complex series of ledges and deep blue waters; and Giantess Geyser is known for its violent eruptions.

1.4 miles round-trip. Easy. Access: Trail head is at the Old Faithful boardwalk.

Lonestar Geyser Trail ★   The popularity of this trail detracts from the pleasure of walking a fairly level, forested trail along the Firehole River, interrupted now and then by broad riverbank meadows. The geyser itself sits in a meadow pocked by steam vents and thermal features. About every 3 hours, it spouts water some 50 feet in the air from a vanilla-and-chocolate-colored cone. The path is partially paved and open to bicycles as far as the geyser (hikers can go farther, over Grants Pass). In the winter, this is a popular route for cross-country skiers.

4.6 miles round-trip. Easy. Access: Trail head is at the parking lot opposite Kepler Cascades.

Mystic Falls Trail   This trail leads to a waterfall on the Little Firehole River that drops more than 100 feet, one of the steepest in the park. The trail starts at Biscuit Basin, crosses the river, and then disappears into the forest. The total distance to the base of the falls is only 1 mile; there's a trail to the top, and if you want to take a different way home, connect with the **Little Firehole Meadows Trail,** with long-distance views of Old Faithful, back to Biscuit Basin.

2.5 miles round-trip. Easy. Access: Trail head is at Imperial Meadows in Biscuit Basin.

Observation Point Trail–Solitary Geyser ★★ 📷   For a spectacular view of Old Faithful and the geyser basin from above, take this 2-mile loop. While it requires a bit more planning than watching Old Faithful from the bleachers, you'll have a totally different perspective from that of the masses below. The path up to the observation point is just half a mile, and the elevation gain is only 200 feet, an easy 15-minute hike. From the top, you can see most of the major geysers, as well as inaccessible steam vents located in the middle of wooded areas. From the top of the boardwalk, continue to the Solitary Geyser on a downhill slope that leads past the geyser, through the basin, and back to the Old Faithful Inn, which completes the loop.

2 miles round-trip. Easy. Access: Trail head is at the Old Faithful boardwalk.

Old Faithful Area Trails

Mount Haynes

YELLOWSTONE NATIONAL PARK

Old Faithful

0	1 mi
0	1 km

Picnic Area
Ranger Station
Visitor Center

FIREHOLE CANYON

Cascades of the Firehole

SENTINEL MEADOW

PORCUPINE HILLS

LOWER GEYSER BASIN

TWIN BUTTES

Sentinel Creek

Fairy Creek

Fairy Falls Trail

Great Fountain Geyser

Grand Loop Rd.

Fairy Falls

MIDWAY GEYSER BASIN

Fairy Creek Trail

BUFFALO MEADOWS

20

LITTLE FIREHOLE MEADOWS

Firehole River

Little

Summit Lake Trail

UPPER GEYSER BASIN

Mallard Creek Trail

Mallard Lake

BLACK SAND GEYSER BASIN

Old Faithful

Mallard Lake Trail

Old Faithful Inn

Fern Cascades Loop

Grand Loop Rd.

Howard Eaton Trail

Lonestar Geyser Trail

Summit Lake

Lonestar Geyser

EXPLORING THE BACKCOUNTRY

The backcountry of Yellowstone is the real thing, a domain of free-roaming wildlife and natural treasures predominately untouched by the hand of man. The U.S. National Park Service, through its system of permits, designated camping areas, and rules (for more on these, see below), has managed to preserve a true wilderness. Yellowstone has more than 1,200 miles of trails (most of which are in the backcountry) and 300 backcountry campsites.

For information on backpacking and safety, see chapter 10.

Planning Ahead

You can pick up a permit the day before beginning a trip, but if you'll be traveling during peak season, try to make a reservation in advance. It costs $20 to hold a site, and you can begin making reservations for the upcoming year on April 1. *Caution:* The reservation is just that, a reservation; upon your arrival at the park, you'll need to secure the permit, which is valid only on the dates for which it is issued.

INFORMATION BEFORE YOU GO   Contact the **Yellowstone Backcountry Office,** P.O. Box 168, Yellowstone National Park, WY 82190 (**℃ 307/344-2160;** www.nps.gov/yell/planyour visit/backcountrytripplanner.htm) to request the useful *Backcountry Trip Planner,* which has a detailed map showing where the campsites are, as well as information on preparation and making reservations. The planner is also available as a PDF on the website listed above.

BACKCOUNTRY PERMITS   Backcountry permits are free, but you have to have one for any overnight trip, on foot, on horseback, or by boat. Camping is allowed only in designated campsites, many of which are equipped with food-storage poles to keep wildlife out of your stores. Some are also equipped with pit toilets. These sites are primitive and well situated, and you won't feel like you're in a campground.

Pick up your permit in the park within 48 hours of your departure at one of the following stations any day of the week during the summer: Bechler, west entrance, or south entrance ranger stations (no phones); or Canyon, Mammoth, Old Faithful, Grant, or Fishing Bridge visitor centers (see "Essentials," in chapter 3, for phone numbers and information).

WHEN TO GO   Many of the trails into the park backcountry remain covered with snow and become muddy in the first weeks of melt, well into June. At the higher elevations, over 9,000 feet, summer doesn't truly begin until early July, and even then the weather is unpredictable at best. Trail maintenance in the backcountry is much less thorough than on the more public trails near the roads: Creeks and streams described as "intermittent" during summer months might be filled with snowmelt that transforms them into impassable, swiftly running rivers that often drench trails and convert them to mud. Look in the *Backcountry Trip Planner* for approximate dates for when specific campsites will be accessible and habitable.

WILDERNESS U: guided BACKPACKING WITH THE YELLOWSTONE ASSOCIATION INSTITUTE

The **Yellowstone Association Institute (YAI)** uses the park's backcountry as a 2.2-million-acre classroom for many of its 400 annual classes. A number of courses are guided backpacking trips into the Yellowstone wilderness.

I went on a YAI expedition with about 10 other people in August 2004, following the same route the Nez Perce Indians took through Yellowstone in summer 1877 while evading the U.S. Army. Our 4-day adventure (preceded by a day in an indoor classroom in Gardiner) traversed 40 miles under the leadership of an experienced backcountry guide and park historian, Lee Whittlesey. Another guide, Julianne Baker, taught us how to identify wolf tracks and uphold "Leave No Trace" etiquette.

The trip illuminated the obstacles the Nez Perce faced en route to their ultimate place of surrender in Montana. Led by Chief Joseph, 600 to 800 people, including many children and elderly persons, evaded capture from June into October, cutting through a slice of the fledgling national park known as Yellowstone. We also learned that the flight of the Nez Perce has been the key event in the tribe's history since 1877; the 5-month ordeal haunts many of its members to this day. The contemporary Nez Perce are a nostalgic tribe, and thus—for better or for worse—quite different from other typically modern Americans.

The "Flight of the Nez Perce" backcountry course has become a staple in the YAI catalog, along with guided backpacking classes about wolves, grizzly bears, waterfalls, photography, and the microbes that inhabit the park's thermal features. Taking a course is a great way to learn the ins and outs of backpacking, and to meet a bunch of like-minded Yellowstone lovers in the process. Trips typically last 3 days to a week and cost $700 to $1,000 per person. You need to bring most of your own gear. Call (✆ **406/848-2400** or visit www.yellowstoneassociation. org/institute for a course catalog and other information.

MAPS Park rangers suggest using maps from the Trails Illustrated Map series, published by National Geographic Maps. There are four Yellowstone maps which include about nine of those produced by the U.S. Geological Survey and they are printed on durable plastic; the maps also show backcountry campsite locations. For more

information, contact **National Geographic Maps** (© 800/
962-1643; www.natgeomaps.com/trailsillustrated.html), or the **Yellowstone Association** (© 406/848-2400; www.yellowstone
association.org).

OUTFITTERS　An alternative to venturing into the backcountry
on your own is to go with an outfitter. Outfitters provide most
equipment, which can offset the cost of their services, which
might include setting up tents and making meals.

Based in Emigrant, Montana, **Big Wild Adventures** (© 406/
848-7000; www.bigwildadventures.com) offers guided trips into
Yellowstone's backcountry with a focus on a specific topic, like
waterfalls or wolves. The trips usually last 5 to 9 days and cost
$1,500 to $2,100. **Yellowstone Safari Co.** (© 866/586-1155
or 406/586-1155; www.yellowstonesafari.com) offers guided trips
of varying length, and can provide rental equipment. The rate is
$200 per person per day, with a four-person minimum for a trip.

The Yellowstone Backcountry

If you just can't get your fill of geysers, or if you've had your fill of
people, several trails lead to more isolated backcountry. The **Shoshone Geyser Basin** and **Heart Lake Geyser Basin** contain
active geysers, as do **Ponuntpa Springs** and the **Mudkettles** in
the Pelican Valley area, **Imperial Geyser** in the Firehole area, and
the **Highland Hot Springs** on the Mary Mountain Trail. If you
head in these directions, be careful about walking on unstable
surfaces: A young man died in 1988 when he fell into a super-
heated pool.

SHOSHONE LAKE

Shoshone Lake is the largest backcountry lake in the lower 48 and
a popular spot for backcountry hikers. The shortest route to the
lake is via the **DeLacy Creek Trail** (see "Old Faithful Area,"
under "Day Hikes," earlier in this chapter), which begins 8 miles
east of Old Faithful. From here, the trail winds 3 miles along
DeLacy Creek through moose country to the lake. At this point, it's
a tossup: You can head around the lake in either direction. Assum-
ing that you take a clockwise track around the lake—a distance of
18 miles—you'll continue 4.5 miles on the DeLacy Creek Trail to
its intersection with **Dogshead Trail,** and then head west on the
Shoshone Lake Trail until it intersects with the **North Shoshone Trail** and returns to your starting point.

A detour: At the western end of the lake, you'll arrive at the
1-mile **Shoshone Geyser Basin Trail ★★**, which loops through
a number of geysers, hot springs, and meadows that, during spring

months, are ankle deep in water and mud. **Union Geyser** erupts sporadically and is impressive in that eruptions occur from three vents simultaneously. Because the crust of the earth is so thin here, your footsteps might sound like thumping on a hollow gourd.

As you travel the lake's loop trail along the **DeLacy Creek Trail,** you'll have views of the lake at the top of a 100-foot rise. Then, on the **Shoshone Lake Trail,** you'll cross the Lewis Channel, which often contains thigh-high water as late as July. Beyond that, the trail is a series of rises that are easily negotiable by the ordinary hiker, passing across shallow Moose Creek and through meadows where you might spot deer or moose early in the morning or evening.

The 8.5-mile **North Shoshone Trail** winds through a lodge-pole-pine forest, over numerous ridges up to 200 feet high. The best views of the lake are from the high points on this trail. The loop trail is especially popular with overnighters because there are 26 campsites on the loop, the largest of which has space for eight campers. (Some of the sites are accessible to paddlers only, however.)

THE BECHLER REGION

This area in the park's southwest section is often referred to as Cascade Corner because it contains a majority of the park's waterfalls. It escaped the fires of 1988 and offers great opportunities to view thermal features. Many backpacking routes cut through this region, including one that leads to Old Faithful on the **Bechler River Trail ★★**.

To begin your hike, drive into the park from Ashton, Idaho, and check in at the Bechler Ranger Station. To reach the ranger station, drive east 17 miles from Ashton on the Cave Falls Road; 3 miles before reaching Cave Falls, you'll find the ranger station turnoff. The ranger station is 1½ miles down the gravel road.

The **Bechler Meadows Trail ★★** takes you into this southwest corner, rich in waterfalls, cascades, and thermal areas that rarely have human visitors. About 6 miles into the journey, the trail fords the river several times as it enters Bechler Canyon, where it passes Colonnade and Iris falls. There are places on this trail where you can view the Tetons in the distance and the hot springs that warm the creeks. You can cover a good 30 miles in 3 or 4 days, depending on what turns you take. It's a camping trip best made late in the summer, to avoid high water during creek crossings. For a shorter trip, hike 3.5 miles along the **Bechler River Trail** to the **Boundary Creek Trail,** and then return to the station via the **Bechler Meadows Trails,** a round-trip of 7 miles.

The most adventurous and scenic route takes you 30 miles from the ranger station to the end of the trail at the **Lonestar Geyser**

Trailhead, near Old Faithful. Beyond Iris Falls and then Ragged Falls, you'll reach a patrol cabin at Three Rivers Junction at the 13-mile mark, a popular camping area. If you continue toward Old Faithful, you'll intersect the **Shoshone Lake Trail** at the 23.5-mile mark and exit 6.5 miles later. Hikers should be able to cover from 6 to 12 miles a day, depending on experience.

HEART LAKE LOOP

Heart Lake is another popular backcountry lake that attracts plenty of paddlers and anglers—not to mention wildlife. It's a 7.5-mile hike on the **Heart Lake Trail** ★ to the lakeshore, where numerous campsites are nestled near the forested banks. There is a 32-mile loop around the lake, which has long stretches in a burn area well away from the water but makes for an excellent 3- to 4-day backpack. Day hikers can tack on the hike up Mount Sheridan, which looms above the lake with a fire lookout at its summit, 10,308 feet above sea level—about 3,000 feet above the lake via a strenuous 3.9-mile trail.

THOROFARE AREA

When you enter this country in the park's southeast corner, you're venturing into the most remote, roadless area in the lower 48. You can make an excursion of around 70 miles round-trip deep into the wilderness, or you can take shorter hikes, such as a trip from the park's East Entrance Road to the Yellowstone River inlet on Yellowstone Lake's southeast arm. The remoteness of this country discourages many hikers, so you'll have it mostly to yourself. Along the way, tepee rings and lean-tos are reminders that Indians once used this trail as the main route between Jackson Hole and points north.

The **Thorofare Trail** ★★ follows first the eastern shore of Yellowstone Lake and then the Yellowstone River up into some of the most remote and beautiful backcountry in the Rockies. It's a lot of miles and a lot of climbing, but you'll be rewarded with spectacular views of the Upper Yellowstone Valley and Two Oceans Plateau, and there's a good chance of seeing some wildlife. You'll reach the Thorofare Ranger Station at 32 miles, and a few miles farther you'll come to Bridger Lake, outside the park, and a gorgeous alpine valley with a ranger station known as Hawk's Rest. Fishermen love this area, as do grizzly bears, especially during the cutthroat trout spawning season in early summer. You'll be a good 35 miles from the trail head at the lake, and even the most capable hikers should consider riding with an outfitter. You can cut 9 miles off the trip by getting a boat shuttle (about $350 round-trip, with a maximum capacity of six people) to the mouth of the lake's southeast arm (call the **backcountry shuttle office** at ℭ **307/242-3893**), or you can come in through **Bridger-Teton National Forest** to the south (check with the forest's district office in Moran, Wyoming; ☎ **307/543-2386**). Other than bears, the major obstacle to early-season trips in the Thorofare is water; you'll encounter knee-deep water at **Beaverdam Creek** and at **Trapper Creek** as late as July.

THE SPORTSMAN LAKE TRAIL

This trail begins near Mammoth Hot Springs and extends west toward U.S. Hwy. 191 to Sportsman Lake: a moderate, 14-mile trail that displays a diverse combination of flora and fauna. From the Glen Creek Trailhead, 5 miles south of Mammoth Hot Springs, you'll spend 2 miles on the Glen Creek Trail as you traverse a mostly level, wide-open plateau covered with sagebrush that is the home of herds of elk and a bear-management area. At the 3-mile mark of the **Sepulcher Mountain Trail ★★**, the terrain becomes steeper as you continue northwest on the **Sportsman Lake Trail ★★**. The trail eventually enters the forest and descends to a log that is used to cross Gardner River. Then it's uphill for another 4 miles to **Electric Divide,** another 2,000-foot gain in elevation. From there, the trail descends 2,100 feet in 3 miles to Sportsman Lake, which is located in an area burned by the 1988 conflagration. The lake, which sits in a meadow populated by moose and elk, is teeming with cutthroat trout. Two campsites provide overnight spaces for a total of 30 visitors.

THE SLOUGH CREEK TRAIL

Beginning in the Lamar Valley of the park's northeast corner, the **Slough Creek Trail ★★** takes hikers through some of the best wildlife habitat in the park. You can see elk, bison, trumpeter swans, sometimes grizzly bears, and now gray wolves that have quite happily taken up residence among abundant prey. The presence of wolves has made this area much more popular, and the trail is also used by horse-packers. The trail starts from the road to Slough Creek campground, following the creek's valley north, and then crosses a ridge to a second valley. You can hike a few miles or take your camping gear and head for the park boundary, 11 miles to the north.

OTHER ACTIVITIES

BIKING Considering the vast expanse of real estate that the parks cover, the challenging terrain, and the miles of paved roads and trails, a cyclist might conclude that the parks are prime areas for biking, on or off the roads.

It looks good on paper, but the reality is more harrowing. The roads are narrow and twisty; there are no bike lanes, so bikers continually fight for elbowroom with wide-bodied RVs and trailers, some of which have side-view mirrors that seem designed to decapitate cyclists. Off-road opportunities are limited because of the small number of trails on which bikes are allowed.

Nevertheless, plenty of bicyclists take the challenge. The following trails are available, but you'll be sharing them with hikers. The **Mount Washburn Trail,** leaving from Old Chittenden Road, is a strenuous trail that climbs 1,400 feet. The **Lonestar Geyser Trail,** accessed at Kepler Cascade near Old Faithful, is an easy 1-hour ride on a user-friendly, partly paved road. Near Mammoth Hot Springs, **Bunsen Peak Road** and **Osprey Falls** trails present a combination ride/hike: The first 3 miles circle Bunsen Peak; getting to the top requires a hike. A hike down to Osprey Falls adds another 2.8 miles. There are also a number of old roads and railroad beds available for biking.

Bike rentals are available in the gateway towns of West Yellowstone at **Free Heel and Wheel** (© 406/646-7744; www.free heelandwheel.com) and Jackson at **Hoback Sports** (© 307/733-5335; www.hobacksports.com). Rental fees for a full-suspension mountain bike are $25 to $50 a day.

BOATING The best place to enjoy boating in Yellowstone is on **Yellowstone Lake,** which has easy access and beautiful, panoramic views. The lake is also one of the few areas where powerboats are allowed. Xanterra rents rowboats and outboard motorboats at **Bridge Bay Marina** (© 866/439-7375). The cost for rowboats is about $45 per day or $10 per hour; an 18-foot outboard, with room for six, rents for $47 per hour. Sea kayakers and canoeists should stay close to the shore on Yellowstone Lake because of high winds that can easily capsize a small craft. Motorboats, canoes, and kayaks can be used on Lewis Lake as well. In West Yellowstone, kayak rentals ($49–$65 a day) and guided kayaking are available from **Lava Creek,** 433 Highway Ave. (© 406/646-5145; www.lavacreekadventures.com).

FISHING   Seven varieties of game fish live in the parks: cutthroat trout, rainbow trout, brown trout, brook trout, lake trout, Arctic grayling, and mountain whitefish. Of the trout, only the cutthroats are native, and they are being pressured in the big lake by the larger lake trout. As a result, you can't keep any pink-meat cutthroat caught anywhere in Yellowstone, and you *must* keep every single lake trout. This policy has done little to discourage fly-fishing purists who are more interested in the sport than in its spoils.

The Yellowstone season typically opens on the Saturday of Memorial Day weekend and ends on the first Sunday in November. Yellowstone Lake has a slightly shorter season, and the lake's tributaries are closed until July 15 to avoid conflicts between humans and grizzly bears, both of which are attracted to spawning trout.

Many fine anglers come to Yellowstone, and they are well informed about which seasons are best on which stretches of river. In June, try the **Yellowstone River** downstream of Yellowstone Lake, where the cutthroat trout spawn. Fish the **Madison River** near the west entrance in July, and fish again in late fall for rainbow and some brown trout. In late summer, you can try to hook the cutthroats that thin out by September on the **Lamar River,** in the park's beautiful northeast corner.

Fishing on **Yellowstone Lake** was popular until recent years, when regulations designed to bring back the waning population of cutthroat trout began to send some of the trolling powerboats elsewhere. The problem is the introduced lake trout, which compete with, and eat, the cutthroat. As is the case anywhere in the park, if you catch a lake trout, you *must* kill it, and if you catch a cutthroat, you *must* throw it back. Certain areas of the lake, such as the southeast arm, are closed to motorized boats; this makes the Yellowstone River inlet a wonderful area to canoe, camp, and fish.

You can fish the **Yellowstone River** below the Grand Canyon by hiking down into **Seven-Mile Hole,** a great place to cast (not much vegetation to snag on) for cutthroat trout from July to September. You'll have the best luck around Sulphur Creek. Other good fishing stretches include the **Gibbon and Firehole rivers,** which merge to form the Madison River on the park's west side, and the 3-mile **Lewis River Channel** between Shoshone and Lewis lakes during the fall spawning run of brown trout.

There is access on the **Madison River** for anglers with disabilities, 3½ miles west of Madison Junction at the Haynes Overlook, where you'll find a wheelchair-accessible fishing platform over the river's edge along 70 feet of the bank.

4

YELLOWSTONE HIKES — Other Activities

Suggested Reading   Two reference guides present excellent information about park fishing opportunities and requirements: *Fishing Yellowstone National Park,* by Richard Parks (Falcon Press, 2007), and *Flyfisher's Guide to Yellowstone National Park,* by Ken Retallic (Wilderness Adventures Press, 2005). Both can be purchased from the **Yellowstone Association** (𝒞 **406/848-2400;** www.yellowstoneassociation.org).

Permits   Park permits are required for Yellowstone anglers ages 16 and older; the permit costs $15 for 3 days, $20 for 7 days, and $35 for the season. Children 15 and under don't need a permit if they are fishing with an adult, but need to pick up a free permit if they're fishing without supervision. Permits are available at any ranger station or visitor center, Yellowstone General Store, and most fishing shops in the gateways. The season usually begins on the Saturday of Memorial Day weekend and continues through the first Sunday in November. Exceptions to this rule are Yellowstone Lake, its tributaries, and sections of the Yellowstone River.

Supplies & Fishing Guides   If you need supplies or a guide in Gardiner, stop at **Parks' Fly Shop,** 202-A Hwy. 89 (𝒞 **406/848-7314;** www.parksflyshop.com). In West Yellowstone, check **Bud Lilly's Trout Shop,** 39 Madison Ave. (𝒞 **406/646-7801;** www.budlillys.com). Full-day trips typically cost about $400 to $500 for two people.

Several Jackson, Wyoming–based fishing guides also lead trips into Yellowstone. See "Fishing," in the "Other Activities" section of chapter 6, and the "Getting Outside" section, in chapter 8.

HORSEBACK RIDING   People who want to pack their gear on a horse, llama, or mule must either get a permit to enter the Yellowstone backcountry or hire an outfitter with a permit (see below). Other visitors who want to get in the saddle but not disappear in the wilderness can put themselves in the hands of the concessionaire, **Xanterra Parks & Resorts** (𝒞 **866/439-7375;** www.travelyellowstone.com). Stables are located at Canyon Village and Roosevelt Lodge. Choices are 1- and 2-hour guided trail rides (the prices are $38 and $58, respectively) aboard well-trained, tame animals. Wranglers refer to these as "nose-and-tail" tours, and an experienced rider is likely to find them awfully dull.

If you're looking for a longer, overnight horse-packing experience, contact the park and request a list of approved concessionaires who lead backcountry expeditions. Most offer customized, guided trips, with meals, horses, and camping and riding gear provided. Costs run from $250 to $500 per day per person, depending on the length of the trip and number of people. One good outfitter is **Rockin' HK Outfitters** (𝒞 **307/333-4505;**

www.rockinhk.com), offering 3- to 10-day trips for about $450 per person per day. Out of Bozeman, **Greater Yellowstone Flyfishers** (© **406/585-5321;** www.gyflyfishers.com) offers custom, 3-day/2-night fly-fishing pack trips in the park.

WINTER SPORTS & ACTIVITIES

The average snowfall in a Yellowstone winter is about 150 inches (and up to 300 in. at high elevations), creating a beautiful setting for sightseers and a wonderful resource for outdoor winter recreation. The steaming hot pools and geysers generate little islands of warmth and clear ground, attracting not just tourists but wildlife as well. Nearby trees are transformed into "snow ghosts" by frozen thermal vapors. Bison become frosted, shaggy beasts, easily spotted as they take advantage of the more accessible vegetation on the thawed ground. Yellowstone Lake's surface freezes to an average thickness of 3 feet, creating a vast ice sheet that sings and moans as the huge plates of ice shift. But the ice is thinner where hot springs come up on the lake bottom, and you'll see otters surfacing at the breaks in the ice. Waterfalls become astounding pieces of frozen sculpture. Snow-white trumpeter swans glide through geyser-fed streams under clear-blue skies of clean, crisp mountain air.

Only two of the park's hostelries, **Mammoth Hot Springs Hotel** (p. 128) and the **Old Faithful Snow Lodge** (p. 133), provide accommodations (and rental hot tubs) from December to March. The only road that's open for cars is **Mammoth Hot Springs–Cooke City Road.** Most visitors come into Yellowstone in winter from the west or south by snowcoach or snowmobile.

For additional information on all of the following winter activities and accommodations, as well as snowcoach reservations, contact **Xanterra Parks & Resorts** (© **866/439-7375;** www.travelyellowstone.com). There are also many activities, outfitters, and rental shops in the park's gateway towns.

The **Yellowstone Association Institute** ★★★ (© **406/848-2400;** www.yellowstoneassociation.org) offers winter courses at various park locations. Past offerings have included 3-day classes devoted to wintertime photography in the park, cross-country skiing, and the ecology of wolf reintroduction.

CROSS-COUNTRY SKIING There are 40 miles of cross-country trails in the Old Faithful area, including the popular **Lonestar Geyser Trail,** an 8-mile route that starts at the Old Faithful Snow Lodge, and the **Fern Cascades Trail,** which winds for 3 miles through a rolling woodland landscape close to the Old

winter **ROAD CONDITIONS**

Due to the high elevation and the abundance of snow, most roads in Yellowstone are closed to all wheeled vehicles in winter. The only major park area that is accessible by car is Mammoth Hot Springs; cars are allowed to drive in the village there. Signs will alert you as to how far south into the park you can go (usually to Tower Junction, 18 miles away). From Tower Junction, it's another 29 miles to the northeast entrance. This entrance is open but not accessible from Red Lodge, Montana, and points east (because the Beartooth Hwy. is closed in winter). You can go only as far as Cooke City, Montana, and the roads are kept open specifically so that the folks in Cooke City aren't stranded during the long winters. **Snowmobiles, snowcoaches,** and **cross-country skiers,** however, use park roads regularly throughout the winter season. For up-to-the-minute information on weather and road conditions, call © **307/344-7381.**

Basing yourself in **West Yellowstone** is another option. From the West Yellowstone entrance, it's only 14 miles to Madison Junction, which presents opportunities to head south to Old Faithful or north to the Grand Canyon and Mammoth Hot Springs. Because this is the most popular way to access the park, plan on making reservations early.

Faithful area. Also near Old Faithful, try the **Fairy Falls Trail** (about 6 miles), which some say is the best in Yellowstone.

Equipment rentals (about $20 per day for skis, boots, and poles), ski instruction, ski shuttles to various locations ($15 per adult), and other services are all available at the **Old Faithful Snow Lodge** and the **Mammoth Hot Springs Hotel,** the park's two winter lodging options. Discounts are available for multiday rentals of skis or snowshoes. Ski instruction costs around $30 per person for a 1-hour private lesson; a full-day guided excursion costs $140 per adult (lunch may or may not be included). Guided snowshoe trips are also available.

ICE SKATING The **Mammoth Hot Springs ice rink** is located behind the Mammoth Hot Springs Recreation Center. On a crisp winter's night, you can borrow a pair of skates (free for guests and nonguests alike) and glide across the ice while seasonal melodies are broadcast over the PA system. It's cold out there, but there's a warming fire at the rink's edge. There is also an Old Faithful rink; skates are likewise free. Call © **866/439-7375** for more information.

SNOWCOACH TOURS It is possible to enjoy the sights and sounds of Yellowstone without raising a finger—except to write a check or sign a credit card voucher—by taking one of the scenic snowcoach tours that originate at the south and west entrances, as well as at Mammoth and Old Faithful. One-way and wildlife-watching trips range from about $30 to $70, while round-trips cost about $120 to $140.

If you've never seen a snowcoach, you're in for a treat. Don't be fooled into thinking that this distinctively Yellowstone mode of transportation is merely a fancy name for a bus that provides tours during winter. Imagine instead an Econoline van with tank treads for tires and water skis extending from its front, and you won't be surprised when you see this unusual-looking vehicle. The interiors are toasty warm, with seating for a large group, and they usually allow each passenger two bags. They aren't the fastest, smoothest, or most comfortable form of transportation, but they do allow large groups to travel together, and they're cheaper and warmer than snowmobiles. They're also available for hire by groups at many snowmobile locations. Guides provide interesting and entertaining stories of the areas as you cruise the park trails, and they give you opportunities to photograph scenery and wildlife.

For snowcoach information, contact **Xanterra Parks & Resorts** (© 866/439-7375). Out of West Yellowstone, **Yellowstone Vacations** (© 800/426-7669 or 406/646-9564; www.snowcoachyellowstone.com) and **Yellowstone Alpen Guides** (© 800/858-3502 or 406/646-9591; www.yellowstoneguides.com) provide service as well.

SNOWMOBILING This is an excellent way to sightsee at your own pace, but note that the courts are still debating long-term snowmobile policies for the parks. A driver's license and guide are required for rental at **Mammoth Hot Springs Hotel** or **Old Faithful Snow Lodge.** Day tours with **Xanterra** (© 866/439-7375) cost about $275 for a single rider or $300 double; custom tours are also available, but considerably more costly. A helmet is included with the snowmobile, as is a clothing package for protection against the bitter cold. **Warming huts** are located at Mammoth, Indian Creek, Canyon, Madison, West Thumb, and Fishing Bridge. They offer snacks, a hot cup of coffee or hot chocolate, and an excellent opportunity to recover from a chill.

Snowmobile rentals and guide service are also available in the **gateway communities** of Gardiner, Cooke City, and West Yellowstone. In West Yellowstone, try **Yellowstone Arctic/Yamaha,** 208 Electric St. (© 406/646-9636; www.yellowstonearcticyamaha.com or www.yellowstonesnowmobiles.com), or **Yellowstone**

4

YELLOWSTONE HIKES | Winter Sports & Activities

Adventures, 131 Dunraven St. (© **406/646-7735;** www.yellow stoneadventures.com). Most rental shops accept reservations weeks in advance; reserving at least 2 weeks ahead is a good idea. Guided tours run $175 to $250 per person per day.

For snowmobile rentals in Jackson, contact **Leisure Sports,** 1075 S. Hwy. 89 (© **307/733-3040;** www.leisuresportsadventure. com), which charges $145 and up per day. For a guided trip, call **Wyoming Adventures,** 1050 S. Hwy. 89 (© **800/637-7147** or 307/733-2300; www.wyomingsnow.com), which offers rentals and three different loop trips through Yellowstone for $269 to $375.

EXPLORING GRAND TETON NATIONAL PARK

Although Grand Teton National Park is much smaller than Yellowstone, there is more to it than just its peaks, a dozen of which climb to elevations greater than 12,000 feet. The park's manageable length—54 miles from north to south—allows visitors to get a good look at the highlights in a day or two. But you'd also be missing a great deal: the beautiful views from its trails, an exciting float on the Snake River, and the watersports paradise that is Jackson Lake.

5

Whether your trip is half a day or 2 weeks, the park's proximity to the town of Jackson, Wyoming, allows for an interesting trip that combines the outdoors with the urbane. You can descend Grand Teton and be living it up at the Million Dollar Cowboy Bar or dining in a fine restaurant that evening. The next day, you can return to the peace of the park without much effort at all.

ESSENTIALS

ACCESS/ENTRY POINTS Grand Teton National Park runs along a north-south axis, bordered on the west by the Teton Range. Teton Park Road, the primary thoroughfare, skirts along the lakes at the mountains' base. From the **north,** you can enter the park from Yellowstone National Park, which is linked to Grand Teton by an 8-mile stretch of highway (U.S. Hwy. 89/191/287) running through the **John D. Rockefeller, Jr. Memorial**

Grand Teton National Park

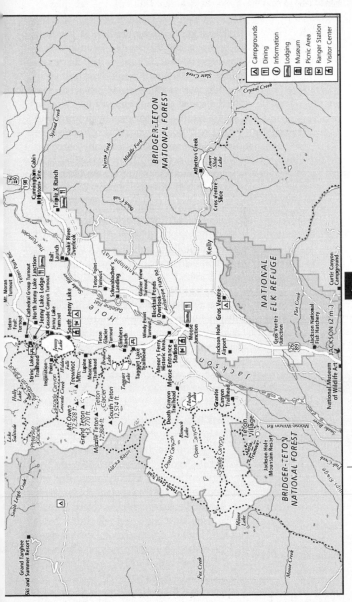

Parkway, along which you might see some bare and blackened trees from the 1988 fires. If you enter this way, you will already have paid your entrance fee to both parks, but you can stop at the park information center at Flagg Ranch, just outside Yellowstone, to get Grand Teton information. From December to mid-March, Yellowstone's south entrance is open only to snowmobiles and snowcoaches.

You can also approach the park from the **east,** via U.S. Hwy. 26/287. This route comes from Dubois, 55 miles east on the other side of the Absaroka and Wind River ranges, and crosses **Togwotee Pass,** where you'll get your first (and one of the best) views of the Tetons towering over the valley. Travelers who come this way can continue south on U.S. Hwy. 26/89/191 to Jackson without paying an entrance fee, although they are within the park boundaries, and enjoy spectacular mountain and Snake River views.

Finally, you can enter Grand Teton from Jackson in the **south,** driving about 12 miles north on U.S. Hwy. 26/89/191 to the Moose Junction turnoff and the park's south entrance. Here you'll find the park headquarters and the Craig Thomas Discovery and Visitor Center, plus a small community that includes restaurants and shops.

VISITOR CENTERS & INFORMATION There are three visitor centers in Grand Teton National Park. Opening in 2007, the dazzling **Craig Thomas Discovery and Visitor Center** (✆ 307/739-3399) is a half-mile west of Moose Junction at the southern end of the park. Featuring exhibits on alpinism, geology, and wildlife, an art gallery, a "video river" and other multimedia installations, free Wi-Fi, and a theater, it's open daily 8am to 7pm from June to Labor Day, 8am to 5pm early May to early June and Labor Day through October, and 9am to 5pm the rest of the year. The **Colter Bay Visitor Center** (✆ 307/739-3594), the northernmost of the park's visitor centers, is open daily 8am to 7pm from early June to Labor Day, and 8am to 5pm early May to early June and after Labor Day through early October. There is also **Jenny Lake Visitor Center** (✆ 307/739-3343), open daily 8am to 7pm from early June to Labor Day, and 8am to 5pm mid-May to early June and after Labor Day through late September. Maps and ranger assistance are available at all three centers, and there are bookstores and exhibits at Moose and Colter Bay.

On the Moose-Wilson Road, you'll find the **Laurance S. Rockefeller Preserve Center** (✆ 307/739-3654), open daily early June to Labor Day from 8am to 6pm and late May to early June and Labor Day to late September from 8am to 6pm. Finally, there is an information station at the **Flagg Ranch** complex

(✆ **307/543-2327**), which is located approximately 5 miles north of the park's northern boundary, open daily 9am to 3:30pm from early June through early September, although it may be closed for lunch.

To obtain park maps before your arrival, contact **Grand Teton National Park,** P.O. Drawer 170, Moose, WY 83012-0170 (✆ **307/739-3300;** www.nps.gov/grte).

FEES There are no park gates on U.S. Hwy. 26/89/191, so you can get a free ride through the park on that route; to get off the highway and explore, you'll pay $25 per automobile for a 7-day pass (admission is good for both Yellowstone and Grand Teton). If you expect to visit the parks more than once in a year, buy an annual pass for $50. And if you visit parks and national monuments around the country, purchase an **Interagency Annual Pass** for $80 (good for 365 days from the date of purchase at nearly all federal preserves). Anyone ages 62 and older can get an **Interagency Senior Pass** for a one-time fee of $10, and people who are blind or who have a permanent disability can obtain an **Interagency Access Pass,** which is free. All passes are available at any entrance point to the parks. While the Interagency Senior and Interagency Access passes must be obtained in person (to verify age or disability), Interagency Annual Passes are also available online at **http://store.usgs.gov/pass**.

Most of the money from entrance fees goes back into the park where it was collected, so consider it a contribution worth making: In Grand Teton, this revenue has been spent on renovating the Jenny Lake Overlook, maintaining trails, and restoring the lakeshore at Jenny Lake, among other things.

Fees for **tent camping** are between $20 and $21 per night at all the park campgrounds ($8 for hike- and bike-in sites). For recorded information on campgrounds, call ✆ **307/739-3603.** For more information on camping, see "Where to Camp in Grand Teton," in chapter 7. It is not possible to make advance reservations at campgrounds in Grand Teton.

SPECIAL REGULATIONS & WARNINGS See chapter 3 for a summary of the major park regulations, which are nearly identical in both parks.

THE HIGHLIGHTS

No matter what you do in Grand Teton, you are nearly always in view of the big granite peaks dominating the western skyline. They define the park and, therefore, deserve top billing of all of its highlights.

THE PEAKS The **Cathedral Group ★★★** comprises **Grand Teton** (elevation 13,775 ft.), **Mount Owen** (elevation 12,928 ft.), and **Teewinot** (elevation 12,325 ft.). Nearby, almost as impressive, are **South Teton** (elevation 12,514 ft.) and **Middle Teton** (elevation 12,804 ft.). To the north, **Mount Moran,** at 12,605 feet, is the fourth largest of the Tetons (on a clear day, though, you can take a great photograph of this peak all the way from Colter Bay to North Jenny Lake Junction). If you come from the east, you will pass no tollbooths on your way south on U.S. Hwy. 26/89/191, but there are frequent pullouts on the west side of the road that give you a panoramic overview of the Snake River and the Tetons. For that matter, you get a more distant but equally spectacular perspective of the mountains coming over **Togwotee Pass** on U.S. Hwy. 26/287. **Signal Mountain,** reached off Teton Park Road by Jackson Lake, is less a peak to look at than to look off—you can drive or hike to the top for a grand view.

COLTER BAY At the north end of the park, alongside Jackson Lake, Colter Bay offers a busy mix of information, services, activities on and off the water, and shopping. The visitor center provides wildlife videos, slide programs, natural history hikes, and evening amphitheater programs. Most remarkable is the **Indian Arts Museum ★**, which houses a collection of American Indian crafts, clothing, and beadwork, covering rooms on two floors.

JACKSON LAKE ★ The biggest of the park's lakes was dammed to provide more water for potato farmers in Idaho, but that also makes it a good place to sail, fish, and ride around on powerboats. Several lodges dot its shores, but the one that bears its name, **Jackson Lake Lodge,** is set back from the lake, bordered by Willow Flats and marshlands—prime moose habitat. The views are striking, and some good hikes begin here.

SIGNAL MOUNTAIN AREA ★ The **Signal Mountain campground** is a favorite of park visitors, conveniently located on the lakeshore for folks with watercraft, and the **Signal Mountain Lodge** is a fine place to stop for a meal with a view or a room for the night. Across the road, you can climb the mountain, by foot or by car, and get a panoramic view of the valley and mountains—the best way to get a perspective on the glacier-carved area known as Jackson Hole.

JENNY LAKE ★★ A loop off Teton Park Road takes you close to String and Jenny lakes and the exclusive **Jenny Lake Lodge** (home to what is probably the finest restaurant in any national park). Day visitors should head to the south end of the lake, the launch point for boat rides and the point of origin of the popular trail to **Inspiration Point and Hidden Falls ★★**, on the west side of the lake. There's also a small store. If you've got your wide-angle lens handy, stop at the **Cathedral Group Turnout,** a terrific spot for taking pictures.

MOOSE   You'll find plenty of services and shops and even a fine wine store in this small community, as well as the **park headquarters** and a **visitor center.** It's been a service area since the days of Bill Menor, who ran a river ferry and a country store here a century ago. Half a mile from the park offices, the store and ferry have been re-created at the **Menor/Noble Historic District.** The nearby **Chapel of the Transfiguration** is a log church built in 1925. The altar window frames a view of the Grand Teton.

SNAKE RIVER ★★   Below Jackson Lake Dam, the Snake River winds its way east and south, eventually turning west toward Idaho in the Snake River Canyon. There are beautiful stretches of river in the park, such as Oxbow Bend, a destination for canoeists and kayakers because of frequent appearances by trumpeter swans and moose. To the east and up on the flats, U.S. Hwy. 26/89/191 follows the river from Moran Junction to Jackson, with several pullouts and overlooks.

IF YOU HAVE ONLY 1 DAY

A 1-day trip around this park is not unreasonable, given its size, and you can do a loop in which you'll see many major attractions without having to retrace your steps. For more complete information on what you'll see along the way, read the next section on touring the park. Although this 1-day itinerary assumes that you are entering Grand Teton from the north, after visiting Yellowstone, you could just as easily begin your itinerary in Jackson, which is 8 miles south of the Moose Entrance Station.

Begin at the south entrance of Yellowstone National Park, driving through the **John D. Rockefeller, Jr. Memorial Parkway** (U.S. Hwy. 89/191/287) south past **Flagg Ranch** and to Grand Teton park. As you drive south, you'll find yourself skirting the northern shore of Jackson Lake, with a view of **Mount Moran** to the west, and, farther south, the stunning **Cathedral Group.**

On the northeast shore, **Colter Bay Village** is one of the park's busiest spots. You can rent boats, take scenic cruises, embark on guided fishing trips, buy fishing licenses and supplies, rent a cabin, or camp. Several popular hiking trails start here. If you turn right at Colter Bay Junction, you'll be at the **Colter Bay Visitor Center** a half-mile later; stop here to take in the **Indian Arts Museum ★**.

The **Lakeshore Trail** begins at the marina entrance and runs along the harbor for an easy 2-mile round-trip. It's level, paved,

The LSR Preserve

In 2007, the Rockefeller family donated to the U.S. National Park Service their former private retreat, the 1,106-acre JY Ranch, on the shore of Phelps Lake in the southern reaches of the park. Buildings came down, and an 8-mile trail system was constructed, as well as a staffed "reflection center" to allow visitors to make a personal connection with nature. Parking is limited; arrive early if you want a spot.

shady, and wheelchair accessible; it's the best opportunity for a hike in this area if you don't have much time. Nearby, on the shore of the lake, is an amphitheater where ranger-naturalists conduct evening programs. The Douglas firs and pine trees here are greener and healthier than the lodgepole pines that you see at higher elevations in Yellowstone.

A few minutes' drive south of Colter Bay, you'll pass Jackson Lake Lodge (you might want to look in the lobby and out the big picture window) and then **Jackson Lake Junction,** where a right turn puts you on **Teton Park Road,** the beginning of a 43-mile loop tour. You'll be driving parallel to the mountain range, with Grand Teton as the 13,770-foot centerpiece. You'll see lakes created by glaciers thousands of years ago, bordering a sagebrush valley inhabited by pronghorn and elk.

Just 5 miles down the road along Jackson Lake, a left (east) turn will take you up **Signal Mountain,** where you'll have a 360-degree view of the valley. Then continue down Teton Park Road to **South Jenny Lake,** where there is a huge parking area (which fills quickly in peak season) for the many people who stop to either hike around the lake or take a boat ride across. If you have time, get to the other side (it's a 2-mile hike) and make the short climb to **Hidden Falls ★★**. Another good day hike in this area is the **Taggart Lake Trail** (p. 117).

When you leave South Jenny Lake, you'll drive along a flat, sagebrush-dotted stretch to Moose, the southernmost of the park's service centers. A half-mile before Moose Junction is the **Craig Thomas Discovery and Visitor Center,** which features exhibits of the Greater Yellowstone area's rare and endangered species, a video room, and an excellent bookstore. While you're in Moose, you might want to visit the **Menor/Noble Historic District** and the **Chapel of the Transfiguration.**

Coming out of Moose, take a left (north) turn on U.S. Hwy. 26/89/191, which crosses the open flats above the Snake River to

Moran Junction. The best views along this road are the **Glacier View Turnout** and the **Snake River Overlook ★**, both of which are right off the road and well marked. At Moran Junction, turn left for a final 5-mile drive back to Jackson Lake Junction, past **Oxbow Bend,** a great spot for wildlife-watching.

Worn out? Catch the dramatic sunset behind the Tetons, and then head for your campsite (if you're tenting, stake out a spot early) or room, either in the park or in Jackson.

TOURING GRAND TETON

A 1-day whirlwind tour of Grand Teton is far from ideal. Like Yellowstone, this park demands a visit of 2 days or more. An extended stay allows for some relaxed hiking, picnicking, and sightseeing—you'll gain a greater appreciation for the park and the area's culture and history. A day at the Jenny Lake area, for instance, will provide awe-inspiring views of the peaks and a chance to walk the trails around the lake, to Inspiration Point or beyond up Cascade Canyon. You could also easily spend a day in the Jackson Lake Lodge area, where there are several wildlife viewing spots, trails, and places for a secluded picnic.

As with the short tour in the previous section, I begin at the northern end of the park, but you could just as easily start exploring from the southern end near Jackson. From Jackson, it's about 13 miles to the Moose Entrance Station, then another 8 miles to the Jenny Lake Visitor Center, another 12 miles to the Jackson Lake Junction, and 5 more miles to Colter Bay.

Jackson Lake & the North End of the Park

Many people enter Grand Teton National Park from the north end, emerging from Yellowstone's south entrance with a 7-day park pass that is good for admission to Grand Teton as well. Yellowstone is connected to Grand Teton by a wilderness corridor called the **John D. Rockefeller, Jr. Memorial Parkway** that runs north-south for 8 miles past meadows sometimes dotted with elk, over the Snake River, above Jackson Lake, and through forests that in some places still show the mosaic burns of the 1988 fires.

Along the parkway, not far from Yellowstone, you'll come to the lone outpost of **Flagg Ranch** (see "Flagg Ranch Village Area," in chapter 7), with gas, restaurants, lodging, and other services.

Giant **Jackson Lake ★**, a vast expanse of water filling a deep gouge left 10,000 years ago by retreating glaciers, dominates the north end of the park. While it is a natural lake, it was dammed

Jackson Lake: Colter Bay Area

nearly a century ago, encroaching the surrounding forest and dismaying conservationists. It empties east into the Snake River, curving around in the languid **Oxbow Bend**—a favorite wildlife-viewing float for canoeists. The water eventually turns south and then west through Snake River Canyon and into Idaho. Stream flow from the dam is regulated both for potato farmers downstream in Idaho and for rafters in the canyon. Elsewhere on the lake, things look quite natural, except when water gets low in the fall.

As the road follows the east shore of the lake from the north, the first development that travelers encounter is **Leeks Marina,** where boats launch, gas up, and moor from mid-May to mid-September. A casual restaurant here serves pizza during the summer; and there are also numerous scenic pullouts along the lake that are good picnic spots.

Just south of Leeks is **Colter Bay,** a busy outpost of park services where you can get groceries, postcards and stamps, T-shirts, and advice. At the **Colter Bay Visitor Center,** you can view park and wildlife videotapes and attend a park orientation slide program throughout the day. Ranger-led activities include museum tours, park-orientation talks, natural-history hikes, and evening

Jackson Lake: Signal Mountain Area

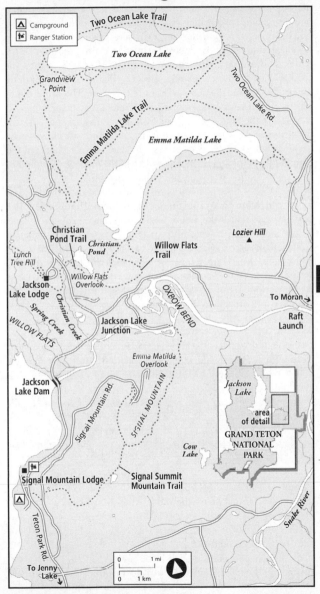

amphitheater programs. Colter Bay has plenty of overnight options, from cabins and old-fashioned tent camps to a trailer park and campground (see chapter 7). There are also a general store, a laundry facility, two restaurants, a boat launch and boat rentals, and tours. You can take pleasant short hikes in this area, including a walk around the bay or out to **Hermitage Point** (see chapter 6).

The **Indian Arts Museum ★ (✆ 307/739-3594)** at the Colter Bay Visitor Center is worth a visit, although it is not strictly about the Native American cultures of this area. The artifacts are mostly from Plains Indian tribes, but there are also some Navajo items from the Southwest. The collection was assembled by David T. Vernon and includes pipes, shields, dolls, and war clubs sometimes called "skull crackers." There are large historic photos in the exhibit area. Visiting Indian artists work in the museum all summer long and sell their wares on-site. Admission is free.

From Colter Bay, the road curves eastward and then south again, passing **Jackson Lake Lodge** (p. 143), a snazzy 1950s-style resort with a great view of the Tetons and brushy flats in the foreground where moose and coyotes often roam. Numerous trails emanate from here, both to the lakeshore and east to **Emma Matilda Lake** (see chapter 6). The road then comes to **Jackson Lake Junction,** where you can either continue west along the lakeshore or go east to the park's Moran entrance station. If you exit via the Moran entrance, you are still in the park, and can turn south on U.S. Hwy. 26/89/191 and drive along the Snake River to Jackson, making the most of your journey within the park's borders. However, you're probably here to enjoy the park, so you should turn right (west) on **Teton Park Road** at Jackson Lake Junction. After only 5 miles, you will arrive at **Signal Mountain.** Like its counterpart at Colter Bay, this developed recreation area, on Jackson Lake's southeast shore, offers camping sites, accommodations in cabins and multiplex units, two restaurants, and a lounge with one of the few televisions in the park. If you need to stock up on gas or food, do so at the small convenience store here. Boat rentals and scenic cruises of the lake are also available.

If you turn east instead of west off Teton Park Road at Signal Mountain, you can drive up a narrow, twisty road to the top of the mountain, 700 feet above the valley, where you'll have a fine view of the ring of mountains—Absarokas, Gros Ventres, Tetons, and Yellowstone Plateau—that create Jackson Hole. Clearly visible are the "Kettles": potholes in the valley's hilly moraines that are the mark of long-gone glaciers. Below the summit, about 3 miles from the base of the hill, is **Jackson Point Overlook,** a paved path 300 feet long leading to the spot where legendary photographer William Henry Jackson shot his famous landscapes of Jackson Lake and the

Tetons in the 1870s—proof to the world that such spectacular places really existed.

Looking for a hideaway? On the right (west) side of the road between Signal Mountain and North Jenny Lake Junction, approximately 2 miles south of the Mount Moran turnout, is an unmarked, unpaved road leading to **Spalding Bay.** It's a sheltered little camping area and boat launch area with a primitive restroom. There are only three sites, but it's a great place to be alone with spectacular views of the lake and mountains. If you decide to camp, a first-come, first-served backcountry permit is required (despite the fact it's accessible by road). An automobile or SUV will have no problem with this road, but speed had better not be of the essence to you. Passing through brush and forest, you might just spot a moose.

Jenny Lake & the South End of the Park

Continuing south along Teton Park Road, you move into the park's southern half, where the tallest peaks rise abruptly above a succession of small, crystalline lakes—**Leigh Lake,** the appropriately named **String Lake,** and **Jenny Lake ★★**, beloved by many visitors. At North Jenny Lake Junction, you can take a turnoff west to **Jenny Lake Lodge** (see chapter 7). The road then continues as a one-way scenic loop along the lakeshore before rejoining Teton Park Road about 4 miles later.

In summer, beautiful **Jenny Lake** attracts its share of crowds—hikers who circumnavigate the lake on a 6-mile trail, as well as more sedentary folks who pay for a boat ride across the lake to Hidden Falls and the short steep climb to Inspiration Point (see chapter 6). The parking lot at **South Jenny Lake** is often jammed, and there can be a long wait for the boat ride, so you might want to get there early in the day. Or you can save your money by taking the 2-mile hike around the lake—it's level and easy. There is also a tents-only campground, a visitor center, and a general store stocked with a modest supply of prepackaged foods and an even smaller selection of fresh produce. You'll have to buy a ticket and wait in line for the trip across the lake in a powerboat that holds about 30 people. Contact **Jenny Lake Boating Company** (© **307/734-9227;** www.jennylakeboating.com); round-trips cost $10 for adults and $5 for children 5 to 12.

South of the lake, Teton Park Road passes through wide-open sagebrush plains with spectacular views of the mountains. You'll pass the **Climbers' Ranch**—an inexpensive dormlike lodging alternative for climbers, run by the **American Alpine Club**

(© **307/733-7271;** www.americanalpineclub.org)—and some trail heads for enjoyable hikes to a handful of pristine alpine lakes. Look closely in the sagebrush for the shy pronghorn, more commonly (and incorrectly) labeled antelope. This handsome animal, with tan cheeks and black accent stripes, can spring up to 60 mph. Badgers also roam the brush here; you might encounter one of the timid-but-ornery creatures in the morning or at twilight.

The **Teton Glacier Turnout** presents a view of a glacier that grew for several hundred years until, pressured by the increasing summer temperatures of the past century, it reversed course and began retreating.

The road arrives at the park's south entrance at **Moose,** home to the stunning new **Craig Thomas Discovery and Visitor Center,** as well as park headquarters. If you are approaching the park from the south rather than the north, this is where you'll find maps, advice, and some interpretive displays.

Near the visitor center is **Menor's Ferry.** Bill Menor had a country store and operated a ferry across the Snake River at Moose back in the late 1800s. The ferry and store have been reconstructed, and you can buy items like those once sold here. Nearby is a historic cabin where a group of locals met in 1923 and planted the seed for the protection of the natural and scenic quality of the area, an idea that eventually led to the creation of the national park.

Also in this area is the **Chapel of the Transfiguration.** In 1925, this chapel was built in Moose so that settlers wouldn't have to make the long buckboard ride into Jackson. It's still in use for Episcopal services from spring to fall and is a popular place for weddings, with a view of the Tetons through a window behind the altar.

Dornan's is a small village area just south of the visitor center on a private holding of land owned by one of the area's earliest homesteading families. There are a few shops and a good grocery store, a post office, rental cabins, a bar with occasional live music, and, surprisingly, a first-rate wine shop.

The East Side of the Park

At Moose Junction, just east of the visitor center, drivers can rejoin the highway and either turn south to Jackson and the Gros Ventre turn or cruise north up U.S. Hwy. 26/89/191 to Moran Junction. This 18-mile trip is the fastest route through Grand Teton National Park and, being farther from the mountains, offers views of a broader mountain tableau.

Jenny Lake Area & Trails

The junction of U.S. Hwy. 89 with **Antelope Flats Road** is 1¼ miles north of the Moose Junction. The 20-mile route beginning here is an acceptable biking route. It's all on level terrain, passing by the town of Kelly and the Gros Ventre campground before looping back to U.S. Hwy. 26/89/191 at the Gros Ventre Junction to the south. (For more information on the Gros Ventre slide area, see "Farther Afield: Southeast of Moose," in chapter 6.)

Less than a mile down U.S. Hwy. 26/89/191, on the left, **Blacktail Ponds Overlook** offers an opportunity to see how beavers build dams and the effect these hard-working creatures have on the flow of the streams. The area is marshy early in summer, but it's still worth the .3-mile hike down to the streams where beaver activity can be viewed more closely.

Two miles farther along U.S. Hwy. 26/89/191, you'll reach the **Glacier View Turnout,** which offers views of an area that 140,000 to 160,000 years ago was filled with a 4,000-foot-thick glacier. The view of the gulch between the peaks offers vivid testimony of the power of the glaciers that carved this landscape. Lower **Schwabacher Landing** is at the end of a 1-mile, fairly well-maintained dirt road that leads down to the Snake River; you'll see the turnoff 4½ miles north of the Moose Junction. The road winds through an area filled with glacial moraine (rocks, sand, and gravel left behind by glaciers), the remnants of the ice age. At the end of the road is a popular launch site for float trips and for fly-fishing. It's also an ideal place to retreat from the crowds. Don't be surprised to see bald eagles, ospreys, moose, river otters, and beavers, all of which regularly patrol the area.

The **Snake River Overlook ★**, approximately 4 miles down the road beyond the Glacier View Turnout, is the most famous view of the Teton Range and the Snake River, immortalized by Ansel Adams. From this overlook, you'll also see at least three separate, distinctive 200-foot-high plateaus that roll from the riverbed to the valley floor, a vivid portrayal of the power of the glaciers and ice floes that sculpted this area. In the early 1800s, this was a prime hunting ground for John Jacob Astor's Pacific Fur Company and a certain David E. Jackson, for whom the lake and valley are named. But by 1840, the popularity of the silk hat had put an end to fur trapping, and the hunters disappeared. Good thing—by the time they departed, the beaver population was almost decimated.

A half-mile north of the Snake River Overlook is the newly repaved road to **Deadman's Bar,** a peaceful clearing on the riverbank. Many float trips launch here (multiday trips also camp in the area), and there is a limited amount of fishing access.

Cunningham Cabin, 1¼ miles north of Deadman's Bar, is a nondescript historic site at which homesteaders Pierce and Margaret Cunningham built their ranch in 1890. By 1928, they had been defeated by the elements and sold out to Rockefeller's Snake River Land Co. You can visit it at any time for a peek into the rough life of early Jackson Hole ranchers.

If you head down the highway in the other direction (south) from Moose Junction, on U.S. Hwy. 26/89/191, you can turn east on the **Gros Ventre River Road** 5 miles before you reach Jackson and follow the river east into its steep canyon; a few miles past the little town of Kelly, you'll leave the park and be in **Bridger-Teton National Forest.** In 1925, a huge slab of mountain broke off the north end of the Gros Ventre Range on the east side of Jackson Hole, a reminder that nature still has an unpredictable and violent side.

The slide left a gaping open gash in the side of Sheep Mountain, sloughing off nearly 50 million cubic yards of rock and forming a natural dam across the Gros Ventre River half a mile wide. Two years later, the dam broke, and a cascade of water rushed down the canyon and through the little town of Kelly, taking several lives. Today, **Kelly** is a quaint and eccentric town containing a large number of yurts (tentlike homes) and the **Teton Science Schools.** Up in the canyon, formed by the Gros Ventre River, there is a roadside display with photographs of the slide area and a short nature walk from the road down to the residue of the slide and **Lower Slide Lake.** Here, signs identify the trees and plants that survived or grew in the slide's aftermath.

ORGANIZED TOURS & RANGER PROGRAMS

The **Grand Teton Lodge Company** (© **800/628-9988** or 307/ 543-2811 for information; www.gtlc.com) runs half-day bus tours of Grand Teton ($45 for adults, $20 for children 3–11) and full-day tours of Yellowstone ($75 for adults, $43 for children 3–11) from late May to early October, weather permitting.

The **Teton Science Schools** ★★, 700 Coyote Canyon Rd., Jackson, WY 83001 (© **307/733-1313;** www.tetonscience.org), has an excellent curriculum for students of all ages, from integrated science programs for junior-high kids to adult seminars covering everything from botany to astronomy. Classes take place at campuses in Jackson and Kelly, and at other locations in Jackson Hole. The school's **Wildlife Expeditions** (© **877/404-6626**) offers tours that bring visitors closer to the park's wildlife. These trips range from a half-day to a week, covering everything from bighorn sheep to the wolves of Yellowstone.

Scenic Safaris (© **888/734-8898;** www.scenic-safaris.com) offers tours of Grand Teton and Yellowstone out of Jackson in comfortable luxury vans. Often centering on a hike in the park, the tours are half- and full-day affairs that range from $125 to $205 for adults and $85 to $125 for kids ages 12 and under. In the winter, the company offers snowcoach and snowmobile tours of both parks for $189 to $299; additional snowmobile riders cost $99 to $149.

Within the park, there are several interesting ranger programs. These include a ranger-led 3-mile hike from the Colter Bay Visitor Center to Swan Lake, as well as a relaxed evening chatting with a ranger on the deck of the Jackson Lake Lodge while you watch for moose and birds through a spotting scope. There are numerous events during the summer at Colter Bay, South Jenny Lake, and the Craig Thomas Discovery and Visitor Center at Moose. Check the daily schedules in the park's newspaper, *The Teewinot,* which is available at any visitor center.

From Moose, rangers lead visitors out to the lek—the mating ground of the strutting grouse, whose males' displays are dramatic, to say the least, during the springtime mating season. In winter, **guided snowshoe hikes** begin at the visitor center in Moose.

There are guided morning hikes to Phelps Lake at the Laurance S. Rockefeller Preserve and Inspiration Point from Jenny Lake (you take the boat across the lake), among other activities.

Children ages 8 to 12 can join the **Junior Ranger program** at Colter Bay or Jenny Lake and learn about the natural world for 2 hours while hiking with a ranger. Signups are at the visitor centers (the fee is a mere $1), and the kids will need basic hiking gear.

There are also evening campfire gatherings at most of the campground amphitheaters on a variety of park-related topics.

HIKES & OTHER OUTDOOR PURSUITS IN GRAND TETON NATIONAL PARK

Beyond the watersports on its lakes and rivers, Grand Teton National Park is a hiker's dream. The varied trail system—more than 250 miles in all—offers short, level trails around the valley floor as well as more demanding trails to the Teton Range that escape the crowds and challenge the body.

For a more extensive and detailed list of trails than what follows here, pick up *Teton Trails,* by Katy Duffy and Darwin Wile (Grand Teton Natural History Association, 1995). It's available for $6.95 from the **Grand Teton Association,** P.O. Box 170, Moose, WY 83012 (*©* **307/739-3403;** www.grandtetonpark.org).

DAY HIKES

The park's many trails vary greatly in length and level of difficulty, so you'll want to consult with rangers before tackling the trails. The rangers can suggest hikes suited to your ability and update you on everything from bear activity to trail damage (such as bridge outages) to

Photo Op

Not far from the trail head, the **Hermitage Point Loop** ★ opens to a broad, sagebrush-carpeted meadow. In the summer, the area blooms with wildflowers, offering one of the most spectacular views of colossal **Mount Moran,** which is as impressive in its own way as the Grand Teton. To avoid retracing your steps past Heron Pond, bear right at the third creek intersection and continue straight ahead to the corrals at Colter Bay—this route adds no distance to the hike.

weather concerns. They also conduct guided walks. *Remember*: If you are planning to hike for more than 30 minutes, carry a supply of water and some rain gear.

Turn to chapter 5 for **maps** showing the major trails described in this section. Trails are generally very well marked. I recommend that those who have only a brief time at Grand Teton choose the **Signal Mountain Summit Trail** ★★ or the **Inspiration Point Trail** ★★ in the Jenny Lake area.

Colter Bay Area

For a map showing the trails in this area, see chapter 5.

Lakeshore Trail This short jaunt starts at the marina and leads out to pebble beaches on the west side of Jackson Lake. The trail is wide and shady, and you can stop to look over the boats moored at the marina. Views of the entire Teton Range leap out at you from across Jackson Lake when you arrive at the end of the trail. The sounds of water lapping at the shore extend a peaceful atmosphere, as traffic and crowd noise are left well behind. The loop can be completed in about 1 hour of brisk walking.

2 miles round-trip. Easy. Access: Trail head is at the Marina entrance.

TRAILS FROM THE HERMITAGE POINT TRAILHEAD

The **Hermitage Point Trailhead,** near the marina, is the starting point for an interesting variety of trips ranging from 1 to 9 miles. With careful planning, it's possible to start the day with a hike beginning at Colter Bay that leads past **Cygnet Lake** across **Willow Flats** to **Jackson Lake Lodge,** where you can stop for lunch. Then, after a break, take the same path and return to Colter Bay in time for the evening outdoor barbecue. All told, that's 10 miles round-trip. While the topography is fairly level, the numerous trail options here can be confusing, so carry a map.

Hermitage Point Loop ★ From the trail head, this footpath heads through a thickly forested area to the isolated Hermitage Point, a peninsula jutting into Jackson Lake. Beyond the timber, the terrain consists of gently rolling hills, passing ponds, streams, and meadows. If you're seeking solitude, this is an excellent place to find it, although you should check with rangers before leaving—this is bear country.

9.4 miles round-trip. Moderate. Access: Trail head is just south of the Colter Bay Ranger Station; there are directional signs near the Swan Lake/Heron Pond Trail intersection.

Heron Pond Trail You journey through dense stands of lodge-pole pine to this pond, inhabited by beavers most likely to be seen in the early morning. This is bear territory and a haven for Canada geese, trumpeter swans, and moose. Wildflowers are part of the show in the early summer: Look for lupine, *Gilia,* heartleaf arnicas, and the Indian paintbrush. Don't be put off by the fact that the first 600 feet of the trail are steep; after reaching the top of a rise, it levels out and has only moderate elevation gains from that point on.

3 miles round-trip. Easy. Access: Trail head is at Hermitage Point Trailhead, Colter Bay.

Swan Lake Trail Finding swans at Swan Lake requires a trip to its southern shore, where a small island offers them isolation and shelter for nests. From Swan Lake, it's only .3 mile through a densely forested area to the intersection with the trail to Heron Pond. Hermitage Point is 3 miles from this junction along a gentle path that winds through a wooded area that's popular with bears. If you circumnavigate the lake, expect to spend roughly 2 hours on this hike.

3 miles round-trip. Easy. Access: Trail head is at Hermitage Point Trailhead, Colter Bay.

Willow Flats Trail ★ An alternative to the park's mountainous, forested trails, this trip from Colter Bay to Jackson Lake Lodge takes you across marshy flats where you'll have an idyllic view of the Tetons and a good chance of seeing a moose. Unfortunately, you begin by skirting the sewage ponds at Colter Bay, but it gets better. Pick up a trail east to Cygnet Lake and, instead of looping back to Colter Bay, you take a spur that crosses Pilgrim Creek going east across the flats. You can hike in either direction, but drop a car at each end if you don't want to double back on foot.

10 miles round-trip. Easy. Access: Horse corrals at Colter Bay.

A wide-open meadow near the summit of Signal Mountain presents an excellent opportunity to look to the west for photos of both **Mount Moran** and the **Teton Range**. The best time to take those photos is before 11am, when the sun will be mostly at your back, or in the early evening, when the sun will be lower in the sky to the west.

Jackson Lake Lodge Area

For a map showing the trails in this area, see chapter 5.

Christian Pond Trail   Starting with a .5-mile walk through a grassy, wet area to a pond with nesting trumpeter swans and other waterfowl, this is a short trail for all skill levels. If you're more ambitious, you can circumnavigate the pond, adding another 3 miles to the trip. In May and June, this is a great wildflower walk; but the area is also prime habitat for bears, so check with rangers before venturing onto the trail. The south end of the pond is covered with little grassy knolls upon which the birds build their nests and roost, and beavers have constructed a lodge here, too. It's a restful sanctuary, but one that's often infested by gnats and mosquitoes, so be sure to apply a coat of insect repellent.

1 mile round-trip. Easy. Access: Trail head is some 600 feet south of the entrance to Jackson Lake Lodge, most easily accessed from the Jackson Lake Lodge corrals. It's unmarked, so look carefully.

Signal Mountain Summit Trail ★★   Venturing up this uneven trail will give you a few fine hours of quiet trail time with views of the mountains, wildflowers, and, at the pinnacle, a grand panorama of the glacially carved valley. After negotiating a steep climb at the beginning of the trail, you'll come upon a broad plateau covered with lodgepole pine, grass, and seasonal wildflowers. Cross a paved road to a lily-covered pond, and just beyond you'll come upon two different trails up the mountain—for variety, take the right one up (ponds, maybe moose and bear) and the left one down (open ridges with views).

8 miles round-trip. Moderate. Access: Trail head is near the entrance to the Signal Mountain Lodge, or you can drive 1 mile up Signal Mountain Rd. to a pond on the right and pick up the trail there.

Two Ocean & Emma Matilda Lake Trails

You can arrive at these lakes from the east or west: From the west you begin at the Grand View Point Trailhead, 1 mile north of Jackson Lake Lodge, or at the Christian Pond Trailhead, just east of Jackson Lake Lodge. From the east, you go up Pacific Creek Road, 4 miles east of Jackson Lake Junction on the road to the Moran entrance. There is a pullout for Emma Matilda Lake 2 miles up this road, or you can go a half-mile farther, take a left on Two Ocean Lake Road, and go to the Two Ocean Lake Trailhead parking lot, from which trails lead to both lakes.

Emma Matilda Lake Trail   Circumnavigating this lake involves a pleasant up-and-down trek with great views of the mountains and a good chance of seeing wildlife. Emma Matilda Lake was named after the wife of Billy Owen, reputedly the first climber to reach the peak of Grand Teton. The hike winds uphill for a half mile from the parking area to a large meadow favored by mule deer. The trail follows the northern side of the lake through a pine forest 400 feet above the lake and then descends to an overlook where you'll have inspiring views of the Tetons, Christian Pond, and Jackson Lake. The trail on the south side of the lake goes through a densely forested area populated by Engelmann spruce and subalpine fir. Be watchful and noisy because this is bear country. It's possible to branch off onto the Two Ocean Lake Trail along the northern shore of the lake. Expect to spend 6 hours on this hike.

11.8 miles round trip. Easy to moderate. Access: Emma Matilda Lake Trailhead on Pacific Creek Rd. or trail head off Two Ocean Lake Rd. north of Jackson Lake–Moran Rd.

Two Ocean Lake Trail ★ 🎁   Take your time and take a picnic on this delightful, underused trail around Two Ocean Lake. You can start at either end. The walk around the lake is fairly level, and ducks, swans, grebes, and loons are commonly seen on the water. The variety of habitat—marshes, lakes, woodlands, and meadows—means that you'll not only see these birds, but also wildflowers, butterflies, and possibly bears, beavers, elk, deer, and moose. As usual, awesome views of the Tetons abound; for the best perspective, take the 1.3-mile trip up 600 feet to Grand View Point, a somewhat difficult climb through lodgepole pine and fir en route to a hilltop covered with orange arrowleaf balsamroot. You'll look

ESPECIALLY FOR kids

Children (ages 8–14) visiting the park are encouraged to explore and experience Grand Teton as members of the **Junior Ranger** program. To participate, pick up a copy of the Junior Ranger activity brochure at any visitor center, and then complete the projects outlined in the booklet during your stay. When you present a completed project (and $1) to a ranger at the Moose, Jenny Lake, or Colter Bay visitor centers, you'll be awarded a Young Naturalist patch.

Two trails within Grand Teton are especially kid-friendly. At 7 miles round-trip, the entire Jenny Lake Loop Trail is a bit long for kids, but take the boat shuttle across Jenny Lake to the **Inspiration Point Trail** ★★ portion, which is less than a mile long. The **Christian Pond Trail,** a level, 1-mile round-trip from the corrals at Jackson Lake Lodge, is also a nice diversion, offering great views and a chance to see myriad waterfowl.

down on lakes, meadows, and volcanic outcrops, and in the distance, you'll gaze at the Tetons, the Mount Leidy Highlands, and Jackson Lake. It's possible to branch off onto the Emma Matilda Lake Trail at the east end of Two Ocean Lake. The hike around the lake takes about 4 hours; allow an extra hour for the side trek up to Grand View Point.

6.4 miles round-trip, or 8 miles round-trip with the Grand View Point side trek. Easy to moderate. Access: Two Ocean Lake Trailhead on Two Ocean Lake Rd., or Grand View Point Trailhead.

Jenny Lake Area

A map showing the trails in this area is in chapter 5.

Amphitheater Lake Trail ★★   Here's a trail that can get you in and out of the high mountains in a day, presuming that you're in good shape and acclimated to the altitude—it's a strenuous 3,000-foot climb. You'll cross glacial moraines and meadows quilted with flowers, and enter forests of fir and pine (including whitebark pine, a delicacy for grizzly bears—be alert!). Finally, you clear the trees and come into a ring of monstrous rock walls topped by Disappointment Peak, with Grand Teton and Teewinot in view. Surprise Lake and Amphitheater Lake sit in this dramatic setting above timberline, with a few gnarled trees struggling to survive on the slopes.

9.6 miles round-trip. Difficult. Access: Lupine Meadows Trailhead. From the Moose entrance station on Teton Park Rd., drive 6½ miles to the Lupine Meadows

Junction and follow signs to the trail head; if you're coming from Jenny Lake, the trail head is at the end of a road less than 1 mile south of South Jenny Lake.

Cascade Canyon Trail ★★★ 📷 Cascade Canyon Trail is the most popular trail in the park for intermediate and expert hikers. You can begin the hike from South Jenny Lake, but you can also shave 2 miles off each way by riding the boat shuttle across the lake and beginning your hike at the boat dock. At this point, you're only a steep mile from Inspiration Point (see "Hidden Falls & Inspiration Point Trail," below), which is as far as most visitors ever get. From here, you make a brief climb up a sharp grade to the glacially rounded canyon. The trail flattens, allowing for a relaxing exploration of a true wonderland of nature: Wildflowers, waterfowl, and busy pikas abound. On a nice day, the warblers will be singing, and you could see moose and bears.

If you want to go farther, you have two choices when you reach forks of North and South Cascade Canyon: Follow the South Fork to Hurricane Pass or the North Fork to Lake Solitude. At 23 and 18 miles, respectively, these are overnight trips for most mortals, so you'll need camping gear and a backcountry permit.

A less taxing alternative to the Cascade Canyon trip mentioned above is a detour to **Moose Ponds,** which begins on the Inspiration Point Trail. The ponds, located 2 miles from either west or east boat docks, are near the south end of Jenny Lake and are alive with birds. The stretch near the base of Teewinot Mountain, which towers over the area, is populated with elk, mule deer, black bears, and moose. The trail is flat (at lake level), short, and easy to negotiate in 1 to 1½ hours. The best times to venture forth are early morning and evening.

9.1 miles round-trip. Moderate to difficult. Access: Inspiration Point.

Hidden Falls & Inspiration Point Trail ★★ ☺ Many people cross Jenny Lake, either by boat or on foot around the south end, and then make the short, forest-shaded uphill slog to **Hidden Falls** (less than 1 mile of hiking if you take the boat; 5 miles round-trip if you walk around), which tumbles down a broad cascade. Some think that's enough and don't go another steep half-mile to **Inspiration Point.** Up there you get a great view of Jenny Lake below, and you can see the glacial moraine that formed it. If you're going to only these two overlooks, I recommend a relaxed hike around the south end of the lake.

Whichever route you take to Inspiration Point, start early in the day to avoid the crowds. Then pace yourself. And once you've reached Inspiration Point, what's to stop you from proceeding on to Cascade Canyon?

1.8–5.8 miles round-trip. Moderate. Access: Trail heads are at the east shore boat dock or at the west shore boat dock of Jenny Lake (if you take the boat shuttle).

Jenny Lake Loop Trail ★★ This trail circumnavigates the lake, following the shore. You can cut it in half by taking the Jenny Lake Boat Shuttle from the east shore boat dock to the west shore boat dock. The unblemished lake, which is 2.5 miles long, is in an idyllic setting at the foot of the mountain range, so it presents excellent views throughout the summer, and is a good spot to see moose.

Keep in mind that Jenny Lake is one of the most popular spots in the park; to avoid the crowds, travel early or late in the day. The trails to Hidden Falls, Inspiration Point, and the Moose Ponds branch off of this trail on the southwest shore of the lake. The trails to String and Leigh lakes branch off of this trail on the northern shore of Jenny Lake.

6.5 miles round-trip. Easy to moderate. Access: Trail head is at the east shore boat dock.

Leigh Lake Trail ★ This trail begins at String Lake, which is a small, finger-shaped lagoon connecting Leigh and Jenny lakes. The trail for Leigh Lake is well marked and relatively flat, and it passes through a forested area that is always within sight of the lake. Picnickers willing to expend the energy necessary to hike roughly 1 mile from the String Lake picnic area to the end of the lake will find themselves eating in a less congested area with spectacular views of Mount Moran. The trail continues along the eastern shore of Leigh Lake to a meadow with typically wonderful views and then continues on to small Bearpaw Lake. A better option, if time allows, is to return to the picnic area, cross the String Lake inlet, and explore the western edge of Jenny Lake along the trail that circumnavigates its shoreline (see the "Jenny Lake Loop Trail," above).

7.5 miles round-trip. Easy. Access: Trail head is adjacent to the String Lake picnic area.

String Lake Trail This easy hike along the eastern shore of String Lake has two things going for it: It provides easy access to Leigh Lake, and it's in a forest that is a better alternative for a lunch break than the crowded picnic area. You'll wander in the shade of a pine forest along the shore with excellent views of Mount Moran above. However, because this is a heavily trafficked area, you should not count on seeing much wildlife, if any. This is also the starting point for a more ambitious trip up Paintbrush Canyon (see "Exploring the Backcountry," below).

3.3 miles round-trip. Easy. Access: Trail head is at the Leigh Lake Trailhead.

Taggart and Bradley Lakes Trail ★★ Want to get away from the crowds on Jenny Lake trails? Just down the road from South Jenny is the trail head to Taggart and Bradley lakes, named for two members of the 1872 Hayden expedition. This hike winds through a burned-out area, in the midst of recovery, to Taggart Lake, which was created by glacial movements. The hike from the parking lot to the lake (where you can fish from the shore) is only 1.5 miles along the southern (left) fork of the trail. Swimming in these cold waters is not recommended. From the lake, you can return by the same trail or continue north to **Bradley Lake** for a round-trip of 5 miles. This route adds 1.8 miles to the trip, and the elevation gain is 467 feet; the payoff is that, at its highest point, the trail overlooks all of Taggart Lake and the stream flowing from it. Like other hikes in Grand Teton, this one is best made during the early-morning or early-evening hours, when it's cooler and there's less traffic.

5 miles round-trip. Moderate. Access: Trail head is west of Teton Park Rd., approximately 6 miles south of Jenny Lake, and is well marked.

Farther Afield: Southeast of Moose

Although it is situated near Kelly, outside the park boundaries, the **Gros Ventre Slide Area** is an interesting hiking area and historical site. You can get to the slide area by traveling east from the Gros Ventre Junction on U.S. Hwy. 26/89/191, 6 miles north of Jackson; alternately, 1 mile north of the Moose Junction on U.S. Hwy. 26/89/191, take the Antelope Flats Road to the second right turn, then take the second left. (There is a sign for the slide area.)

It was at this spot, in June 1925, that the side of Sheep Mountain broke loose and created one of the largest earth movements ever observed. Nearly 50 million cubic yards of sandstone formed a dam 225 feet high and a half-mile wide across the Gros Ventre River. Then, in 1927, the upper 60 feet of the dam gave way, creating a raging river that flooded the town of Kelly, 3½ miles downstream.

Informational brochures and maps of this interpretive trail, which is in the Bridger-Teton National Forest, are available from the U.S. Forest Service. Stop in at the **Greater Yellowstone Visitor Center,** at 532 N. Cache St. in downtown Jackson, where you can pick up all the information you'll need to hike in this area, or call the **Forest Service** at © 307/739-5500.

EXPLORING THE BACKCOUNTRY

Grand Teton might seem small compared to Yellowstone, but there are more than 250 miles of trails in the backcountry and plenty of opportunities for solitude and adventure. As in Yellowstone, a permit is required for camping in the backcountry—the permits are free and are essentially for keeping track of campers and for making sure that no one area is overused. Rather than receiving a specific site reservation, the permits allow you to establish camp in one of several camping "zones," where you'll have a choice of sites.

For **general information** on backpacking and safety, see chapter 10.

INFORMATION BEFORE YOU GO   For background information, write for the *Grand Teton Backcountry Camping* brochure, Grand Teton National Park, P.O. Drawer 170, Moose, WY 83012, or print it out from **www.nps.gov/grte**. For recorded backcountry information, call © **307/739-3602.**

BACKCOUNTRY PERMITS   Backcountry permits from the National Park Service are required to use an overnight campsite; the permits themselves are free, but an advance reservation entails a nonrefundable $25 fee. To avoid the fee, you may pick up a permit the day before you commence your trip. Reservations are accepted only from January 1 to May 15; it's wise to reserve a camp area during this period if you're going in July or August. The permit is valid only on the dates for which it is issued.

Warning: The reservation is just that, a reservation; upon your arrival at the park, you'll need to secure the permit. Permits are issued at the Moose and Colter Bay visitor centers and at the Jenny Lake Ranger station; you may make reservations by writing the **Permits Office,** Grand Teton National Park, P.O. Drawer 170, Moose, WY 83012, or faxing 307/739-3438. Reservations can also be made online at **www.nps.gov/grte**.

WHEN TO GO   Remember that this region has a short summer and virtually no spring. While the valley floor of the park is open in May, some of the high-country trails might not be clear of snow or high water before late June or early July. Look in the *Backcountry Camping* brochure (see above) for approximate dates when specific campsites are habitable.

MAPS   Topographic maps of Grand Teton are available from the U.S. Geological Survey and National Geographic Maps (© **800/ 962-1643;** www.natgeomaps.com), as is the *Grand Teton Hiking and Climbing* map, which includes maps of Granite and Moran canyons and a trip planner; it is available from the **Grand Teton Association,** P.O. Box 170, Moose, WY 83012 (© **307/739-3403;** www.grandtetonpark.org).

The Backcountry in Grand Teton

The premier backcountry activity in Grand Teton is not hiking but rather **mountain climbing,** which you should not attempt alone unless you are an expert. For a complete discussion of mountaineering possibilities and outfitters in Grand Teton National Park, see "Climbing," in the "Other Activities" section below.

Perhaps the most popular backcountry trail in Grand Teton is the 19.3-mile **Cascade Canyon Loop ★★★**. The loop starts on the west side of Jenny Lake, winds northwest 9.3 miles on the **Cascade Canyon Trail** to Lake Solitude and the Paintbrush Divide, and then returns on the 10-mile-long **Paintbrush Canyon Trail** past Holly Lake, tucked into a cirque including Mount Woodring. While there are longer hikes, this is one of the most rigorous in either park because of gains in elevation (more than 2,600 ft.), rocky trails, and switchbacks through loose gravel that can get slippery, especially in years when snow remains until the middle of summer on the north-facing side of Paintbrush Divide.

Rangers recommend the hike for several reasons, the most noteworthy of which is unsurpassed scenery. Moose and black bear are part of the park home, and so hikers are cautioned to be diligent about making noise (strap some bells on your pack). You might also see harlequin ducks, which nest near the trail in Cascade Creek. You'll see many other avians, a whole host of wildflowers, and large stands of whitebark pine trees.

Although it adds 5 miles to the trip (one-way), a detour west from the Cascade Canyon Trail to **Hurricane Pass** will reward you with a view from the foot of **Schoolroom Glacier.** If it's an extended trip you're after, head west into the **Jedediah Smith Wilderness** on a trail that eventually crosses into Idaho. This trail doesn't end anytime soon—you can actually continue trekking all the way to Alaska.

If you are looking to make a *long* day hike out of this, you can trek 7.3 miles on the Cascade Canyon Trail to **Lake Solitude** and return via the same trail. But you're better off planning for a multi-day trip because camping zones are 6 miles west of the trail head on the Cascade Canyon Trail and 8.8 miles northwest on the Paintbrush Canyon Trail at Holly Lake. Be sure to get a reservation.

The quickest way to get up high in these mountains for a backcountry foray is to hitch a ride up **Rendezvous Mountain ★** on the Jackson Hole Ski Resort Tram. Hikers can ride it up to 10,450 feet above sea level in **Bridger-Teton National Forest,** just south of the park, and embark north toward the park's Middle Fork Cutoff. From here, you can head down into **Granite Canyon** to Phelps Lake, which has three lakefront campsites—and is the closest backcountry camping zone to civilization. Alternatively, you can hike north through the high country along the **Teton Crest Trail** to Fox Creek Pass (over 8 difficult miles from the tram) and to Death Canyon and beyond.

If you are hardy enough to make it to **Death Canyon Shelf,** a wildflower-strewn limestone ledge that runs above Death Canyon toward **Alaska Basin,** you'll have an extraordinary, high-altitude view of the west side of the Tetons' biggest peaks. If you are on an extended backcountry trip, you can continue north to Hurricane Pass, where you can come back down to the valley floor by way of Cascade Canyon.

This kind of backcountry trip is truly an expedition and requires a certain level of skill and experience. Go over any such plans with park rangers, who can help you evaluate your ability to take on such a challenge.

OTHER ACTIVITIES

In addition to the activities listed here, check out some of the other options in the Jackson area that are listed in chapter 8.

BIKING   Bikes are banned from all hiking trails in the park, and on the paved roads below. The problem is safety—there are huge RVs careening about, and some roads have only narrow shoulders. Construction has widened Teton Park Road a bit, but traffic on it is still heavy. There's a popular 8-mile multiuse trail between Jenny Lake and Moose. Road bikers should also try **Antelope Flats,** beginning at a trail head a mile north of Moose Junction and going east. Also called **Mormon Row,** this paved route crosses the flats below the Gros Ventre Mountains, past the small town of Kelly. It connects to the unpaved **Shadow Mountain Road,** which leaves the park and continues into national forest. After a total distance of 7 miles and an elevation gain of 1,370 feet, you'll be looking at Mount Moran and the Tetons across the valley.

Mountain bikers have a few more options: Try **Two Ocean Lake Road** (reached from the Pacific Creek Rd. just north of Moran Junction) or the **River Road,** a 15-mile dirt path along the Snake River's western bank. Ambitious mountain bikers might want to load their overnight gear and take the **Grassy Lake Road,** once used by Indians, west from Flagg Ranch on a 50-mile journey to Ashton, Idaho.

Books and maps with bicycle routes are available at visitor centers, or from **Adventure Sports,** at Dornan's in the village of Moose (© **307/733-3307**), which is inside the boundaries of Grand Teton National Park. You can also rent mountain bikes here as well as road and performance bikes for a few dollars more. Children's bikes are also available. Rates run $28 to $36 for a half-day and $36 to $48 for 24 hours.

BOATING   Boaters have more choices in Grand Teton than they do in Yellowstone. Motorboats are permitted on Jenny, Jackson, and Phelps lakes. Bigger boats, even a few yacht-size vessels, find room on Jackson Lake, where powerboats pull skiers, sailboats move noiselessly in summer breezes, and fishermen ply the waters. Those who venture on the big lake need to be aware that the weather can change suddenly, and late afternoon lightning is not uncommon; sailors should be particularly wary of the swirling winds that accompany thunderstorms.

If you bring your own boat, you must register it: For human-powered craft, the fee is $10 for 7 days, or $20 for a yearlong permit; motorized skippers pay $20 for 7 days and $40 for an annual permit, which you can buy at the Colter Bay and Moose visitor centers. Boat and canoe rentals, tackle, and fishing licenses are available at Colter and **Signal Mountain Lodge** (© **307/543-2831;** www.signalmtnlodge.com). Rental fees are $36 to $55 per hour for motorboats; kayaks, canoes, and pontoon boats. Deck cruisers are also available.

Motorized boats are allowed on Phelps, Jackson, and Jenny lakes, but on Jenny Lake the motor can't be over 8 horsepower. Only human-powered vessels are permitted on Emma Matilda, Two Ocean, Taggart, Bradley, Bearpaw, Leigh, and String lakes. Rafts, canoes, dories, and kayaks are allowed on the Snake River within the park. No boats are permitted on Pacific Creek or the Gros Ventre River.

Scenic cruises ★ of Jackson Lake are conducted daily by the **Grand Teton Lodge Company** (© **307/543-2811;** www.gtlc. com). Breakfast cruises run Saturday through Thursday and dinner cruises run Monday, Wednesday, and Friday. Both depart from the **Colter Bay Marina** from May to September. You'll travel to Elk Island, where they cook up a pretty good meal: trout and steak for dinner, and pancakes and eggs for breakfast. The scenic trips are 1½ hours long, and cost $28 for adults and $13 for kids 3 to 11; the meal cruises are twice as long and run $37 (breakfast) and $57 (dinner) for adults, and $22 and $37, respectively, for kids 3 to 11.

Jenny Lake Boating Company (© **307/734-9227;** www.jenny lakeboating.com) takes visitors on scenic cruises in Jenny Lake; the cost is $15 for adults and $7 for children. The tours are scheduled throughout the day and last about an hour. Reservations are strongly recommended. The company also rents kayaks for $15 an hour.

Additionally, you can rent kayaks and canoes at **Adventure Sports** at Dornan's in the town of Moose (© **307/733-3307**), which is in the boundaries of Grand Teton National Park. Rentals run $48 per day.

CLIMBING Mountaineering in Grand Teton National Park is wildly popular, but it's important to stay within the limits of your skill level. Every single year, there are rescues of climbers who fall or get trapped on Teton rock faces, and many years there are fatalities. Yet the peaks have a strong allure for climbers, even inexperienced ones, perhaps because you can reach the top of even the biggest ones in a single day, albeit not without a serious workout. The terrain is mixed, speckled with snow and ice even in midsummer—knowing how to self-arrest with an ice ax is a must—and the weather can change suddenly. The key is to get good advice, know your limitations, and, if you're not already skilled, take some lessons at the local climbing schools (see paragraph below). If you go without a professional guide, you should definitely go with experienced companions who know the mountain.

Climbers who go out for a day do not have to register or report to park officials, but they should be sure to tell friends where they're going and when they'll be back. Overnight climbers must pick up a free permit. Climbing rangers who can lead rescue efforts are on duty at the **Jenny Lake Ranger Station** at South Jenny Lake from late May to late September. The American Alpine Club (AAC) provides inexpensive dormitory beds ($14 nightly for AAC members, $22 for nonmembers) for climbers at the **Grand Teton Climbers' Ranch** (✆ 307/733-7271; www.americanalpine club.org). A pair of long-standing operations offer classes and guided climbs of Grand Teton: **Jackson Hole Mountain Guides** in Jackson (✆ 800/239-7642 or 307/733-4979; www.jhmg.com) and **Exum Mountain Guides** ★ in Moose (✆ 307/733-2297; www.exumguides.com). Expect to pay $700 to $1,000 for a guided 2-day climb of Grand Teton or $150 to $200 for a class.

The **Jenny Lake Ranger Station** (✆ 307/733-3392), which is open only in summer, is the center for climbing information; climbers are encouraged to stop in and obtain information on routes, conditions, and regulations.

FISHING The lakes and streams of Grand Teton are popular fishing destinations, loaded with lively cutthroat trout, whitefish, and mackinaw (lake) trout in Jackson, Jenny, and Phelps lakes. Jackson has produced some monsters weighing as much as 50 pounds, but you're more likely to catch fish under 20 inches, fishing deep with trolling gear from a boat during hot summer months.

The Snake River runs for about 27 miles in the park and has cutthroat and whitefish up to about 18 inches. It's a popular drift-boat river for fly fishermen. If you'd like a guide who knows the holes, try **Jack Dennis Fishing Trips** (✆ 307/690-0910; www.jackdennis fishingtrips.com), **Triangle X Float Trips** (✆ 307/733-5500;

www.trianglex.com), or **Westbank Anglers** (© 800/922-3474 or 307/733-6483; www.westbank.com). The going rate is $425 to $475 for a full day for two people. **Signal Mountain Lodge** (© 307/543-2831; www.signalmtnlodge.com) offers guided half-day trips on motorized craft in **Jackson Lake** for one or two people for $280. As an alternative, stake out a position on the banks below the dam, where you'll have plenty of company and just might snag something. While special fishing permits are issued by the National Park Service in Yellowstone, a **Wyoming fishing license** is required of anglers in Grand Teton (nonresident fees are $14 per day, $92 for the season for adults; $3 per day, $15 for the season for teenagers 14–18; no license is required for kids ages 13 and under). A $13 Conservation Stamp is also required for all licenses except the 1-day variety.

FLOAT TRIPS The upper end of the Snake River in the park can be deceptive—its smooth surface runs fast during the spring, and there are deadly snags of fallen trees and other debris. Without a local guide or past experience, you might want to think twice about dropping your personal raft in. Check in with rangers, and let them discourage you if they think your skills might not match the river. There are plenty of commercial-rafting outfitters that will help you get acquainted (see paragraph below). If you want white water, there are a dozen commercial outfitters offering white-water trips down Snake River Canyon, outside the park (see "Jackson, Wyoming," in chapter 8).

The park's 27-mile stretch of river attracts all sorts of wildlife, with moose, eagles, and other animals coming to the water's edge. There are many commercial float operators in the park that generally run trips from mid-May to mid-September (depending on weather and river flow conditions). These companies offer 5- to 10-mile scenic floats, some with early-morning and evening wildlife trips. Try **Solitude Float Trips** (© 888/704-2800; www.grand-teton-scenic-floats.com), **Barker-Ewing Float Trips** (© 800/365-1800 or 307/733-1800; www.barkerewing.com), **Grand Teton Lodge Company** (© 307/543-2811; www.gtlc. com), or **Signal Mountain Lodge** (© 307/543-2831; www. signalmtnlodge.com). Scenic float trips cost about $50 to $70 for adults, with discounts for children ages 11 and under.

HORSEBACK RIDING Horseback riding is as popular in Grand Teton as it is in Yellowstone. The **Grand Teton Lodge Company** (© 307/543-2811; www.gtlc.com) offers tours from corrals at Colter Bay and Jackson Lake Lodge. Guided 1- and 2-hour trail rides run $37 to $75; pony rides for kids are $5. An experienced rider might find these tours too tame; wranglers refer to them as "nose and tail" tours. For the names of several other companies that organize horseback trips in Jackson Hole, see "Jackson, Wyoming," in chapter 8.

WINTER SPORTS & ACTIVITIES

Park facilities pretty much shut down during the winter, except for a skeleton staff at the Moose Visitor Center, and the park shows no signs of becoming a winter magnet, à la Yellowstone. That may be just as well—you can enjoy some quiet, fun times in the park without the crowds.

WINTER ROAD CONDITIONS Teton Park Road opens to conventional vehicles and RVs around May 1. The **Moose-Wilson Road** opens to vehicles about the same time. Park roads close on November 1 for the winter season. They are open to snowshoers and cross-country skiers after mid-December.

SPORTING GOODS & EQUIPMENT RENTALS Jackson has enough sporting equipment places to keep everyone in Wyoming outfitted. The **Jack Dennis Outdoor Shop,** on the south side of Town Square (© 800/570-3270 or 307/733-3270; www.jackdennisoutdoors.com), has all the skis and outdoor clothing you can possibly need. **Teton Mountaineering,** 170 N. Cache St. (© 800/850-3595; www.tetonmtn.com), is the equipment shop of choice for the knowledgeable and advanced skier or ice climber; **Hoback Sports,** 520 W. Broadway Ave. (© 307/733-5335; www.hobacksports.com), is another good option. **Skinny Skis,** at 65 W. Deloney Ave. off the Town Square (© 888/733-7205 or 307/733-6094; www.skinnyskis.com), is a year-round specialty sports shop focusing on Nordic skiing. For a great supply of seconds (same quality of material as "firsts"), stop at **Moosely Seconds** (© 307/739-1801) in Moose.

CROSS-COUNTRY SKIING You can ski on flat or steep terrain in Grand Teton; the two things to watch out for are hypothermia and avalanches. As with climbing, know your limitations, and make sure you're properly equipped. Check with local rangers and guides for trails that match your ability. Among your options is the relatively easy **Jenny Lake Trail,** starting at the Taggart Lake Parking Area, about 13km (8 miles) of flat and scenic trail that follows Cottonwood Creek. A more difficult ski is the **Taggart Lake–Beaver Creek Loop,** a 5km (3.1-mile) route that has some steep and icy pitches coming back. About 6.5km (4 miles) of the **Moose-Wilson Road**—the back way to Teton Village from Moose—is unplowed in the winter and is an easy trip through the woods. You can climb the windy, unplowed road to the top of **Signal Mountain**—you might encounter snowmobiles—and have some fun skiing down. There is an easy ski trail from the Colter Bay Ranger Station area to **Heron Pond**—about 4km (2.5 miles), with a great view of the Tetons and Jackson Lake. Get a ski trail map from the visitor centers. Rangers also offer guided snowshoe tours.

SNOWMOBILING   Snowmobiling is a popular winter option. Snowmobiling is allowed on the frozen surface of Jackson Lake and in the nearby **Bridger-Teton National Forest,** immediately east of Grand Teton National Park.

WHERE TO STAY & EAT IN THE PARKS

7

Before picking up the phone to make a reservation, take some time to study maps of the parks (see ours in chapters 3 and 5). While the parks are small enough that you can drive practically anywhere in a day, you'll want to be acquainted with the locations of the park attractions that you most want to see and their proximity to accommodations. For instance, if you want to see Old Faithful at different hours of the day and night, or if you want to hike the Lonestar Geyser Trail, try to get a room at the Old Faithful Inn or the Old Faithful Snow Lodge. If you find large bodies of water soothing, check in at the Lake Yellowstone Hotel or Colter Bay Village.

Also keep in mind that the characteristics of the lodgings vary considerably, and request specific information about the type of rooms available before making a reservation. If you are bedding down in one of the historic hotels or cabins in the parks, be aware that they offer fewer modern conveniences than your typical commercial motel.

One final bit of advice: Try to spend at least 2 nights within park boundaries, whether you prefer campgrounds or hotels. When the sun dips below the horizon, you'll see a summer sky that sparkles more brightly than in the gateway cities (weather permitting), and you might hear coyotes and other wildlife. And you will discover that the hours just after daybreak are an ideal time for exploring: The trails are empty, animals go about their early-morning routines oblivious to visitors, and the silence is deafening.

WHERE TO STAY IN YELLOWSTONE NATIONAL PARK

To book a room within Yellowstone, you need to contact **Yellowstone National Park Lodges,** operated by Xanterra Parks & Resorts, P.O. Box 165, Yellowstone National Park, WY 82190 (*(℗)* **866/439-7375** or 307/344-7311; www.yellowstonenational parklodges.com). Most Yellowstone accommodations are open from early May to mid-October. During Yellowstone's winter season, which begins in mid-December and runs through early March, accommodations and meals for snowmobilers, cross-country skiers, and other visitors can be found at either Mammoth Hot Springs Hotel or Old Faithful Snow Lodge. There are also special packages in winter and summer that bundle activities and lodging; visit the Xanterra website for current specials. Because operations are heavily dependent on weather conditions, it's best to call ahead.

It's easier to find a vacant room before June 20 and after September 25, and the week before Labor Day weekend is usually slow. The more popular lodges and campgrounds in the parks are typically fully booked during the peak season, so reservations should be made a few months in advance. At Old Faithful Snow Lodge, Lake Yellowstone Hotel, Grant Village, and Mammoth Hot Springs Hotel, the rates sometimes drop early in the season and in October, and visitors making reservations before April 1 can also get significant discounts.

If you want television, air-conditioning, and other modern amenities typical of American hotels, stay in a gateway town rather than in the park. Some of the inns are close to a century old, and the park has encouraged the concessionaires to keep technology to a minimum. Although some of the park lounges now have televisions, and telephones have been added to many rooms, you'll find only two in-room TVs in the entire park (in the suites at Mammoth, but reception wavers). Most of the accommodations do have heat, although in some cases—in the cabins at Roosevelt Lodge Cabins, for example—it's generated by a wood stove.

Mammoth Hot Springs Area

5 miles from the Gardiner (north) entrance to Yellowstone

This area is open year-round and houses the park headquarters. It's a 5-mile drive from the park's north entrance, and you can often find a room here, even during the height of its peak summer and winter seasons. Besides easy access, the area has quite a bit to

WHAT YOU'LL really PAY

The prices quoted here are rack rates, the maximum that the hotels charge; it is likely that you'll end up paying these rates in Yellowstone and Grand Teton unless you arrive in spring or fall. The concessionaires do not offer a great deal of discounts, thanks to the short summer season in both parks and the fact that occupancy is near 100% all summer long. During slow times, however, it's not impossible to obtain a room at an expensive property for the same rate as at a more moderate one.

In both parks, April and October are the bargain months, but the sheer number of visitors the rest of the year overwhelms the capacity. If you're looking for a bargain, your best bets are the gateway cities of Cooke City and Gardiner, Montana (see chapter 8). In Cody, Wyoming, you'll be lucky to get a room for less than $100 per night in peak season; in Jackson, Wyoming, $200 is a more realistic baseline for in-town lodgings. You'll want to shop online for deals, but I tend to look hard in Teton Village in summer: You still have easy access to Jackson (and better access to Grand Teton National Park), but the supply of rooms here is meant to contain the winter ski crowd, and summer vacancies are the norm. In winter, you'll save money by staying in Jackson instead and taking the free shuttle to the slopes at Jackson Hole Mountain Resort.

Note: Quoted discount rates almost never include breakfast, hotel tax, or any other fees.

offer: the park's best visitor center; colorful, travertine limestone terraces; a historic hotel with one of the park's better restaurants; and a campground.

Mammoth Hot Springs Hotel and Cabins ★ Below the steaming terraces of Mammoth Hot Springs, this is one of two Yellowstone hotels open during both summer and winter seasons. (The other is the Old Faithful Snow Lodge.) Established in 1911, the hotel itself is less distinguished than the Lake Yellowstone Hotel or the Old Faithful Inn, but it manages to blend a wide range of rooms into a satisfying whole. The only truly high-end accommodations are the suites. Standard rooms and cabins offer minimal amenities, but make up for it with a fair amount of charm. Some have tubs only, some have showers only, and some have a shared bathroom down the hall. The cottage-style cabins are clustered in rings adjacent to the hotel, and vary in quality, but are generally good picks for families and those who want a little more elbowroom. Make sure you drift into the **Map Room** (named for the massive inlaid map of the United States on one of the walls), a great place to spend an evening reading or listening to one of the pianists who sometimes play here.

At Mammoth Hot Springs, P.O. Box 165, Yellowstone National Park, WY 82190. www. yellowstonenationalparklodges.com. © **866/439-7375** or 307/344-7311. Fax 307/344-7456. 212 units. $87–$120 double; $81–$112 cabin; $217 hot tub cabin; $439–$449 suite. AE, DISC, MC, V. Closed Oct to mid-Dec and early Mar to early May. **Amenities:** 2 restaurants; lounge. *In room:* No phone (cabins).

Canyon Village Area

40 miles from the West Yellowstone (west) entrance; 38 miles from the Gardiner (north) entrance

This is one of the busiest areas in the park because the Grand Canyon of the Yellowstone is, like Old Faithful, on everyone's itinerary. Accommodations here are in lodge rooms, modestly priced cabin units, or a large campground, and there are restaurants and coffee shops to fit most palates and pocketbooks, as well as a visitor center, general store, and post office. With the many amenities available here, it won't matter that you're 40 miles from the nearest gateway town.

Canyon Lodge and Cabins This complex is one of the newer facilities in the park (both Cascade and Dunraven lodges were completed in the 1990s). While you won't entirely escape the bustle of Canyon Village here, the lodges are located a mere half-mile from the Grand Canyon of the Yellowstone and Inspiration Point, one of the most photographed spots in the park. Cascade Lodge offers simple rooms appointed with tasteful log furnishings in the three-story building; the newer Dunraven is similar, although it is more modern (with an elevator). Both are located adjacent to woodlands. The cabins are single-story duplex and fourplex structures with private bathrooms that are among the largest in the park. They're a bit weathered but generally acceptable, though, given the sheer number of units involved (over 600), this isn't the place to "get away from it all."

In Canyon Village, P.O. Box 165, Yellowstone National Park, WY 82190. www. yellowstonenationalparklodges.com. © **866/439-7375** or 307/344-7311. Fax 307/344-7456. 605 units. $170 double; $96–$179 cabin. AE, DISC, MC, V. Closed late Sept to early June. **Amenities:** Restaurant; lounge. *In room:* No phone.

Tower-Roosevelt Area

23 miles from the Gardiner (north) entrance; 29 miles from the northeast entrance

This is a throwback to the early days of Yellowstone: no big complex of shops and services, and a certain cowboy philosophy. Out of the way and far from the crowds, the lodge here offers easy access to the hiking trails and the beautiful corridor of the Lamar Valley. The basic cabins are an affordable (and apt) choice for families who want to "rough it" without pitching a tent.

Roosevelt Lodge Cabins ★ ☺ This is considered the park's family hideaway, a low-key operation with dinky, primitive cabins; stables; and a lodge restaurant that feels like a big ranch house. The bare-bones cabins are called **Roughriders,** and they're each furnished with two simple beds, clean linens, a writing table, and a wood stove. A step up, the **Frontier** cabins have their own bathrooms and showers. The lodge is a rugged-but-charming stone edifice; its large, inviting porch is outfitted with rockers so guests can sit back and watch the world go by. Stagecoach rides, horseback trips, and Western trail cookouts give this place a cowboy flavor. It's a less hectic scene than the other park villages—and it's also the one with the best access to the Lamar Valley and its incomparable wildlife.

At Tower Junction (at junction of Mammoth-Tower Rd. and Tower-Canyon Rd.), P.O. Box 165, Yellowstone National Park, WY 82190. www.yellowstonenational parklodges.com. ℂ **866/439-7375** or 307/344-7311. Fax 307/344-7456. 80 cabins, 14 with private bathroom. $65–$110 cabin. AE, DISC, MC, V. Closed early Sept to early June. **Amenities:** Restaurant; lounge. *In room:* No phone.

Lake Village Area

27 miles from the east entrance; 56 miles from the West Yellowstone (west) entrance; 43 miles from the south entrance

More elegant than the Old Faithful Inn, this cluster of structures on the lake has the feel of a Victorian-era resort. There are accommodations in a historic hotel, motel and cabin units, and waterfront camping sites, all of which provide access to the lake's numerous recreational opportunities and the nearby hiking trails. The hotel's dining room is the finest in the park, although there are also cheaper alternatives in the neighborhood.

Lake Lodge Cabins ★ These cabins surrounding Lake Lodge stand a little ways from the lake in a relatively quiet, traffic-free area. The old Western lodge's most attractive feature is a large porch with wicker rockers that invite visitors to sit and gaze out across the waters. The accommodations are in well-preserved, clean, freestanding cabins near a trout stream that threads through a wooded area. (Access is usually restricted when grizzlies emerge from hibernation.) The cabins come in three grades: Motel-style **Western** cabins provide electric heat, paneled walls, two double beds (and, in some cases, an extra twin), and combination bathrooms, while historic **Frontier** and **Pioneer** cabins are smaller and sparsely furnished. Both Frontier and Pioneer cabins have one or two double beds each and small shower-only bathrooms, but the Frontier cabins have been modernized. Because the dining room here is a tad short on atmosphere, you might want to make the short trek to the Lake Yellowstone Hotel for a more sumptuous meal in a more appetizing setting.

On Yellowstone Lake, P.O. Box 165, Yellowstone National Park, WY 82190. www. yellowstonenationalparklodges.com. © **866/439-7375** or 307/344-7311. Fax 307/344-7456. 186 cabins. $69 Pioneer cabin; $106 Frontier cabin; $179 Western cabin. AE, DISC, MC, V. Closed mid-Sept to early June. **Amenities:** Restaurant; lounge. *In room:* No phone.

Lake Yellowstone Hotel and Cabins ★★

The Ionic columns, dormer windows, and deep porticos on this classic yellow building faithfully recall the year it was built: 1891. It's an entirely different world from the rustic Western style of other park lodgings. The facility was restored in the early 1990s, and its better rooms are the most comfortable and roomy in the park, with soul-stirring views of the massive lake. The three- and four-story wings house the hotel rooms, and there's also a motel-style annex and an assortment of cabins. The upper-end rooms here are especially lavish for Yellowstone, with stenciled walls and traditional spreads on one queen-size or two double beds. Smaller rooms in the annex are fitted with two double beds and bring to mind a typical motel chain. The freestanding yellow-clad cabins here are passable, decorated with knotty pine paneling, and furnished with double beds and a writing table.

On the north side of the lake, P.O. Box 165, Yellowstone National Park, WY 82190. www.yellowstonenationalparklodges.com. © **866/439-7375** or 307/344-7311. Fax 307/344-7456. 300 units. $149–$223 double; $130 cabin; $549 suite. AE, DISC, MC, V. Closed late Sept to mid-May. **Amenities:** 2 restaurants; lounge. *In room:* No phone (cabins).

Grant Village Area

22 miles from the south entrance; 47 miles from the West Yellowstone (west) entrance

This relatively modern addition doesn't have the romantic ambience of the Old Faithful Inn or Lake Yellowstone Hotel. Regardless, it's reasonably priced and has a good location, on the south shores of beautiful Yellowstone Lake near West Thumb, with a good visitor center and access to various sights.

Grant Village The southernmost of the major overnight accommodations in the park, Grant Village was completed in 1984 and is one of the more contemporary choices in Yellowstone. It's not as architecturally distinctive as the Old Faithful options, consisting of six condo-style units (with motel-style rooms), but it's also less touristy and more isolated. Rooms are tastefully furnished, most outfitted with light wood furniture, track lighting, electric heat, and laminate counters. Nicer and more expensive rooms affording lake views have mullioned windows, one queen-size or one or two double beds, and full bathrooms.

On the West Thumb of Yellowstone Lake, P.O. Box 165, Yellowstone National Park, WY 82190. www.yellowstonenationalparklodges.com. © **866/439-7375** or 307/344-7311. Fax 307/344-7456. 300 units. $152 double. AE, DISC, MC, V. Closed early Oct to late May. **Amenities:** Restaurant; lounge.

Old Faithful Area

30 miles from the West Yellowstone (west) entrance; 39 miles from the south entrance

Despite the crowds, the Old Faithful area is probably the best spot to center a hotel-based visit to the park. First of all, you'll spend a night in the midst of the most famous geyser basin in the world. You'll also have more choices of rooms, restaurants, and services— including a visitor center, a gas station, and a large Yellowstone General Store—than anywhere else in the park. And, from a logistical point of view, you'll have excellent access to attractions in every direction.

Old Faithful Inn ★★★   There are three hotels within viewing distance of the geyser, but this is undoubtedly the crown jewel of Yellowstone's man-made wonders. Seven stories tall with dormers peaking from a shingled, steep-sloping roof, it's an architectural marvel designed by Robert Reamer to blend into the natural environment, first welcoming guests in 1904.

The cavernous, log-laden lobby is striking, with an ambience that is half elegant palace and half rugged wilderness lodge. You can climb the stairs to its internal balconies, but seismic activity eventually closed the crow's nest, where a chamber orchestra once performed for the well-dressed guests below. Within 40 miles of the west and south entrances, this is the first stop for many visitors, so make reservations well in advance.

Guest rooms are basic, appointed with conservative fabrics and park-theme art, and they don't all have private bathrooms; the wing rooms offer better facilities and more privacy.

At Old Faithful, P.O. Box 165, Yellowstone National Park, WY 82190. www. yellowstonenationalparklodges.com. © **866/439-7375** or 307/344-7311. Fax 307/344-7456. 327 units. $126–$236 double with private bathroom; $96–$183 double with shared bathroom; $399–$499 suite. AE, DISC, MC, V. Closed early Oct to early May. **Amenities:** 2 restaurants; lounge. *In room:* No phone.

Old Faithful Lodge Cabins ✦   These are the leftovers from the days when crude cabins littered the landscape around the world's most famous geyser. The ones closest to the geyser were hauled away years ago, but you still get a sense of what tourism was like in the park's early days, especially if you rent one of the **budget cabins,** which are only slightly less flimsy than tents and have basic beds and sinks, no more. Showers and restrooms are a short walk away. **Frontier cabins** are the better units, adding a private bathtub to other amenities. If amenities are irrelevant, these rustic, thin-walled cabins are an economical way to put a roof over your head in the park. The lodge itself is perhaps the busiest spot in the geyser area, featuring several snack shops and a huge cafeteria dishing up varied fast-food items.

At Old Faithful, P.O. Box 165, Yellowstone National Park, WY 82190. www.yellow stonenationalparklodges.com. ℭ **866/439-7375** or 307/344-7311. Fax 307/344-7456. 96 units, some with shared bathroom. $67–$110 double. AE, DISC, MC. V. Closed late Sept to mid-May. **Amenities:** 2 restaurants. *In room:* No phone.

Old Faithful Snow Lodge and Cabins ★★
This is the newest and most modern property in Yellowstone. The dormitory-style lodge was torn down in 1998, replaced the next year by this new, award-winning structure. Its contemporary big-beam construction and high ceiling in the lobby echo the Old Faithful Inn, and a copper-lined balcony curves above the common area, where guests can relax in wicker furniture. Public areas have a contemporary (but appropriate) style, some of the lodge's wood was recycled from the same mill that provided the lumber for the Old Faithful Inn in 1904, and wrought-iron bears abound on everything from lamps to fireplace grates. The modern rooms are spacious and comfortable, second only to the upper-end accommodations at the Lake Yellowstone Hotel. There are also a few surrounding cabins with motel-style furnishings, many of which were built after the 1988 fires.

At Old Faithful, P.O. Box 165, Yellowstone National Park, WY 82190. www.yellow stonenationalparklodges.com. ℭ **866/439-7375** or 307/344-7311. Fax 307/344-7456. 134 units. $197–$206 double; $96–$149 cabin. AE, DISC, MC, V. Closed late Oct to mid-Dec and early Mar to late Apr. **Amenities:** Restaurant; lounge. *In room:* No phone (cabins).

WHERE TO CAMP IN YELLOWSTONE

Camping at Yellowstone's 12 developed campgrounds can be a happy affair, with the stars overhead, the scent of pine, and friendly neighbors from all over the world. The campgrounds are spaced throughout the park.

For those who carry their tents on their backs and want no neighbors other than their hiking buddies, there's plenty of room out there. Some areas in the Yellowstone backcountry are delicate habitat—the southeast arm of Yellowstone Lake is an example—and visitors must camp in designated areas for a limited time only. This in no way diminishes the sense of being in a true wilderness. Check with the **Yellowstone Backcountry Office** (*©* **307/344-2160**) for rules, reservations, and advice.

GETTING A CAMPSITE The National Park Service has shifted management of five major campgrounds to Xanterra Parks & Resorts, which means, predictably, higher fees, but thankfully it also means you can make reservations. The other seven campgrounds still managed by the park are available only on a first-come, first-served basis. These **lower-cost campgrounds** are at Indian Creek, Lewis Lake, Mammoth, Norris, Pebble Creek, Slough Creek, and Tower Fall. I happen to like the Norris and Lewis Lake sites, which tend to be available when others are full. Check with rangers about campsite availability when you enter the park; generally, you need to arrive early to get a site—some campgrounds completely fill up as early as 8am.

Xanterra Parks & Resorts operates the large campgrounds at Bridge Bay, Canyon, Grant Village, Madison, and Fishing Bridge. Some are rather barren of trees unless you get a site on the fringes. You can make reservations by calling *©* **866/439-7375** or 307/344-7311, or by writing Xanterra Parks & Resorts, P.O. Box 165, Yellowstone National Park, WY 82190.

REGULATIONS You can set up your tent only in designated areas, and stays are limited to 14 days between June 15 and September 15, and to 30 days the rest of the year, except at Fishing Bridge, where there is neither a summer nor a yearly limit. Check-out time at all campgrounds is 10am. Quiet hours are enforced between 8pm and 8am (10pm–7am at Fishing Bridge). No generators or loud music are allowed during these hours.

THE CAMPGROUNDS For exact information on prices, opening dates, and amenities, refer to the chart "Amenities for Each Campground: Yellowstone National Park," below.

These are campgrounds, not motels, so the amenities are sparse; but some have laundry facilities, showers, bathrooms, and potable water, which are luxuries to campers who've experienced the world's more primitive campgrounds.

In the northeast area of the park, the campground at **Tower Fall** is near a convenience store, restaurant, and gas station at Tower Lodge, 19 miles north of Canyon Village, and 18 miles east of Mammoth. **Slough Creek Campground** ★ is in a remote section of the Lamar Valley near the northeast entrance; the good news is that there are fewer people, good fishing, and the possibility of wolf sightings; the bad news is that restroom facilities are pit toilets.

Canyon Campground is the busiest in the park. Sites are in a heavily wooded area; the store, restaurants, visitor center, and laundry at Canyon Center are all nearby.

Because it's in an area of spring bear activity, attempts have been made over the years to close the **Fishing Bridge RV Park.** It's still open, but only hard-sided camping vehicles are allowed here.

Bridge Bay is located near the shores of Yellowstone Lake, so you get tremendous views, especially at sunrise and sunset. Unfortunately, though surrounded by the forest, much of the area is wide open, so there's not a whole lot of privacy. It's close to the marina (where fishing charters originate) and the boat-rental operation.

Madison ★ is in a wooded area just south of the river, a popular spot with good access to fishing and hiking. **Norris ★** is one of the park's better camping areas, with an attractive, wooded location in the heart of the park, close to wildlife activity and the Gibbon River. These camp areas seem less like outdoor motels than the big campgrounds on the park's east side.

WHERE TO CAMP NEAR YELLOWSTONE

There are three U.S. Forest Service campgrounds in the **West Yellowstone** area, all located in the Gallatin National Forest (see the chart "Amenities for Each Campground: Yellowstone National Park," above, for amenities, prices, and opening dates). They accommodate both RVs and tents, but during some periods in late summer they accept hard-sided vehicles only. All three are first-come, first-served, so it's best to stake out a spot early. The heavily forested **Bakers Hole,** just 3 miles north of West Yellowstone on U.S. Hwy. 191, is popular because of its fishing access. Both tents and RVs are accepted, and 30 sites have electric hookups. **Lonesomehurst,** 8 miles west of the park on U.S. Hwy. 20, and then 4 miles north on Hebgen Lake Road, is only a third of the size of Bakers Hole and fills up quickly in summer. It has tent and RV sites, some of them right on the shore of Hebgen Lake. You can reach **Rainbow Point** by driving 5 miles north of West Yellowstone on U.S. Hwy. 191, then 3 miles west on Forest Service Road 610, and then north for 2 miles on Forest Service Road 6954. Tucked away in the forest near Hebgen Lake, it accommodates both tents and RVs (no hookups) and has boating and fishing access. For further information on these campgrounds, call concessionaire **Hebgen Basin Campgrounds (✆ 877/646-1012**

Amenities for Each Campground: Yellowstone National Park

CAMPGROUND	TOTAL SITES	RV HOOK-UPS	DUMP STATION	TOILETS	DRINKING WATER	SHOWERS
INSIDE THE PARK						
Bridge Bay*	425	No	Yes	Yes	Yes	No
Canyon*	272	No	No	Yes	Yes	Yes
Fishing Bridge RV Park*	346	Yes	Yes	Yes	Yes	Yes
Grant Village*	425	No	Yes	Yes	Yes	Yes
Indian Creek	75	No	No	Yes	Yes	No
Lewis Lake	85	No	No	Yes	Yes	No
Madison*	275	No	Yes	Yes	Yes	No
Mammoth	85	No	No	Yes	Yes	No
Norris	100	No	No	Yes	Yes	No
Pebble Creek	30	No	No	Yes	Yes	No
Slough Creek	28	No	No	Yes	Yes	No
Tower Fall	31	No	No	Yes	Yes	No
NEAR THE PARK						
Bakers Hole	73	Yes	No	Yes	Yes	No
Lonesomehurst	27	Yes	No	Yes	Yes	No
Rainbow Point	85	Yes	No	Yes	Yes	No

*Reserve through Xanterra Parks & Resorts; Fishing Bridge RV Park accepts only hard-sided vehicles.

or 406/646-1012; www.hebgenbasincampgrounds.com) or the **Hebgen Lake Ranger District** (© **406/823-6961;** www.fs.fed. us/r1/gallatin).

In addition, there are a few RV parks in or near West Yellowstone. While these parks have full utility hookups and are generally designed for hard-sided vehicles, if there's space left over and you're willing to pay the price for a utility hookup that you won't be able to fully utilize, an owner of an RV park might allow you to pitch your tent. The excellent **Grizzly RV Campground,** 210 S. Electric St. (© **406/646-4466;** www.grizzlyrv.com), has cable TV hookups, Wi-Fi, a game room, a playground, and showers. Rates are $49 to $60 for sites with hookups, and $40 for tents; cabins run $89 to $125. The **Madison Arm Resort** on the south shore of Hebgen Lake (© **406/646-9328;** www.madisonarmresort.com) has RV and tent sites ($37–$39 and $28 per night, respectively), cabins ($150–$170), a marina, and a peaceful setting. Both are open from mid-May to early October.

WHERE TO EAT IN YELLOWSTONE

While they're not world-class establishments, Yellowstone's restaurants are well suited to their location and the appetites of their patrons: The portions definitely won't leave anyone going hungry.

FIRE PITS/ GRILLS	LAUNDRY	RESERVE	FEES	OPEN
Yes	No	Yes	$20	Late May to mid-Sept
Yes	Yes	Yes	$20	Early June to early Sept
Yes	Yes	Yes	$28–$37	Mid-May to late Sept
Yes	Yes	Yes	$20	Late June to late Sept
Yes	No	Yes	$12	June–Sept
Yes	No	No	$12	Early June to early Nov
Yes	No	Yes	$20	Early May to mid-Oct
Yes	No	No	$14	Year-round
Yes	No	No	$14	Late May to late Sept
Yes	No	No	$12	Mid-June to late Sept
Yes	No	No	$12	Late May to late Oct
Yes	No	No	$12	Mid-May to late Sept
Yes	No	Yes	$16–$22	Late May to mid-Sept
Yes	No	Yes	$16–$22	Late May to mid-Sept
Yes	No	Yes	$16–$22	Late May to mid-Sept

Most of the menus include a selection of unadventurous, all-American meat-and-potatoes grub alongside a few more creative entrees. Consistency can be a problem because the volume is high and the kitchen staffs are seasonal.

If you're not up for restaurant dining but you don't want to cook over your camp stove the whole time, there is counter-style fast-food service at the **Yellowstone Park General Stores,** as well as snack shops and cafeterias at Canyon, Mammoth, Grant Village, Lake Lodge, and Old Faithful.

Mammoth Hot Springs

You'll find the **Terrace Grill** at the opposite end of the building in which the **Mammoth Hotel Dining Room** is located. Here fast-food fare is served in a less-formal and less-pricey dining room; reservations are not accepted.

Mammoth Hotel Dining Room ★ SEAFOOD/STEAKS   The dining room at Mammoth is a good balance of casual and formal: comfortable and pleasant without too much of the hotel's Victorian past. The view of the Old Fort Yellowstone buildings and surrounding slopes is also quite enjoyable. The breakfast buffet is essentially identical to what you'll find at other locations, featuring eggs, French toast, and the like. The lunch menu focuses on an array of sandwiches, including smoked turkey on Parmesan-crusted sourdough, trout tacos, and a smoked salmon club. The dinner menu includes bison top sirloin, Idaho trout, and tasty pork chops, and the vegetarian entrees are creatively inspired and surprisingly good.

At Mammoth Hot Springs. ℂ **307/344-7311.** www.yellowstonenationalpark lodges.com. Reservations recommended in winter. Main courses $4–$12 breakfast, $8–$16 lunch; $11–$25 dinner. AE, DISC, MC, V. Mid-May to early Oct daily 6:30–10am, 11:30am–2:30pm, and 5–10pm; late Dec to early Mar daily 6:30–10am, 11:30am–2:30pm, and 5:30–8pm. Closed early Oct–late Dec and early Mar to mid-May.

Canyon Village Area

Not unlike many other park centers, the eating options at Canyon Village consist of three choices: a casual soda fountain, a fast-food cafeteria, and a conventional dining room.

The **Canyon Glacier Pit Snack Bar,** which is operated by Yellowstone Park General Stores, is in the same building as the grocery store and souvenir shop. Seating is on stools in the fashion of a 1950s soda fountain. Breakfast consists of egg dishes, lunch is soup and sandwiches, and dinner is traditional Western food.

The **Canyon Lodge Cafeteria** is a fast-food alternative managed by Xanterra Parks & Resorts and is across the parking lot in the Canyon Lodge area. Hours are the same as at the snack bar, and the menu bears some striking similarities—but you might get through the cafeteria line faster than you would get a stool at the soda fountain. Next door is an inexpensive **deli** with sandwiches, salads, and other light fare.

Canyon Lodge Dining Room ☺ SEAFOOD/STEAKS   This is a spacious dining area, a tad sterile perhaps, and when it fills up, it's noisy. The salad bar is long and loaded, but otherwise the dinner fare is largely geared toward the carnivore, with a wide selection of steaks alongside some seafood and pasta selections. The breakfast buffet is a good way to start your day, with all the standard American fixings. The crowds can be large at Canyon Village, but there is a relaxed and unhurried feel to this place that you don't find at some of the park's other busy points. Families, in particular, might appreciate the ability to take their time with meals.

At Canyon Lodge. ℂ **307/344-7311.** www.yellowstonenationalparklodges.com. Reservations are not accepted. Main courses $5–$12 breakfast, $7–$10 lunch, $12–$26 dinner. AE, DISC, MC, V. Early June to late Sept daily 7–10am, 11:30am–2:30pm, and 5–10pm.

Tower-Roosevelt Area

Roosevelt Lodge Dining Room SEAFOOD/STEAKS   This is supposed to be the cowboy alternative to the fancier cuisine served at the bigger Yellowstone hotels, but the unadventurous menu will win over only the most naive city slickers. For breakfast, it's eggs and flapjacks; lunch is burgers and sandwiches. Come suppertime, the menu is dominated by barbecue and steaks. A better idea: Join Roosevelt's Old West Dinner Cookout, and ride by horse or wagon through the Pleasant Valley to a chuck-wagon dinner that includes cornbread, steak, watermelon, those famous beans, and apple crisp. It's a daily summer event (reservations required) that costs $68 to $84 for an adult, depending on the route of your horseback ride, or $57 if you go by wagon. Children pay about $10 less.

At Tower Junction. ✆ **307/344-7311.** www.yellowstonenationalparklodges.com. Reservations are not accepted for the dining room; required for Old West cook outs. Dining room main courses $5–$10 breakfast; $7–$11 lunch, $9–$25 dinner. AE, DISC, MC, V. Mid-June to early Sept daily 7–10am, 11:30am–3pm, and 4:30 9pm.

Yellowstone Lake

For the eat-on-the-run traveler, a **deli** in the Lake Yellowstone Hotel serves lighter fare in an area that is slightly larger than a broom closet. Just down the road, the **Yellowstone Park General Store** offers three meals in a section of the store that is shared with tourist items; the best bet here is breakfast or a burger. There is also a basic but busy **cafeteria** serving three meals a day at Lake Lodge, but the ambience is minimal compared to the hotel's flagship dining room.

Lake Yellowstone Hotel Dining Room ★★ CONTINEN-
TAL This represents the finest dining Yellowstone has to offer, with a view of the lake stretching south from a vast dining room that doesn't feel crowded even when it's full. One of the best ways to start your day is with a generous breakfast buffet, but the polenta corn cakes with hazelnut-huckleberry butter are also quite good. Lunch entrees are gourmet sandwiches and burgers. The dinner menu is the most adventurous in the park. Appetizers include velvet corn soup and lobster ravioli, while entrees include vegetable paella, bison tenderloin, and blackened salmon.

On the north side of the lake. ✆ **307/344-7311.** www.yellowstonenationalpark lodges.com. Dinner reservations recommended. Main courses $6–$14 breakfast, $8–$14 lunch, $13–$30 dinner. AE, DISC, MC, V. Mid-May to early Oct daily 6:30– 10am, 11:30am–2:30pm, and 5–10pm.

Grant Village

The casual choice here is the **Lake House,** footsteps away from the Grant Village restaurant. It specializes in inexpensive fish entrees, as well as burgers and beer. No reservations are accepted. The **grill** at the Yellowstone General Store here also serves three meals daily from a basic menu.

Grant Village Dining Room ★ AMERICAN Breakfast and lunch at the Grant Village restaurant are much like those at other restaurants in the park, although the chef often surprises diners with interesting dinner items that stray from the norm. Lunch includes pan-fried trout covered with toasted pecans and lemon butter, huge burgers, and Monte Cristo sandwiches. The dinner menu ranges from herb-roasted chicken to penne with balsamic-roasted veggies to prime rib, but the specialty is trout, pan-fried with pecans. Quality and ambience here are comparable to those of the better dining rooms at the major park hotels.

At Grant Village. ⓒ **866/439-7375.** www.yellowstonenationalparklodges.com. Dinner reservations required. Main courses $5–$12 breakfast, $8–$11 lunch, $10–$27 dinner. AE, DISC, MC, V. June–Sept daily 6:30–10am, 11:30am–2:30pm, and 5:30–10pm.

Old Faithful Area

Choices abound here. For quick and inexpensive, the year-round **Geyser Grill** at the Old Faithful Snow Lodge and the **Old Faithful Lodge Cafeteria and Bake Shop** serve lunch and dinner in a fast-food environment that fits the mood of a crowd on the move; the **Bear Paw Deli,** an ice-cream stand in the lobby of the Old Faithful Inn, is your best choice for dessert. The **Yellowstone General Store** also has a lunch counter.

Obsidian Dining Room ★ SEAFOOD/STEAKS In the snazzy new Old Faithful Snow Lodge, a spacious restaurant provides a comparatively contemporary alternative to the dining room at the Old Faithful Inn. It's a little quieter, a little less expensive, and a little less formal. It still has some flash on the menu—braised bison short ribs shank and linguine with shrimp or chicken, for instance—and the vegan breakfast burrito is a gem.

At the Old Faithful Snow Lodge. ⓒ **307/344-7311.** www.yellowstonenational parklodges.com. Reservations not accepted in summer. Main courses $5–$12 breakfast, $7–$20 lunch, $10–$30 dinner. AE, DISC, MC, V. Early May to mid-Oct daily 6:30–10:30am and 5–10:30pm; mid-Dec to mid-Mar daily 6:30–10am, 11:30am–3pm, and 5–9:30pm.

Old Faithful Inn Dining Room ★ SEAFOOD/STEAKS The gnarled log architecture of this distinguished historic inn and the rather extensive menu make dining here a pleasurable experience. Breakfast is buffet or a la carte, and there's a lot to choose from. There's another buffet at lunchtime (headlined by pan-fried trout and barbecue chicken), as well as a generous assortment of salads and sandwiches. Dinnertime brings yet another buffet (prime rib being the headliner), along with menu entrees like steak, fish, and a vegetarian dish. The fare has gotten more distinguished in recent years, with such creative options as bison ravioli and pan-seared elk medallions making regular appearances on the menu.

At the Old Faithful Inn. ℭ **307/344-7311.** www.yellowstonenationalparklodges. com. Dinner reservations required. Main courses $5–$15 breakfast and lunch, $15–$26 dinner. AE, DISC, MC, V. Early May to early Oct daily 6:30-10:30am, 11:30am–2:30pm, and 5–10pm. Closed in winter.

WHERE TO STAY IN GRAND TETON NATIONAL PARK

The three concessionaires that operate lodgings within Grand Teton provide a range of accommodations that can suit any budget or taste, but not every schedule. I say fairly often in this guide that fall and spring are the best times to have the parks to yourself, but these are not the easiest times to find a room. If you come in early May, you'll find padlocks on the doors everywhere but at Flagg Ranch, which technically isn't in Grand Teton but on the John D. Rockefeller, Jr. Memorial Parkway. Likewise, by mid-October, you'll be bunking in Jackson.

You can get information about or make reservations for Jackson Lake Lodge, Jenny Lake Lodge, and Colter Bay Village through the **Grand Teton Lodge Company,** P.O. Box 250, Moran, WY 83013 (ℭ **800/628-9988** or 307/543-2811; www.gtlc.com), or **Signal Mountain Lodge,** P.O. Box 50, Moran, WY 83013 (ℭ **307/543-2831;** www.signalmountainlodge.com). Reservations at **Headwaters Lodge and Cabins at Flagg Ranch** can be made by contacting P.O. Box 187, Moran, WY 83013 (ℭ **800/443-2311;** www.gtlc.com).

Rooms in Grand Teton National Park properties have telephones but no televisions or air-conditioning. You'll find televisions in the lounge areas at Jackson Lodge, Signal Mountain Resort, and Flagg Ranch.

Flagg Ranch Village Area

2 miles from the south entrance to Yellowstone; 5 miles from the northern boundary of Grand Teton

Like Grant Village in Yellowstone, Flagg Ranch offers travelers the full gamut of services: cabins, tent and RV sites, an above-average restaurant, and a gas station. Also, because it's situated in a stand of pines in the middle of nowhere, there's not much to do in the immediate vicinity except watch the Snake River (and the cars en route to both parks) roll by.

Headwaters Lodge and Cabins at Flagg Ranch At this resort on the Snake River with log-and-luxury ambience, accommodations are duplex and fourplex log cabins that were constructed in the 1990s. The rooms feature patios with rocking chairs, king- and queen-size beds, spacious sitting areas with writing desks and chests of drawers, and bathrooms with tub/shower combinations and separate vanities. There are float trips, horseback rides, and excellent fishing in Polecat Creek and the Snake River. The lodge is a locus of activity, with its double-sided fireplace, fancy dining room, gift shop, espresso bar and pub with large-screen television, convenience store, and gas station. A campground is situated on the grounds amid a stand of pine trees.

P.O. Box 187, Moran, WY 83013. www.gtlc.com. (C) **800/443-2311** or 307/543-2861. Fax 307/543-2356. 92 cabins, 171 campsites. $180–$250 cabin double; $64 RV site; $35 tent site. AE, DISC, MC, V. Closed mid-Oct to mid-May. **Amenities:** Restaurant; lounge. *In room:* No phone.

Colter Bay Village Area

11 miles from the park's northern boundary; 10 miles from the Moran (east) entrance

The village provides an excellent base of operations for visitors who want to hike or enjoy the lake. It encompasses two restaurants, a visitor center, an amphitheater, a museum, a general store, a post office, a sporting-goods shop, and laundry facilities. Scenic cruises, fishing charters, and boat rentals of all kinds can be arranged at the marina. The village operates from mid-May to early October.

Colter Bay Village ★ ☺ You might call this the people's resort of Grand Teton, with simpler lodgings, lower prices, and a lively, friendly atmosphere that seems particularly suited to families. Situated on the eastern shore of Jackson Lake, Colter Bay Village is a full-fledged recreation center. Guest accommodations are in rough log cabins perched on a wooded hillside; they are clean and simply furnished with area rugs on tile floors and reproductions of pioneer furnishings—chests, oval mirrors, and extra-long bedsteads with painted headboards. If you want to take a trip back to the early days of American auto travel, when car camping involved unwieldy canvas tents on slabs by the roadside, you can spend an inexpensive night in tent cabins. The shower and bathroom are communal. Overall, the village provides an excellent base of operations for visitors because it has the most facilities of any area in the park.

P.O. Box 250, Moran, WY 83013. www.gtlc.com. (C) **800/628-9988** or 307/543-2811. 166 units. $65 cabin with shared bathroom; $165–$219 cabin with private bathroom; $52 tent cabin. MC, V. Closed late Sept to late May. **Amenities:** 2 restaurants; Wi-Fi (free). *In room:* No phone.

Jackson Lake Lodge ★★ Much the way that Old Faithful Inn or the Lake Yellowstone Hotel captures historic eras of Yellowstone tourism, Jackson Lake Lodge epitomizes the architectural milieu of the period when Grand Teton became a park. That era was the 1950s, an age of right angles, flat roofs, and big windows. While not as distinctive as Yellowstone's standouts, the lodge is more functional and comfortable than its northern counterparts. The setting is sublime, overlooking Willow Flats with the lake in the distance, and, towering over it without so much as a stick in the way, the Tetons and Mount Moran. You don't even have to go outside to see this impressive view—the lobby has 60-foot-wide windows showcasing the panorama. A few guest rooms are in the three-story main lodge, but most are in cottages scattered about the property, some of which have large balconies and mountain views. Newly remodeled in 2009, rooms are spacious and cheery, and most offer double beds, electric heat, and newly tiled bathrooms. For a premium, the view rooms provide guests with a private picture window facing the Tetons.

P.O. Box 250, Moran, WY 83013. www.gtlc.com. © **800/628-9988** or 307/543-2811. 385 units. $229–$319 double; $625–$750 suite. MC, V. Closed mid-Oct to mid-May. **Amenities:** 2 restaurants; lounge; pool; Wi-Fi (free). *In room:* Hair dryer.

Signal Mountain Area

15 miles from the north entrance; 9 miles from the Moran (east) entrance

Signal Mountain Lodge ★ 🏕 Signal Mountain has a different feel—and different owners—from the other lodgings in Grand Teton, adding to the sense that any place you choose to stay in this park is going to offer a fairly unique atmosphere. What they all have in common is the Teton view, and this lodge, located right on the banks of Jackson Lake, might have the best. To top it off, it's got lakefront retreats, which you can really inhabit, with stoves and refrigerators and foldout sofa beds for the kids. Other accommodations, mostly rustic log cabins, come in a variety of flavors, from motel-style rooms in four-unit buildings set amid the trees to beachfront family bungalows. These carpeted units feature handmade pine furniture, electric heat, covered porches, and tiled bathrooms; some have fireplaces, and all are nonsmoking. Recreational options include rafting, fishing, and sailboat tours on the lake. A convenience store and a gas station are also on-site.

P.O. Box 50, Moran, WY 83013. www.signalmountainlodge.com. © **307/543-2831.** 80 units. $131–$300 double. AE, DISC, MC, V. Closed late Oct to early May. Pets accepted ($15/night). **Amenities:** 2 restaurants; lounge; Wi-Fi (free). *In room:* Kitchenette.

Jenny Lake Area

28 miles from the northern boundary; 17 miles from the Moran (east) entrance; 16 miles from the south entrance

Jenny Lake Lodge ★★★ My favorite property in any national park, this lodge justifiably prides itself on seclusion, award-winning food, and the individual attention that comes with a cabin resort kept intentionally small. Catering to an older, affluent, and exceedingly loyal clientele, the style here is a throwback: a blend of peaceful rusticity and occasional reminders of class and formality. The property is a hybrid of mountain-lake resort and dude ranch, with various extras included in its prices, such as horseback rides, meals, walking sticks, umbrellas, and cool cruiser bicycles. The cabins, each named for a resident flower, are rustic on the outside and luxurious within—decorated with bright braided rugs, dark wood floors, beamed ceilings, cushy plaid armchairs, and tiled bathrooms. Rooms have one queen-size, one king-size, or two double beds. Some were old dude-ranch cabins from the 1920s, and some were built on the property in the 1990s; the latter have larger bathrooms and more modernity, but less character.

P.O. Box 250, Moran, WY 83013. www.gtlc.com. **℡** **800/628-9988** or 307/543-2811. 37 units. $620 double; $800–$885 suite. Extra person $150 a night. Rates include breakfast and dinner, horseback riding, and use of bicycles. AE, MC, V. Closed mid-Oct to May. **Amenities:** Restaurant; lounge; Wi-Fi (free). *In room:* Fridge.

Moose Area

36 miles south of the northern boundary; 18 miles from the Moran (east) entrance; 8 miles south of Jenny Lake

Moulton Ranch Cabins ✎ A century-old homestead now offers an off-the-beaten-track alternative to the bustling developments on Jackson and Jenny lakes. The small but comfortable cabins here are a few miles west of Moose Junction, scattered around a verdant, private acre entirely surrounded by the park. The cabins, built in stages from the 1930s to 2004, range from dinky to family-size, and packages are available for those who require numerous cabins. The Granary, Grand, and Bunkhouse are larger, with kitchenettes and space for six to sleep.

Mormon Row, Kelly, WY 83011. www.moultonranchcabins.com. **℡** **307/733-3749.** 5 units. $95–$249 double. MC, V. Closed Oct–Apr. *In room:* Kitchenette, no phone.

Spur Ranch Cabins ★ An outfitter's camp since the 1940s, Dornan's is now a collection of year-round cabins built in the 1990s and nicely renovated in 2010. Located at a family-owned operation in Moose that also includes a market, a wine shop, an outdoors store, guide services, and dining, the dozen cabins here are a good option for families and larger groups. All the units have tub/shower combinations, fitting lodgepole-pine furnishings, and fully equipped kitchens. Two are right on the Snake River, but they're often booked a year in advance during peak season.

P.O. Box 39, Moose, WY 83012. www.dornans.com. 🕾 **307/733-2522.** 12 units. $175–$250 for up to 6 people. Lower rates fall–spring. AE, DISC, MC, V. **Amenities:** 2 restaurants; lounge. *In room:* Kitchen.

WHERE TO CAMP IN GRAND TETON

Because Grand Teton is so much smaller than its counterpart to the north, distances between campgrounds are reduced substantially. As a consequence, choosing between the seven campgrounds in the park becomes a matter of preference (rather than geography) and availability. There are seven campgrounds in Grand Teton: The Grand Teton Lodge Company operates Gros Ventre, Jenny Lake, and Colter Bay; Signal Mountain Lodge runs Signal Mountain and Lizard Creek; and park concessionaires operate the Colter Bay Trailer Village and the Flagg Ranch campground. The Colter Bay Trailer Village and the Flagg Ranch campground are the only facilities with RV hookups (Flagg Ranch has sites suitable for RVs as well as tents, while the Colter Bay Trailer Village is for RVs only). The only campground in the park where RVs are not allowed is Jenny Lake Campground, which permits tents only.

GETTING A CAMPSITE Campgrounds operate on a first-come, first-served basis, but reservations are available to groups of 10 or more from the **Grand Teton Lodge Company,** P.O. Box 250, Moran, WY 83013 (🕾 **800/628-9988** or 307/543-2811; www.gtlc.com). You may also make reservations for **trailer sites** at the Colter Bay campground by contacting the Grand Teton Lodge Co. Additionally, there is a concessionaire-operated campground located in the Flagg Ranch complex on the John D. Rockefeller, Jr. Memorial Parkway. The area has 97 sites with utility hookups, 74 tent sites, showers, and a launderette. For reservations, contact **Flagg Ranch,** P.O. Box 187, Moran, WY 83013 (🕾 **800/443-2311;** www.gtlc.com).

THE CAMPGROUNDS For exact information on prices, opening dates, and amenities, refer to the chart "Amenities for Each Campground: Grand Teton National Park," below. Note that for campgrounds that accommodate RVs, they are not given a separate section away from tent campers.

Amenities for Each Campground: Grand Teton National Park

CAMPGROUND	TOTAL SITES	RV HOOKUPS	DUMP STATION	TOILETS	DRINKING WATER
INSIDE THE PARK					
Colter Bay	350	No	Yes	Yes	Yes
Colter Bay Trailer Village	112	Yes	Yes	Yes	Yes
Gros Ventre*	350	No	Yes	Yes	Yes
Jenny Lake**	51	No	No	Yes	Yes
Lizard Creek	60	No	No	Yes	Yes
Signal Mountain	81	No	Yes	Yes	Yes
NEAR THE PARK					
Flagg Ranch	171	Yes	Yes	Yes	Yes
Snake River Park KOA	90	Yes	Yes	Yes	Yes

*Gros Ventre is undergoing a renovation through 2012; sites are being removed and showers and laundry are on the agenda.

**Tents only are allowed here.

All the campgrounds except Jenny Lake can accommodate tents, RVs, and trailers, but there are no utility hookups at any of them. **Jenny Lake Campground ★★**, a tents-only area, is situated in a quiet, wooded area near the lake. You have to be here first thing in the morning to get a site. There are also sites for those without a car for $8.

The largest campground, **Gros Ventre,** is the last to fill, if it fills at all—probably because it's located on the east side of the park, a few miles from Kelly on the Gros Ventre River Road. If you arrive late in the day and you have no place to stay, go here first.

Signal Mountain Campground ★, with views of the lake and access to the beach, is another popular spot that fills first thing in the morning. It overlooks Jackson Lake and Mount Moran, as well as a pleasant picnic area and boat launch. There are a store and a service station nearby.

Colter Bay Campground and Trailer Village has access to the lake but is far enough from the hubbub of the village to offer a modicum of solitude; spaces are usually gone by noon. There are also sites for those without a car for $8.

Lizard Creek Campground, at the north end of Grand Teton National Park near Jackson Lake, offers an aesthetically pleasing wooded area near the lake with views of the Tetons, bird-watching, and fishing (and mosquitoes—bring your repellent). It's only 8 miles from facilities at Colter Bay, and its sites fill by 2pm.

SHOWERS	FIRE PITS/ GRILLS	LAUNDRY	RESERVE	FEES	OPEN
Yes	Yes	Yes	No	$20	Late May to late Sept
No	Yes	Yes	Yes	$56	Late May to late Sept
No	Yes	No	No	$20	Early May to mid-Oct
No	Yes	No	No	$20	Mid-May to early Oct
No	Yes	No	No	$21	Early June to early Sept
No	Yes	No	No	$21	Early May to mid-Oct
Yes	Yes	Yes	Yes	$35–$64	Mid-May to mid-Sept
Yes	Yes	Yes	Yes	$47–$89	Mid Apr to late Nov

WHERE TO CAMP NEAR GRAND TETON

There are several places to park an RV or pitch a tent around Jackson Hole, and a few of them are reasonably priced and not too far away from the park. Most charge around $50 per night, although prices seem to change at the drop of a hat, just like local motel prices. Your best bets are outside of the city limits, away from the crowds and the constant buzz of traffic, such as at **Snake River Park KOA,** 13 miles south of Jackson on U.S. 26/89/191 (© **800/562-1878** or 307/733-7078; www.srpkoa.com). See the chart "Amenities for Each Campground: Grand Teton National Park," above, for amenities, prices, and opening dates.

WHERE TO EAT IN GRAND TETON

Just as in Yellowstone, there are not enough places at the table for all of the travelers in Grand Teton during the busiest mealtimes of July and August, but the higher-end options are the best restaurants in any of the national parks. Because there is more than one concessionaire operating the full-service dining rooms, there is no central number for making reservations.

Near the Northern Boundary

Tasty gourmet pizzas are available at **Leeks Marina** (📞 **307/543-2494**), which is located inside the park, a few miles north of Colter Bay. At the **Headwaters Lodge and Cabins at Flagg Ranch** (p. 142) on the John D. Rockefeller, Jr. Pkwy., **The Steakhouse** (📞 **800/443-2311**) is open for breakfast lunch, and dinner.

Colter Bay

Colter Bay Village AMERICAN   Here you'll find two sit-down restaurants (although there's also a snack shop in the grocery store). Three meals are served daily during the summer months. **John Colter Café Court** serves sandwiches, burgers, and pretty good Mexican fare. Breakfasts at the new **Ranch House** are hearty; lunch is a soup-and-salad bar and hot sandwiches; dinner is more of an event but nonetheless family-friendly. Among the dinner entrees are trout, pasta, and beef and buffalo steaks. The bar is worth a look, emblazoned with the brands of a number of Jackson Hole–area ranches.

Across from the visitor center and marina in Colter Bay Village. 📞 **307/543-2811**. Reservations accepted for parties of 8 or more at the Ranch House. Main courses $5–$13 breakfast and lunch, $6–$25 dinner. MC, V. John Colter Café Court: Daily 11am–10pm. Ranch House: Daily 6:30–10:30am, 11:30am–1:30pm, and 5:30–9pm. Closed early Sept to May.

Jackson Lake Junction

The **Blue Heron** cocktail lounge at the Jackson Lake Lodge is one of the nicest spots in either park to enjoy a drink—especially a huckleberry margarita. Featuring indoor and outdoor seating, the lounge here offers the same views as at the **Mural Room** (see below). There are barbecues at Jackson Lake Lodge's outdoor pool Sunday through Friday evenings with live Western entertainment.

The Mural Room ★★ STEAKS/WILD GAME   Jackson Lake's main dining room is quiet and fairly formal, catering to a more sedate crowd as well as corporate groups; it's also more expensive than other park restaurants. The floor-to-ceiling windows provide stellar views across a meadow inhabited by moose to the lake and the Cathedral Group. (The staff applauds sunset every night.) Interior walls are adorned with hand-painted Western murals created by Carl Roters. The food is the perfect complement to the view, and markedly superior to most of what you'll find in Yellowstone. Three meals are served daily in summer. Breakfast items include a "healthy start" breakfast, organic granola, and fruit smoothie, as well as a breakfast buffet. Dinner might be a grand five-course event that includes buffalo carpaccio, lobster and brie bisque, and house salad, followed by an entree of Idaho trout, slow-roasted prime rib, vegetable Wellington, or molasses-spiced elk loin. Dessert includes delicious homemade ice cream and a rich fudge cake. Aside from the dining room at Jenny Lake Lodge and Lake Yellowstone Hotel, this is the most romantic and upscale eatery in either park.

At Jackson Lake Lodge. *C* **800/628-9988** or 307/543-2811. Reservations recommended. Main courses $6–$15 breakfast, $9–$17 lunch, $18–$38 dinner. MC, V. Summer daily 7–9:30am, 11:30am–1:30pm, and 5:30–9pm.

Pioneer Grill ☺ AMERICAN   Bedecked with regional homesteading antiques and photos, this 1950s-style luncheonette, with its curving counter and old-fashioned soda fountain, offers hearty meals and a casual, friendly atmosphere. Breakfasts are basic but ideal for hiking appetites: bagels, eggs, flapjacks, and the like. For lunch, try one of the Grill's ever-popular buffalo burgers or a plump turkey sandwich. Dinner is similarly laid-back and traditional—you can't miss with the pan-fried rainbow trout. (And don't miss the huckleberry milkshakes for dessert.) When a tour bus stops at the lodge, the restaurant is often overrun, so you might want to head next door to the Mural Room if you're looking for peace or romance. If you're looking for convenience, good service, and a relatively quick meal, though, this spot is hard to beat.

At Jackson Lake Lodge. *C* **800/628-9988** or 307/543-2811. Reservations not accepted. Main courses $4–$9 breakfast, $7–$10 lunch, $9–$18 dinner. MC, V. Summer daily 6am–10pm.

Signal Mountain Lodge ✦ AMERICAN/MEXICAN   There are actually two restaurants here, serving delicious food in the friendliest style in the park. The fine dining room and lounge are called **Peaks** and **Deadman's Bar,** respectively, and the **Trapper Grill** supplements the continental fare with Mexican entrees, pizzas, and plump sandwiches. You eat up the scenery, too, with a view of Jackson Lake and Mount Moran.

Bargain hunters flock to the bar for the decadent nachos supreme: a foot-tall mountain of chips, cheese, chicken, beef, beans, and peppers that runs a mere $15. You'll easily fill four people for that price, leaving you plenty of change for the bar's signature blackberry margaritas. Because the bar has one of three televisions in the park and is equipped with cable for sports nuts, the crowd tends to be young and noisy. Full meals are served in the proper dining room, with an emphasis on sustainable cuisine. Entrees include free-range chicken with organic black beans and rice, vegetarian lasagna, and filet mignon served on a potato cake with sautéed spinach, the most expensive entree.

At Signal Mountain Resort. ☎ **307/543-2831.** Reservations required for break-fast and dinner. Main courses $7–$10 breakfast, $8–$16 lunch, $19–$35 dinner. AE, DISC, MC, V. Summer daily 7–10am and 11:30am–10pm.

Jenny Lake

Jenny Lake Lodge Dining Room ★★★ CONTINEN-TAL   The finest meals in either park (or, for that matter, in *any* park) are served here, where a talented chef creates culinary delights for guests and, occasionally, a president of the United States. Breakfast, lunch, and dinner are served here, and all are spectacular. (Nonguests should have lunch here if they can.) The five-course dinner is the bell ringer, though. Guests choose from appetizers that might include elk carpaccio; salads with organic greens, pecans, and dried cherries; and entrees such as buffalo short ribs, braised rabbit leg, or a venison strip loin. Desserts are equally creative and tantalizing. Price is no object, at least for guests, because meals are included in the room charge; nonguests should expect a hefty bill. Casual dress is discouraged, with jackets requested for dinner.

At Jenny Lake Lodge. ☎ **307/733-4647.** Reservations required. Prix-fixe break-fast $23; lunch main courses $9–$14; prix-fixe dinner $78, not including alcoholic beverages. AE, MC, V. Summer daily 7:30–9am, noon–1:30pm, and 6–8:45pm.

Moose

Chuck-wagon fare (three meals a day) and pasta dishes and pizzas (lunch and dinner) are available at two separate facilities at **Dor-nan's** (☎ **307/733-2415**). The outdoor **bar** here is a great place to watch the sun set and enjoy a cocktail.

GATEWAYS TO YELLOWSTONE & GRAND TETON NATIONAL PARKS

Yellowstone and Grand Teton National Parks are accessible from all four points of the compass. One of the biggest decisions facing you will be where to commence your journey and base yourself while you're in the area, if you choose not to stay in one of the parks themselves.

WEST YELLOWSTONE, MONTANA

At the west entrance of Yellowstone National Park

Yellowstone's west entrance is a bastion for tourism, chock-full of accommodations, restaurants, souvenir shops, and outfitters. The personality of the town has changed since the popularity of snowmobile excursions increased winter traffic on Yellowstone's roads; it now offers more, and better, year-round facilities.

Originally called Riverside, and then Yellowstone, the name was officially changed to West Yellowstone in 1920 when Gardiner residents grudgingly complained that people would assume that the town was the park. Regardless of its name, this place is about shopping, not nature, and its biggest attraction is a zoolike look at regional wildlife in the **Grizzly and Wolf Discovery Center.**

Essentials

GETTING THERE   For information on air service and car rentals, see "Getting There & Getting Around," in chapter 10. To drive to West Yellowstone from Bozeman (91 miles), take U.S. Hwy. 191 south to its junction with U.S. Hwy. 287 and head straight into town. From Idaho Falls, take I-15 north about 50 miles to U.S. Hwy. 20, which takes you directly into West Yellowstone, a 53-mile drive.

VISITOR INFORMATION   Contact the **West Yellowstone Chamber of Commerce,** 30 Yellowstone Ave. (P.O. Box 458), West Yellowstone, MT 59758 (© **406/646-7701;** www.west yellowstonechamber.com).

Getting Outside

Yellowstone is obviously the big draw here, but there is plenty of wilderness west of the park in the Targhee and Gallatin national forests. The area around West Yellowstone ranks among the best **fishing** locales in the country. There are also numerous **hiking** and **kayaking** opportunities near the town. Come winter, **snowcoach tours** and **snowmobiling tours** are huge draws for West Yellowstone, and Yellowstone rangers come into town and lead **snowshoe walks.** The town also has a gem of a network of groomed cross-country ski trails that interconnect with trails on public lands. Every major hotel and motel in town offers snowmobile packages that include a room and a sled rental; just be sure to book well in advance. For more information on all of these activities, see chapter 4.

Seeing the Sights

Beyond the attractions below, families interested in firefighting will want to drop into the **National Smokejumper Center,** just east of the chamber of commerce (© **406/646-7557;** www.smoke jumpercenter.org). In a cluster of relocated historic log structures, kids can take part in a Junior Smokejumper Program at 9am in summer to learn about smokejumpers' tools, tricks, and training to fight fires in inaccessible corners of the wilderness.

Grizzly and Wolf Discovery Center   Those who haven't the patience to search out and observe the free-ranging wildlife of Yellowstone might want to check out this not-for-profit educational center. The interpretive center gives a detailed explanation of the history of wolves and grizzlies in this country, along with the difficult and controversial efforts to revive them in the wild. This is a closer look than you'll likely get at animals in the park, but did you

really come to Yellowstone to look at grizzlies imported from Alaska in an enclosure?

201 S. Canyon St. (in Grizzly Park). ⓒ **800/257-2570** or 406/646-7001. www.grizzly discoveryctr.org. Admission $11 adults, $9.75 seniors, $5.50 children 5–12, free for children 4 and under. Summer daily 8:30am–8:30pm; shorter hours in winter.

Yellowstone Historic Center ★   Located in the historic 1909 Union Pacific depot, this is the only museum that focuses on Yellowstone's cultural history, providing an interesting look into the ways of the park's first tourists, with scads of memorabilia, postcards, and concessionaire ephemera. There are also displays on the historic Yellowstone railroad and other transportation, covering epochal events such as the 1959 earthquake that created Quake Lake and the 1988 fires, along with a mounted grizzly bear known in his animate days as "Old Snaggletooth."

At Yellowstone Ave. and Canyon St. ⓒ **406/646-1100.** www.yellowstone historiccenter.org. Admission $5 adults, $4 seniors, $3 children and students, free for children 2 and under. Mid-May to mid-Oct daily 9am–6pm. Closed mid-Oct to mid-May.

Yellowstone IMAX Theater   This theater is next door to the **Grizzly and Wolf Discovery Center,** and together they form the centerpiece of a real-estate development on the edge of the park, which includes several new hotels. Regardless, the IMAX concept works pretty well here—there are things an airborne camera can show you on a six-story-tall screen that you'll never see on your own two feet. A film called *Yellowstone* plays fairly often, with swooping views of the canyon, falls, and other sights.

101 S. Canyon St. ⓒ **888/854-5862** or 406/646-4100. www.yellowstoneimax. com. Admission $9 adults, $8.50 seniors, $6.50 children 3–12, free for children 2 and under. Summer 8:30am–9pm; shorter hours in winter. Call or check the website for exact show times.

Where to Stay

Make your reservations early if you want to visit in July or August, or if you're going to spend Christmas or New Year's here. If you're smart, you'll come in the fall, when there are plenty of empty rooms and better rates, and spend your days fishing the Henry's Fork or one of the other great streams in the vicinity. Room rates often reflect the seasonal traffic, and prices fluctuate. Unless noted, all these establishments are open year-round.

You'll find such chains as **Comfort Inn,** 638 Madison Ave. (ⓒ **406/646-4212;** www.comfortinn.com), with summertime doubles for $129 to $229; and **Days Inn,** 301 Madison Ave. (ⓒ **800/548-9551** or 406/646-7656; www.daysinn.com), with summer rates of $119 to $189 for a double. There are three **Best**

Western affiliates, ranging from about $160 to $220 a night for a double during the summer. Call © **800/528-1234,** or go online to **www.bestwestern.com** for information and reservations. The **One Horse Motel,** at 216 N. Dunraven St. (© **800/488-2750** or 406/646-7677; www.onehorsemotel.com), is a top-notch independent across the street from City Park, with doubles for $79 to $129 a night. Another good inexpensive option (with more character than the chains, to boot), the 1912 **Madison Hotel,** 139 Yellowstone Ave. (© **800/838-7745** or 406/646-7745; www. madisonhotelmotel.com), has historic rooms for $59 to $99 for a double or $33 for a bunk in a dormitory, and newer motel doubles for $79 to $139. Another option with historic cachet—and a one-time favorite of broadcasting legend Charles Kuralt—is the **Parade Rest Guest Ranch,** 10 miles north of West Yellowstone at 1279 Grayling Rd. (© **800/753-5934** or 406/646-7217; www. paraderestranch.com), in a serene setting near Hebgen Lake. Rates are about $190 per day for adults and $70 to $150 for kids, all meals and horseback riding included; for lodging only, you'll pay $160 for a cabin sleeping two guests.

Bar N Ranch ★★   One of the oldest brands in Montana, the Bar N is an excellent new lodging option in West Yellowstone, operating a spiffed-up lodge and cabin complex since 2004. Located on 200 acres of unsullied ranchland with 2 miles of the Madison River and a fishing pond, the lodge is an image of the New West, with a great river-rock fireplace and a knotty pine banister leading up to the rooms upstairs. The lodge rooms mix equal parts Ralph Lauren and Old West, exuding a simple but rich style with antler lamps, hardwood floors, and jetted tubs. The cabins are one- and two-bedroom units arranged in a half circle around the lodge, with decor that echoes that of the lodge; all of them have fireplaces and private outdoor hot tubs.

890 Buttermilk Creek Rd. (P.O. Box 250), West Yellowstone, MT 59758. www. bar-n-ranch.com. © **406/646-0300.** Fax 406/646-0301. 15 units. Lodge rooms $235–$250 double; cabins $290–$365 double; 4-bedroom cabin $465. Lower rates late Oct and early May. AE, DC, DISC, MC, V. **Amenities:** Restaurant; Jacuzzi; pool; Wi-Fi (free). *In room:* TV/DVD, fridge, no phone.

Holiday Inn West Yellowstone ★   This is the town's best modern hotel. The rooms are sizable and comfortable, well maintained, and regularly updated. At the tour desk, you can arrange fishing and rafting trips, bike and ATV rentals, and chuckwagon cookouts. The Iron Horse Saloon serves regional microbrews, and the Oregon Short Line Restaurant serves Western cuisine, including game and seafood dishes. At the center of the restaurant sits the restored railroad club car that brought Victorian gents to Yellowstone a century ago.

315 Yellowstone Ave. (P.O. Box 470), West Yellowstone, MT 59758. www.do yellowstone.com. © **800/646-7365** or 406/646-7365. 123 units. $199–$249 double; $279–$319 suite. Lower rates fall to spring. AE, DISC, MC, V. **Amenities:** Restaurant; lounge; bikes; children's program; health club; Jacuzzi; pool; sauna. *In room:* A/C, TV, fridge, hair dryer, Wi-Fi (free).

Moose Creek Cabins ★ 🎁 A 1950s motel complex that got a slick revamp in 2004, Moose Creek Cabins offers comfortable and stylish rooms and cabins in the heart of West Yellowstone. The one-time Ranger Motel—which spent 2 decades as employee housing before becoming Moose Creek—is a good value and one of the better maintained properties in town. There are stand-alone kitchenette cabins (good for families) and cabin-style motel rooms with queen beds; both are laden with pine and charming individual themes. The proprietors also own a good motel, the Moose Creek Inn, a few blocks away with double rooms for $100 to $110 and suites for $180 in summer.

220 Firehole Ave., West Yellowstone, MT 59758. www.moosecreek-cabins.com. © **406/646-9546.** 15 units. $100–$120 double; $190–$200 cabin. Lower rates fall to spring. DISC, MC, V. *In room:* TV, kitchenette, no phone, Wi-Fi (free)

Three Bear Lodge ★ ☺ Rebuilt from the ground up after a 2008 fire, this woodsy, family-friendly inn is located less than 3 blocks from the park entrance. Those familiar with the old Three Bear will be hard-pressed to recognize the slick new incarnation, featuring recycled wood, a striking lobby with a monolithic stone fireplace and scads of taxidermy, and stylish guest rooms. Some rooms are family suites that sleep up to eight people. About half of the rooms survived the fire, but were updated as the main lodge was rebuilt. The Three Bear offers snowmobile and snowcoach tours in the winter, as well as van tours in the summer.

217 Yellowstone Ave. (P.O. Box 1590), West Yellowstone, MT 59758. www.three bearlodge.com. © **800/646-7353** or 406/646-7353. Fax 406/646-4567. 72 units. $159–$219 double. Lower rates fall to spring. AE, DISC, MC, V. **Amenities:** Restaurant; lounge; exercise room; Jacuzzi; pool (seasonal); sauna. *In room:* TV, hair dryer, Wi-Fi (free).

Where to Eat

West Yellowstone is a good place to stop for a quick bite on your way into the park. For coffee and baked goods, visit the espresso bar at the excellent **Book Peddler** in Canyon Square (© **406/646-9358**). **Morning Glory Coffee & Tea,** 129 Dunraven St. (© **406/646-7061**), roasts its own beans on-site and offers a low-key atmosphere for getting going.

Beartooth Barbecue ★ BARBECUE A bustling and funky space that plates up some mean barbecue, this is my pick for a casual meal in West Yellowstone. At the bar or a table in a room adorned with sleds, *ristras,* a traffic light, and sports memorabilia, order a plate of St. Louis–cut spareribs or beef brisket with plenty of tangy sauce. The bar has Montana microbrew on draft and serves wine by the glass, but no liquor is served.

111 Canyon St. ☎ **406/646-0227.** Main courses $10–$27. MC, V. Daily noon–10pm. Closed Oct–Apr.

The Canyon Street Grill 🔔 AMERICAN With checkerboard floors and shiny red booths, this delightful 1950s-style spot serves hearty food for breakfast, lunch, and dinner. Hamburgers and chicken sandwiches are popular, accompanied by milkshakes of hard ice cream or their famous root beer floats.

22 Canyon St. ☎ **406/646-7548.** www.canyonstreetgrill.com. Main courses $5–$12. DISC, MC, V. May–Nov Mon–Sat 11am–10pm; shorter hours rest of year. Closed Apr to mid-May.

Eino's Tavern 🎁 AMERICAN Locals snowmobile out from West Yellowstone to Eino's (there's a trail that follows U.S. Hwy. 191) to become their own chefs at the grill here. There's usually a line out the door, but it's fun to peruse the walls, plastered with dollar bills and other currency as well as bras and funny photos, while you wait. After placing your order for a steak, teriyaki chicken, hamburger, or hot dog, keep a straight face when you're handed an uncooked piece of meat. Go to the grill, slap it on, and stand around, drink in hand, shooting the breeze with other patrons until your food is exactly the way you like it. Steaks and chicken come with your choice of a salad (or their trademark "hot potatoes" in winter), and hamburgers come with chips. The fine view of Hebgen Lake is a plus.

155 Eino's Loop (9 miles north of West Yellowstone on U.S. Hwy. 191). ☎ **406/646-9344.** Main courses $6–$25. No credit cards. Winter daily 9am–9pm; rest of year Mon–Fri 4-9pm, Sat–Sun noon–9pm. Closed Thanksgiving to mid-Dec.

The Outpost Restaurant ☺ AMERICAN Tucked away in a downtown mall, this rustic restaurant laden with Western bric-a-brac serves old-fashioned home-style fare, such as hearty beef stew with fork-size chunks of carrots and potatoes. There's also salmon, steak, trout, liver, and an excellent salad bar. For breakfast, if you're really hungry, you can't beat the Campfire Omelet, smothered in homemade chili, cheese, and onions. There's no video poker, beer, wine, liquor, or smoking, making for a relatively quiet, family-friendly atmosphere. The desserts include pie and a wild huckle-berry sundae.

115 Yellowstone Ave. (in the Montana Outpost Mall). ✆ **406/646-7303.** Main courses $5–$16 breakfast, $6–$14 lunch, $9–$25 dinner. AE, DISC, MC, V. Daily 6:30am–10:30pm. Closed mid-Oct to mid-Apr.

Sydney's Mountain Bistro ★★ NEW AMERICAN The most upscale option in a meat-and-potatoes town, Sydney's offers an intimate setting, an excellent wine list, and a menu that balances seafood and vegetarian fare with beef, poultry, and pork. With creative preparations—such as flash-fried calamari and sweet-chili salmon and butternut squash ravioli—and a breezy patio complementing the upscale atmosphere inside, this is my pick for a special meal in West Yellowstone.

38 Canyon St. ✆ **406/646-7660.** www.sydneysbistro.com. Main courses $15–$38. MC, V. Daily 5–10pm.

GARDINER, MONTANA ★

At the north entrance to Yellowstone National Park

At the other end of the spectrum from West Yellowstone is Gardiner, which provides the only year-round access to Yellowstone on the north side. Although this tiny town (pop. 1,000) booms and busts with the tourist season, full-time residents manage to lead regular lives that include soccer practice, a day on the river, and a night on the town. For these folks, deer, elk, and bison meandering through the streets are no big deal. If you need additional information, contact the **Gardiner Chamber of Commerce,** 222 Park St. (P.O. Box 81), Gardiner, MT 59030 (✆ **406/848-7971;** www.gardinerchamber. com). Across from the landmark Roosevelt Arch is the slick new headquarters of the **Yellowstone Association** (✆ **406/848-2400;** www. yellowstoneassociation.org), a restored historic building by renowned architect Robert Reamer, complete with a terrific store and visitor center. Up the hill from town is the Yellowstone Association Institute's new-for-2010 **Overlook Field Campus,** featuring cabins with superlative views and open to participants in seminars and tours.

Getting Outside

Gardiner is the spot to go for white-water rafting on the Yellowstone River. Several outfitters take guests on half- and full-day trips on routes skirting the park's northern boundary; the best of the bunch is the **Yellowstone Raft Company,** U.S. Hwy. 89 (✆ **800/858-7781** or 406/848-7777; www.yellowstoneraft.com), with half-day trips for $37 and full days for $80; children get on the boat for $27 for a half-day or $60 for a full day. While this is not a **snowmobiling** hub on the magnitude of West Yellowstone, a few motels here rent snow machines or offer snowcoach tours. And

hiking and **fishing** opportunities are bountiful in every direction from town.

Where to Stay

Dinky, personable, and a bit eccentric, Gardiner has long had ultrafriendly lodging—thin-walled motels where, if you show up late, they've gone to bed and left a key in the door. These days it also has some newer, chain-affiliated properties, built to accommodate the ever-increasing traffic to the park. As with all the gateway towns, make your reservations early if you're coming during the peak season. The steep off-season decline in traffic results in discounts that can be considerably less expensive than the high-season rates quoted below, so be sure to ask.

Inexpensive motels are moving in and filling up during the summer months: the **Yellowstone Park Travelodge,** 109 Hellroaring Rd. (© **406/848-7520**), and the **Super 8,** 702 U.S. Hwy. 89 (© **800/800-8000** or 406/848-7401; www.jacksonholesuper8. com), are open year-round with rates during the summer high season between $120 and $160 for a double. The **Best Western by Mammoth Hot Springs,** on U.S. Hwy. 89 (© **800/828-9080** or 406/848-7311; www.bestwestern.com), is another option, with doubles for $149 to $189 in summer.

Of the independents, I like **Yellowstone River Motel,** 14 E. Park St. (© **406/848-7303;** www.yellowstonerivermotel.com) with doubles for $80 to $110 in peak season. Fans of vintage roadside motels and their indelible neon signage might also take a look at the bare-bones cabins at **Jim Bridger Motor Court,** 901 Scott St. (© **406/848-7371**), built in the 1930s around a shady green courtyard. Cabins come with one or two queen beds and range from $50 to $199 nightly.

Absaroka Lodge ★★   Every room in this lodge has its own furnished balcony with jaw-dropping views of the Yellowstone River and the mountain scenery beyond it. The lodge's riverbank location—with a nice slope of lawn overlooking the river gorge—is just a few blocks from the village center, and the rooms are well appointed with queen-size beds. Suites with kitchenettes cost a little more; there is also a pair of cabins without balconies.

U.S. Hwy. 89 at the Yellowstone River Bridge (P.O. Box 10), Gardiner, MT 59030. www.yellowstonemotel.com. © **800/755-7414** or 406/848-7414. Fax 406/848-7560. 41 units. Summer $110–$125 double; winter $45–$60 double. AE, DISC, MC, V. *In room:* A/C, TV, kitchenette, Wi-Fi (free).

Comfort Inn   This log cabin–style hotel looks like it belongs here, unlike a lot of chain operations. The centerpiece is a 3,000-square-foot rustic lobby decorated with wild-game trophies, and a large second-floor balcony with views of Yellowstone scenery and passing wildlife. Family rooms that sleep six and luxurious suites with hot tubs are also available. The Antler Pub and Grill here serves Italian and American dinners in summer only.

107 Hellroaring Dr. (P.O. Box 268), Gardiner, MT 59030. www.yellowstonecomfort inn.com. ✆ **800/424-6423** or 406/848-7536. Fax 406/848-7062. 77 units. Summer $159–$200 double; winter $75–$100 double. AE, DISC, MC, V. **Amenities:** Restaurant; bar; Jacuzzis. In room: A/C, TV, hair dryer, Wi-Fi (free).

Cowboy Lodge & Grille ★   Right in the center of the action in Gardiner, the new-in-2010 Cowboy Lodge & Grille features a hearty American restaurant and a quartet of rooms: a studio, two one-bedrooms, and a three-bedroom. All decorated in attractive "cowboy-chic" style, the units feature comfortable furnishings, gas stoves, and a kitchen or kitchenette. The restaurant is open from 11am to 9pm daily.

303 2nd St. (P.O. Box 415), Gardiner, MT 59030. www.vrbo.com/229756. ✆ **406/848-9175.** 4 units. $150–$275 double. DISC, MC, V. **Amenities:** Restaurant. In room: A/C, TV, Wi Fi (free).

Yellowstone Suites Bed and Breakfast ★ 🎁   This quiet B&B on the south bank of the Yellowstone River is a good alternative to the motels that line U.S. Hwy. 89. Originally built in 1904, legend has it that the second story's quarried-stone exterior is actually a leftover from the Roosevelt Arch. The rooms are frilly and cozy, with a teddy-bear motif in the Roosevelt Room and a Victorian theme in the Jackson Room; the Yellowstone Suite has satellite television and a kitchenette. The real perks here are the impeccably gardened backyard, the views of Electric Peak from the new-in-2011 deck, and the breakfasts, which might feature cinnamon rolls or cheese blintzes.

506 4th St. (P.O. Box 277), Gardiner, MT 59030. www.yellowstonesuites.com. ✆ **800/948-7937** or 406/848-7937. 4 units. Summer $120–$165 double; winter $80–$105 double. Rates include complimentary full breakfast. MC, V. **Amenities:** Jacuzzi. In room: A/C, kitchenette, no phone, Wi-Fi (free).

Where to Eat

An indication that Gardiner has kept in touch with its mining-town roots is the relative dearth of fancy restaurants—you'll find mostly steakhouse fare, hearty breakfasts, and travelers' food. A few upscale eateries have come and gone in recent years, but the dish-clattering local color of the park-side coffee shops is hard to beat.

The Chico Dining Room ★★ CONTINENTAL   The Chico Hot Springs Resort is 30 miles north of Gardiner, but if you're in the area, stop here for some of the best food in the Greater Yellowstone Ecosystem and a soak in this resort's hot springs. The carnivorous traveler will enjoy the selection of top-drawer beef, the pine nut–crusted Alaskan halibut is a seafood aficionado's dream, and wine lovers won't be disappointed by the award-winning list. Many of the fresh veggies originate in the resort's garden and greenhouse, and the menu always includes a vegetarian selection. You may want to consider a night's stay.

Old Chico Rd., Pray, MT (30 miles north of Gardiner). ℂ **406/333-4933.** www. chicohotsprings.com. Reservations recommended. Main courses $25-$40. AE, DISC, MC, V. Summer daily 5:30-10pm; winter Mon-Thurs 5:30-9pm, Fri-Sat 5:30-10pm, Sun 8:30-11:30am (brunch) and 5:30-9pm.

The Corral Drive-In AMERICAN   Since 1960, this place's reputation has rested on burgers that are nothing short of colossal. With a half pound of meat (beef, elk, or buffalo), several slices of American cheese, bacon, and all the usual veggies, these burgers have been known to measure a full 7 inches from bun to bun. The monstrous things garnered the nickname "Helen's Hateful Hamburgers" after a dissatisfied customer wrote a letter to the local paper dubbing them just that. Corral founder Helen Gould ran with it, using the intended insult as a sarcastic slogan in promotions and on T-shirts. Ice cream, chicken and fish sandwiches, and an assortment of fried goods round out the menu.

U.S. Hwy. 89 at Yellowstone St. ℂ **406/848-7627.** Reservations not accepted. Menu items $4-$16. MC, V. May-Sept daily 11am-11pm. Closed mid-Oct to Apr.

Sawtooth Deli ★ AMERICAN/DELI   This stalwart eatery on Park Street is a reliable spot for hearty American breakfasts and plump subs. I like the breakfast burritos in the morning (especially before a big hike) and the Philly cheese steaks and veggie subs for lunch (especially after a big hike). With a basic main room and a breezy patio, there is both wait service and a to-go counter. Dinner features the lunch menu plus nightly specials like pasta and ribs. Beer and wine are served, but not liquor.

222 W. Park St. ℂ **406/848-7600.** Main courses $5-$8 breakfast and lunch, $5-$16 dinner. MC, V. Summer Tues-Sat 8am-4pm and 5-9pm; shorter hours rest of year.

COOKE CITY, MONTANA ★

Near the northeast entrance to Yellowstone National Park

Mining gold and platinum and other precious metals pumped intermittent life into Cooke City for 100 years, but now there is only park tourism. Fewer than 100 residents live year-round in the town today; and Silver Gate, right next to the park entrance, is even smaller.

Contact the **Colter Pass/Cooke City/Silver Gate Chamber of Commerce** at P.O. Box 1071, Cooke City, MT 59020 (© **406/838-2495;** www.cookecitychamber.org), for information. The chamber operates a visitor center at 206 W. Main St. that is open daily in summer.

A room for the night here will be less expensive than in other gateway towns, typically from $60 to $120 a night. The **Soda Butte Lodge,** 209 Main St. (© **406/838-2251;** www.cookecity. com), is the biggest motel in Cooke City, with doubles for $80 to $90 and suites for $120, and it includes the **Prospector Restaurant** and a small casino; or, you can go to the **Alpine Motel,** 105 Main St. (© **888/838-1190** for reservations or 406/838-2262; www.cookecityalpine.com), with doubles for $78 to $85 and suites for $120. The newest property is a woodsy **Super 8,** 303 Main St. (© **877/338-2070** or 406/838-2070; www.cookecitysuper8. com), with doubles for about $100. For a bite to eat and a great selection of beers, try the funky **Beartooth Cafe** (© **406/838-2475**), also on Main Street. I also like the sandwiches and barbecue plates at **Buns 'N' Beds,** 201 Main St. (© **406/838-2030**). In Silver Gate, the **Log Cabin Café and B&B** (© **406/838-2367**) is a rustic-meets-refined eatery specializing in trout dinners.

JACKSON, WYOMING ★★★

Near the south entrance of Grand Teton National Park

More so than any of the other gateway towns to Yellowstone and Grand Teton, Jackson has managed to reap the fruits of tourism and diversify beyond it, thanks in no small part to a white-hot real-estate market. Sure, the heart of Jackson is thick with shops and motels and tourists, and yes, urban sprawl is a serious issue in the surrounding valley; it's admirable, though, that the town has used some of its prosperity to preserve open space and enhance the cultural agenda of the community.

Jackson has a wealth of outdoor recreation to occupy the hordes of visitors. In summer, you can play golf at world-class courses, chase trout in pristine streams or lakes, drift down a river in a raft or kayak, or ride horses at one of the area's dude ranches. Come winter, you can glide down mountain slopes, cross-country ski on the seemingly endless trails, or ride a snowmobile into the forest.

And if you're tired of the great outdoors, well, you can go shopping. Jackson has national brand-name fashion outlets, tourist curio shops, excellent art galleries, clothing stores, antiques shops, and outdoor-equipment suppliers. The retail frenzy concentrates around the town's delightful central square, a grassy park with entryways arched by tangles of elk antlers.

Oh, yeah, and there are a couple of nice parks up the road, too.

Essentials

Air service to Jackson and rental-car agencies are discussed in chapter 10.

GETTING THERE If you're driving, come north from I-80 at Rock Springs on U.S. Hwy. 189/191, or east from I-15 at Idaho Falls on U.S. Hwy. 26, and either travel via Snake River Canyon on that highway or veer north over Teton Pass on Wyo. 32. If you are driving south from Yellowstone National Park, stay on U.S. Hwy. 89, which runs north-south through both parks and into town. Likewise, from I-80, take U.S. Hwy. 189 or U.S. Hwy. 191 north to the park, or U.S. Hwy. 89 from I-15 in Ogden, Utah. For up-to-date weather information and road conditions, contact the Jackson Hole Chamber of Commerce (© **307/733-3316;** www.jackson holechamber.com), call © **888/996-7623** (in state) or 511 (in-state mobile), or visit **www.wyoroad.info**.

VISITOR INFORMATION The **Jackson Hole Chamber of Commerce** is a source of information concerning just about everything in and around Jackson. Along with the Bridger-Teton, Yellowstone, and Grand Teton rangers, chamber representatives can be found at the **Jackson Hole and Greater Yellowstone Visitor Center,** 532 N. Cache St. (no phone), open daily from 8am to 7pm in summer and 9am to 5pm in winter. For information on lodging, events, and activities, contact the chamber at P.O. Box 550, Jackson, WY 83001 (© **307/733-3316;** www.jacksonhole chamber.com). For lodging information and reservations, call **Jackson Hole Central Reservations** (© **888/838-6606;** www. jacksonholewy.com).

GETTING AROUND Taxi service is available from **Buckboard Cab** (© **307/733-1112**) and **Cowboy Cab** (© **307/413-1000**). **Alltrans** (© **800/443-6133** or 307/733-3135; www. jacksonholealltrans.com) offers shuttle service from the airport as well as full-day tours of Yellowstone. Before you call a cab, remember that many of the hotels and car-rental agencies in the Jackson area offer free shuttle service to and from the airport.

The **Southern Teton Area Rapid Transit** (**START;** © **307/733-4521;** www.startbus.com) offers bus transport from Teton Village to Jackson daily for $3 (half price for seniors 60 and over and students; children 8 and under ride free). Service includes about 70 trips a day between downtown and Teton Village in the winter, and 15 in the summer; it shuts down around midnight year-round. Visit their website for schedule information.

Getting Outside

Whether you're a raw beginner, a seasoned pro, or an adrenaline addict, Jackson can make you feel at home. There's mountain biking, hiking, fishing, kayaking, and river running in the summer, and skiing, snowmobiling, and snowboarding in the winter.

SPORTING GOODS & EQUIPMENT RENTALS Serious climbers with serious wallets will appreciate the gear at **Teton Mountaineering** ★, at 170 N. Cache St. (© **800/850-3595** or 307/733-3595; www.tetonmtn.com), a block from the square, where you can get killer Nordic skis and high-grade fleece jackets. **Adventure Sports,** at Dornan's in the town of Moose ((© **307/733-3307**), has a small selection of mountain bike, kayak, and canoe rentals, and advice on where to go with the gear. When snowboards are put away for the summer, the **Boardroom,** 225 W. Broadway (© **307/733-8327;** www.boardroomjacksonhole.com), switches to BMX bikes and skateboards. **Hoback Sports,** 520 W. Broadway (© **307/733-5335;** www.hobacksports.com), has a large selection of skis, boards, and summer mountain bikes for rent and sale. **Skinny Skis,** at 65 W. Deloney Ave., off Town Square (© **888/733-7205** or 307/733-6094; www.skinnyskis.com), is a year-round specialty sports shop with an excellent selection of equipment and clothing. For serviceable factory seconds at steeply discounted prices, head north to the little town of Moose near the entrance to Grand Teton National Park and shop **Moosely Seconds** ★ (© **307/739-1801**).

SUMMER SPORTS & ACTIVITIES

FISHING Yellowstone and Grand Teton national parks have incredible fishing in their lakes and streams; see the "Fishing" sections in chapters 4 and 6 for details.

The Snake River emerges from Jackson Lake Dam as a broad, strong river, with decent fishing from its banks in certain spots—such as right below the dam—and better fishing if you float the river. Fly-fishers should ask advice at local stores on recent insect hatches and good stretches of river, or hire a guide to keep them company. Outdoor gear stores will provide all the tackle you need and more information on fishing conditions in the area than you can likely process. **High Country Flies** ★, 185 N. Center St. (© **866/733-7210** or 307/733-7210; www.highcountryflies. com), has a vast selection of high-quality fishing gear, flies, and fly-tying supplies, along with lessons and guided trips, as well as free advice if you just want to gab about where to cast. If you'd like a guide who knows the holes, try **Jack Dennis Fishing Trips** (© 307/690-0910; www.jackdennisfishingtrips.com), **Triangle X Float Trips** (© 307/733-5500; www.trianglex.com), or **Westbank Anglers** (© 800/922-3474 or 307/733-6483; www.west bank.com). The going rate for guided fishing is about $450 for a full day for two people.

GOLF The semiprivate Robert Trent Jones, Jr.–designed course at **Jackson Hole Golf and Tennis Club** (© 307/733-3111; www.jhgtc.com), north of Jackson off U.S. Hwy. 89, has an 18-hole course that's one of the best in the country—as well as a good restaurant, the **North Grille** (see "Where to Eat," later in this chapter). Seasonal greens fees range from $70 to $145 for 18 holes, cart included. The **Teton Pines Resort,** 3450 N. Clubhouse Dr. (© 800/238-2223 or 307/733-1005; www.tetonpines. com), offers a challenging course, designed by Arnold Palmer and Ed Seay; greens fees range from $65 to $160, cart included, depending on the season. Both courses are open to the public.

HIKING In addition to the myriad trails in Grand Teton National Park (see chapter 6), there are trails in the surrounding forests—they might be less maintained, but they also get less use and provide more solitude. Adjacent to Grand Teton on the east and south is **Bridger-Teton National Forest;** go east and over the Continental Divide, and you're in **Shoshone National Forest.** Together, these forests encompass a huge piece of mountain real estate, including glaciers, 13,000-foot peaks, and some of the best alpine fishing lakes in the world. Among the mountain ranges included in these forests are the **Absarokas,** the **Gros Ventre,** the **Wyoming,** and the **Wind River.** The **visitor center,** located in the sod-roofed A-frame at 532 N. Cache St., provides all the hiking and access information you'll need for Bridger-Teton, including the Gros Ventre and Teton wilderness areas. If you want detailed information in advance, contact the U.S. Forest Service's district office (© 307/739-5500; www.fs.fed.us/r4/btnf).

For those who would like a hiking/backpacking (or snowshoeing/cross-country skiing) guide—for about $120 a day per adult—contact the **Hole Hiking Experience** (© 866/733-4453 or 307/690-4453; www.holehike.com).

HORSEBACK RIDING Trail rides are a staple of the Western vacation experience, and there are several companies in the area that will put you in the saddle. Some hotels, including those in Grand Teton National Park, have stables and operate trail rides for their guests. For details, contact **Jackson Hole Outfitters**

(📞 **307/654-7008;** www.jacksonholetrailrides.com), **Spring Creek Ranch Riding Stables** (📞 **800/443-6139** or 307/733-8833; www.springcreekranch.com), or the **Mill Iron Ranch** (📞 **888/808-6390** or 307/733-6390; www.millironranch.net). Rides typically cost around $50 for 2 hours or $150 for a day.

KAYAKING, CANOEING & SAILING   Several operators in Jackson run schools and guide paddlers of all skill levels. The two major outfits are the **Snake River Kayak and Canoe School,** 260 N. Cache St. (📞 **800/529-2501** or 307/733-9999; www.snakeriverkayak.com), and **Rendezvous River Sports,** 945 W. Broadway (📞 **307/733-2471;** www.jacksonholekayak.com).

RAFTING   There are two parts to the Snake River—the smooth water, much of it running through Grand Teton National Park north of Jackson, and the white water of the canyon, to the south and west. A rafting trip down the upper Snake, usually from Jackson Lake Dam or Pacific Creek to Moose, is not about wild water but about wildlife: Moose, bald eagles, ospreys, and other creatures come to the water just like we do. Several operators provide scenic float trips in the park; see chapter 6 for a list.

The most popular way to experience the Snake River is whitewater rafting; these are wet, wild, white-knuckle tours. Several companies offer adrenaline-pumping day trips down the Snake, but don't plan on being just a passenger—this is a participatory sport. Contact **Barker-Ewing** (📞 **800/448-4202;** www.barker-ewing.com), **Sands Wildwater** (📞 **800/358-8184** or 307/733-4410; www.sandswhitewater.com), **Dave Hansen Whitewater** (📞 **800/732-6295** or 307/733-6295; www.davehansenwhitewater.com), or **Mad River Boat Trips** (📞 **800/458-7238;** www.mad-river.com). Generally, a full-day trip runs $80 to $100, lunch included, and a half-day trip costs about $50 to $70.

WINTER SPORTS & ACTIVITIES

CROSS-COUNTRY SKIING   With five Nordic centers and a couple of national parks at your feet, plus the 3½-million-acre Bridger-Teton National Forest, cross-country skiers have plenty of choices. If you're new to the sport, you might choose to start on the groomed, level trails at one of the Nordic centers. If, however, you have experience in the steep, deep powder of untracked wilderness, visit or call the National Park Service in **Grand Teton National Park** (📞 **307/739-3300;** www.nps.gov/grte) or the **Bridger-Teton National Forest** in downtown Jackson at 340 N. Cache St. (📞 **307/739-5500;** www.fs.fed.us/r4/btnf), and check in before you go.

The local ski shops are excellent sources of unofficial advice about the area's backcountry. Keep in mind that many of the trails used by cross-country skiers are also used by snowmobiles. For those seeking instruction, lessons are available at the Nordic centers, or you can check the schedule of **Teton Parks and Recreation** (✆ **307/733-5056;** www.tetonwyo.org/parks), which takes visitors on various cross-country ski outings from mid-December to mid-March, weather permitting.

The **Jackson Hole Nordic Center,** 7658 Teewinot St., Teton Village (✆ **307/733-2292;** www.jacksonhole.com), on the flats just east of Teton Village, is a small part of **Jackson Hole Mountain Resort** (see below), which is known for offering some of the best downhill skiing around. Trail passes ($14) allow access to 11 miles of groomed trails. **Teton Pines Cross Country Skiing Center** (✆ **800/238-2223** or 307/733-1005; www.tetonpines. com) has 7.5 miles of groomed trails that wind over the Teton Pines Resort's golf course. At **Grand Targhee Resort** (✆ **800/827-4433** or 307/353-2300; www.grandtarghee.com), you can rent or buy anything you need in the way of equipment and take off on the resort's 9.3 miles of groomed trails.

DOG SLEDDING If your idea of mushing is not oatmeal but a pack of yipping dogs, you might want to try your hand at dog sledding, an enjoyable open-air way to tour the high country during the winter. **Jackson Hole Iditarod** (✆ **800/554-7388;** www.jhsled dog.com), associated with Iditarod racer Frank Teasley, offers both half- and full-day trips in five-person sleds (the fifth companion is your guide), and you can take a turn in the driver's stand. The half-day ride costs $245 per person, gives the dogs an 11-mile workout, and includes a light lunch before you head back to the kennels. For $300 a head, you can take the full-day excursion out to Granite Hot Springs, a 22-mile trip total. You get a hot lunch, with your choice of trout or steak.

DOWNHILL SKIING This is one of the premier destinations for skiers in the country. Despite a relatively remote location, chilly temperatures, and a high percentage of black-diamond trails (although still plenty of intermediate trails), skiers flock here in droves. The two largest ski resorts in the area have been putting in faster chairs in recent years, eliminating long waits in lift lines.

Jackson Hole Mountain Resort ★★, 3395 W. Village Dr. (P.O. Box 290), Teton Village, WY 83025 (✆ **888/333-7766** or 307/733-2292; www.jacksonhole.com), is making improvements to move into the elite international ranks; incidentally, prices are moving up, too. Head to the top of **Rendezvous Mountain** and plunge down Tensleep Bowl if you want to get a taste of skiing on the edge, or try the gentler, intermediate runs down the sides of **Apres Vous Mountain.** The resort's renowned tram was shut down in 2006; a new $25-million, 100-passenger tram opened in time for the 2008–09 season. Full-day adult lift tickets are $95 in peak season.

Grand Targhee Resort ★★, 3300 E. Ski Hill Rd. (P.O. Box SKI), Alta, WY 83422 (© **800/827-4433** or 307/353-2300; www. grandtarghee.com), has the best snow in the universe: deep, forgiving powder from November to spring (an average of over 500 in. annually), and a more peaceful, less-crowded village that provides a worthy alternative to Teton Village. Full-day adult lift tickets are $69 (2011–12 rate).

Snow King Resort, 400 E. Snow King Ave. (P.O. Box SKI), Jackson, WY 83001 (© **800/522-5464** or 307/733-5200; www. snowking.com), lights up its hill above Jackson at night; it's the smallest of the valley's resorts, with fairly steep and unvaried terrain, but it's within walking distance of downtown Jackson. Full-day adult lift tickets run $42 (2011–12 rate).

SNOWMOBILING Although West Yellowstone is the most popular base for snowmobiling in the Yellowstone area, Jackson has a growing contingent of snowmobile aficionados and outfitters.

The operators who rent snowmobiles (including the necessary clothing and helmets) also have guides to take you on 1-day and multiday tours of Jackson Hole and the surrounding area. **High Country Snowmobile Tours, Wyoming Adventures,** and **Rocky Mountain Snowmobile Tours** share a website and reservation service (© **800/647-2561;** www.snowmobiletours.net), offering guided trips in Jackson Hole, Yellowstone, and the surrounding wildlands. **Jackson Hole Snowmobile Tours,** 515 N. Cache St. (© **800/633-1733** or 307/733-6850; www.jacksonhole snowmobile.com), offers 1-day trips in Yellowstone and multiday trips along the Continental Divide. A typical guided, full day outing costs from $250 to $300 for a single rider, with pickup and drop-off service, equipment, fuel, a continental breakfast, and lunch at Old Faithful included. Also in Jackson, snowmobiles and relevant gear can be rented at **Leisure Sports,** 1075 S. U.S. Hwy. 89 (© **307/733-3040;** www.leisuresportsadventure.com).

A BIRD'S-EYE VIEW

AERIAL TOURING For a much quicker climb to the mountaintops, call **Teton Aviation** (© **208/354-3100;** www.teton aviation.com), in Driggs, Idaho. You'll actually be looking down at the summits that climbers strain to top, and you'll get a new perspective on the immensity of Grand Teton (although you won't get too close—the park has some airspace restrictions). Teton has

1-hour flights in planes and gliders (starting at $250 per flight) that take you to 11,800 feet on the west side of the Grand.

BALLOONING The folks at the **Wyoming Balloon Company ★** (© **307/739-0900;** www.wyomingballoon.com) like to fire up early, in the still air that cloaks the Teton Valley around 6am. Their "float trips" stay aloft for a little more than an hour, cruising over a 3,000-acre ranch with a full-frontal view of the Tetons. The journey concludes with a champagne toast at the landing site. Prices are $325 for adults and $285 for children ages 6 to 12 (kids 5 and under not allowed).

WILDLIFE-WATCHING

National Elk Refuge ★ It's not exactly nature's way, but the U.S. Fish and Wildlife Service makes sure that the elk in this area eat well during the winter by feeding them alfalfa pellets. It keeps them out of the haystacks of area ranchers and creates a beautiful tableau on the peaceful flats along the Gros Ventre River: thousands of elk, some with huge antler racks, dotting the snow for miles. Drivers along U.S. Hwy. 89 might also see trumpeter swans, coyotes, moose, bighorn sheep, and, lately, gray wolves. As autumn begins to chill the air in September, you'll hear the shrill whistles of the bull elk in the mountains; as snow begins to stick on the ground, about 5,000 animals make their way down to the refuge—the world's largest winter concentration of elk. Although the cultivated meadows and pellets help the elk survive the winter, some biologists say this approach results in overpopulation and the spread of diseases, such as brucellosis.

Regardless, this is a great opportunity to see these magnificent creatures up close. Each winter from mid-December to March, the Fish and Wildlife Service offers **horse-drawn sleigh rides** that weave among the refuge elk. In early winter, you'll find young, energetic bulls banging heads; in late winter (when the Fish and Wildlife Service begins feeding the animals) you'll wander through a more placid scene. Rides embark from the Jackson Hole and Greater Yellowstone Visitor Center (532 N. Cache St.) daily between 10am and 4pm on a first-come, first-served basis. Tickets for the 45-minute rides cost $18 for adults and $14 for children 5 to 12 and can be purchased at the visitor center.

Located 3 miles north of Jackson on U.S. Hwy. 26/89. © **307/733-9212.** http://nationalelkrefuge.fws.gov. Free admission. Visitor center: summer daily 8am–7pm; winter daily 9am–5pm.

Area Attractions

Beyond its role as a staging area for explorations of Grand Teton and Yellowstone national parks, Jackson is a place to relax, shop,

RESTAURANTS ◆

The Blue Lion 29
The Cadillac Grille/
  Billy's Giant Hamburgers 26
D.O.G. 22
Il Villaggio Osteria 5
The Kitchen 27
Koshu Wine Bar 21
Mangy Moose 4
Nani's Genuine Pasta House 33
North Grille 39
Q Roadhouse 10
Rendezvous Bistro 11
Snake River Brewing Co. 16
Snake River Grill 23
Stiegler's 7
Sweetwater Restaurant 19
Trio 20

ATTRACTIONS ●

Cayuse Western Americana 32
Jackson Hole Mountain Resort 3
Jackson Hole Historical Society
  Museum 34
National Elk Refuge 41
National Museum of Wildlife Art 40
Snow King Resort 18
Taylce Piggott Gallery 15
Teton Pines Resort 8
Town Square 24

HOTELS ■

The Alpenhof 3
Alpine House 36
Amangani 13
Anvil Motel 31
Buckrail Lodge 17
Four Seasons Resort
  Jackson Hole 1
The Hostel 6
Hotel Terra 5
Inn on the Creek 37
The Lexington at
  Jackson Hole 35
Rustic Inn 38
Rusty Parrot Lodge
  and Spa 30
Snake River Lodge
  and Spa 2
Spring Creek Ranch 12
Super 8 14
Wildflower Inn 9
Woods Hotel 28
Wort Hotel 25

INFORMATION ℹ

Jackson Hole and
  Greater Yellowstone
  Visitor Center

play some golf, or kick up your heels at an authentic Western saloon. There are also a number of attractions, running the gamut from history and art to pure entertainment. From Memorial Day to Labor Day at **Town Square,** actors reenact an Old West gunfight at 6:15pm every day except Sunday. **Stagecoach rides** are also available from Town Square all summer long; they cost $5 for adults and $3 for kids.

Jackson Hole Aerial Tram ★ After Jackson Hole Ski Resort's legendary tram shut down in 2006, a new tram nicknamed "Big Red" opened for the 2008–09 ski season. From the top, you can see the Tetons from an elevation above 10,000 feet, but don't expect a private tour—during busy summer days, the tram carries 45 passengers, packed in like the skiers that take the lift in the winter. You can hike down, or take the tram, or even paraglide. The top of Rendezvous Mountain offers an incredible view; but it can get pretty chilly, even in the middle of summer, so bring a light coat. Atop the tram, **Corbet's Cabin** offers a place to eat before you head back down.

7658 Teewinot St., Teton Village (at Jackson Hole Ski Resort). © **307/739-2753.** www.jacksonhole.com. Tickets $19–$29 adults and seniors, $10–$20 children 6–17, free for children 5 and under. Early Sept to early Oct and late May to mid-June daily 9am–5pm; mid-June to early Sept daily 9am–6pm. Tram runs approximately every half-hour.

Jackson Hole Historical Society Museum Reopened in a new facility in 2011, the Jackson Hole Historical Society Museum nicely covers the lore and legends of Jackson Hole in its inaugural exhibit, *Playing Hard: Labor and Leisure in Jackson Hole.* On display are exhibits covering everything from skiing and snow planes to gambling, painting, and rodeo in the valley. There are Western getups for kids to try on, as well as a special display dedicated to movies shot on location here, including *Shane, Dances with Wolves,* and *Rocky IV.*

225 N. Cache St. (at the corner of Deloney St.). © **307/733-2414.** www.jackson holehistory.org. Admission $6 adults, $5 seniors, $4 students and children. Mon-Sat 10am–6pm; Sun noon–5pm. Shorter hours fall to spring.

National Museum of Wildlife Art ★★ If you don't spot this museum on your way into Jackson from the north, consider that a triumph of design: Its jagged, red-sandstone facade is meant to blend into the steep hillside facing the elk refuge. Within this 50,000-square-foot castle is some of the best wildlife art in the country. There are 12 exhibit galleries that display traveling shows and collections dating from 2000 B.C. to the present, including a gallery devoted to the American bison and a showcase for local great Carl Rungius. Younger visitors will be entertained by the many interactive exhibits. The facility also houses a repository of internationally acclaimed wildlife films and a good little cafe.

2820 Rungius Rd. (3 miles north of town on U.S. Hwy. 89, across from the National Elk Refuge). (C) **800/313-9553** or 307/733-5771. www.wildlifeart.org. Admission $30 families, $12 adults, $10 seniors, $6 children 5–18, free for children 4 and under. Winter daily 9am–5pm; fall–spring Sun 11am–5pm.

ART GALLERIES

Collectors, tired of bighorn sheep on the crags and weather-beaten cowboys on their horses, often dismiss Western art. But while Jackson has plenty of that genre in stock, some of its two dozen galleries are more adventurous and sophisticated.

Cayuse Western Americana, 255 N. Glenwood St. ((C) **800/ 405-4096** or 307/739-1940; www.cayusewa.com), focuses on antiques of all kinds, from beadwork to spurs to belt buckles to paintings. **Tayloe Piggott Gallery,** 745 W. Broadway ((C) **307/ 733-0555;** www.tayloepiggottgallery.com), showcases contemporary paintings and other edgy work. A mile north of town, at 1975 U.S. Hwy. 89 (toward the park), is the **Wilcox Gallery** ((C) **307/ 733-6450;** www.wilcoxgallery.com), which showcases more than 20 painters and sculptors from across the nation. The **Jackson Hole Galleries Association** (www.jacksonholegalleries.com) is a great resource.

Where to Stay

The thin-walled, dimly lit motels of the past are just memories now—Jackson lodgings these days come with palatial trappings and, in some cases, prices that start at $500 a night. Prices are generally discounted in the off season (spring/fall), but not during ski season.

Clustered together near the junction west of downtown where Wyo. 22 leaves U.S. Hwy. 26/89 and heads north to Teton Village is a colony of chain franchises: a surprisingly chic **Motel 6,** 600 S. U.S. Hwy. 89 ((C) **307/733-1620;** www.motel6.com); a **Super 8,** 750 S. U.S. Hwy. 89 ((C) **307/733-6833;** www.jacksonholesuper8. com); and the more upscale and expensive **Days Inn,** 350 S. U.S. Hwy. 89 ((C) **307/733-0033;** www.daysinn.com), with private hot tubs and fireplaces in the suites. High-season prices for these chain motels range from $150 to $200 double. North of Town Square, the **Lexington at Jackson Hole** (formerly the Trapper Inn), 285 N. Cache St. ((C) **888/771-2648** or 307/733-2648; www.lexjh.com), is a solid pick, with doubles for $229 and suites for $299 in summer.

On the inexpensive end of the scale, the **Anvil Motel,** 215 N. Cache St. (© **800/234-4507** or 307/733-3668; www.anvilmotel. com) offers double rooms for $110 to $148 in summer. I also like the summer-only **Buckrail Lodge,** at the base of Snow King Mountain at 110 E. Karns Ave. (© **307/733-2079;** www.buck raillodge.com), a comfortable independent that's been nicely maintained since it opened in the 1960s. Doubles are $91 to $143.

IN JACKSON

Alpine House ★★ Stylish, environmentally conscious, and melding the best of the B&B and hotel worlds, Alpine House began as a six-room operation in 1996 and expanded nearly fourfold in 2000 when it also opened a spa. Modeled after Scandinavian lodging, the rooms are woodsy and Western but modern and functional. Some have lofts with additional beds; all have a shared or private balcony, a fireplace, and a soaking tub. The public areas, indoors and out, are quiet and serene. New in 2009 are five spacious creek-side cottages a block away from the main building. Owners Hans and Nancy Johnstone are former Olympians and great resources for planning outdoor adventures in Jackson Hole.

285 N. Glenwood St. (P.O. Box 1126), Jackson, WY 83001. www.alpinehouse.com. © **800/753-1421** or 307/739-1570. Fax 307/734-2850. 27 units. $185–$275 double; $295 suite; $325–$400 cottage. Lower rates Oct–May. Rates include full breakfast (inn, not cottages). AE, MC, V. **Amenities:** Lounge; sauna; spa. *In room:* A/C, TV (in most), kitchenette, MP3 docking station, Wi-Fi (free).

Inn on the Creek ★ Tucked into a quiet corner of Jackson, this bed-and-breakfast has an enviable location away from the bustle but within easy walking distance of it. The rooms, many of which feature a great view of Flat Creek lolling along behind the inn, are adorned with nature and wildlife art and nicely balance charm and comfort. The one suite features a working gas fireplace and full kitchen; many rooms have jetted tubs. This is a perfect spot for couples looking for both privacy and access to the town's dining and nightlife.

295 N. Millward St. (P.O. Box 445), Jackson, WY 83001. www.innonthecreek.com. © **800/669-9534** or 307/739-1565. Fax 307/734-9116. 9 units. $179–$425 double; $599 suite. Lower rates spring to fall. Rates include continental breakfast. AE, DISC, MC, V. *In room:* A/C, TV, Wi-Fi (free).

Rustic Inn ★★ ☺ New in 2008, on the creekside former home of the Wagon Wheel Motel, the Rustic Inn is a standout property with something for everybody, especially families. The rooms come in a wide variety of layouts and sizes, from nicely redone historic motel rooms dating back to the Wagon Wheel days to shiny new standalone cabins and fourplexes on Flat Creek. All of the units are decorated in tasteful "New West" style, featuring antler chandeliers and dual-head showers in the bathroom. There is plenty of space here—7 acres in all—and one of the few hotel swimming pools in Jackson proper.

475 N. Cache St. (P.O. Box 14250), Jackson, WY 83002. www.rusticinnatjh.com. ℂ **800/323-9279** or 307/733-2357. Fax 307/733-0568. 152 units. $229–$529 double. Lower rates spring-fall. Rates include full breakfast. AE, DISC, MC, V. **Amenities:** Restaurant; lounge; exercise room; pool; sauna; spa. *In room:* A/C, TV, hair dryer, Wi-Fi (free).

Rusty Parrot Lodge and Spa ★★

This country lodge and spa is ideally located right in the heart of busy Jackson. Located across from Miller Park, the Parrot is decorated in the nouveau Western style of peeled log, with an interior appointed with elegant furnishings and river-rock fireplaces. One very attractive lure is the Body Sage Spa, where you can get yourself treated to all sorts of scrubs, wraps, massages, and facials. Another is the excellent restaurant, the Wild Sage. Rooms are large, and several have private balconies.

175 N. Jackson St. (P.O. Box 1657), Jackson, WY 83001. www.rustyparrot.com. ℂ **800/458-2004** or 307/733-2000. 30 units. $360–$425 double; $625–$750 suite. Lower rates spring and fall. Rates include full breakfast. AE, DISC, MC, V. **Amenities:** Restaurant; lounge; Jacuzzi; spa. *In room:* A/C, TV, Wi-Fi (free).

Woods Hotel ★ 👜

Originally opening in 1950, the Woods Hotel was collecting cobwebs from 1998 to 2006 until new ownership reinvented the place as a boutique lodging in 2007. The brick exterior and vintage sign belie the innlike rooms, which feature spare Western-chic style. Standard rooms are small and lack air-conditioning, but the brick structure stays surprisingly cool; the suites and one family room (with bunk beds) give guests more space to stretch out, plus microwaves and minifridges.

120 N. Glenwood St. (P.O. Box 266), Jackson, WY 83001. www.thewoodshotel. com. ℂ **800/963-2200** or 307/733-2200. 11 units. $129-149 double; $159–$189 suite. AE, MC, V. Closed Oct–May. *In room:* TV, no phone, Wi-Fi (free).

Wort Hotel ★★

Located on Broadway just off the Town Square, the Wort stands like a charming old tree. Opened in the early 1940s by the sons of Charles Wort, an early-20th-century homesteader, the Tudor-style, two-story building was largely rebuilt after a 1980 fire. Nowadays, it has an old-fashioned style, both in the relaxed **Silver Dollar Bar** (distinctively graced with 2,032 silver dollars) and in the quiet, formal dining room. In the manner of an old cattle-baron hotel, the lobby is graced by a warm, romantic fireplace; another fireplace and a huge, hand-carved mural accent a mezzanine sitting area. Comfortable, air-conditioned guest rooms with modern decor and thick carpeting aren't Tudor at all—the Wort labels them "New West." The Silver Dollar Suite features a wet bar inlaid with silver dollars, like the bar downstairs.

50 N. Glenwood St. (at Broadway), Jackson, WY 83001. www.worthotel.com. ℂ **800/322-2727** or 307/733-2190. 59 units. $359 double; $659–$799 suite. Lower rates fall–spring. Valet parking $10 per day. AE, DISC, MC, V. **Amenities:** Restaurant; lounge; exercise room; Jacuzzi. *In room:* A/C, TV, CD player, MP3 docking station, Wi-Fi (free).

NEAR JACKSON

Amangani ★★★　Cut into the side of East Gros Ventre Butte, Amangani's rough rock exterior blends incredibly well so that the lights from its windows and pool appear at night to glow from within the mountain. Understated and rustic, all details are done with high contemporary style. From the high-ceilinged corridors to the idyllic outdoor pool, this place is all about class and privacy, not to mention superlative views. Hotelier Adrian Zecha has resorts like this around the world, from Bali to Bhutan, and while the designs are tailored to the landscape, the approach is the same: personal service, luxury, and all the little touches. To name a few of the latter, there are iPod cradles in every bedroom, plush throws on the daybeds, and stunning slate and redwood interiors.

1535 NE Butte Rd., Jackson, WY 83002 (on top of East Gros Ventre Butte). www. amanresorts.com. ℂ **877/734-7333** or 307/734-7333. 44 units. $725–$1,700 double; $3,400–$7,500 private house. AE, DISC, MC, V. **Amenities:** Restaurant; lounge; health club; Jacuzzi; pool; spa. *In room:* A/C, TV/DVD, hair dryer, MP3 docking station, Wi-Fi (free).

Spring Creek Ranch ★★　Perched atop East Gros Ventre Butte, 1,000 feet above the Snake River and minutes from both the airport and downtown Jackson, this resort commands a panoramic view of the Grand Tetons and 1,000 acres of land populated by deer, moose, and the horses at its riding facility in the valley below. Views aside, Spring Creek has much going for it: The rooms, divided among nine buildings with cabinlike exteriors, all have wood-burning fireplaces, Native American floor and wall coverings, and private decks and balconies. Most rooms have a king- or two queen-size beds, and the studio units boast kitchenettes. In addition to its own rooms, the resort arranges accommodations in the privately owned condominiums and vacation homes that dot the butte—large, lavishly furnished, and featuring full kitchens. The resort also staffs in-house naturalists, who lead guests on "Wildlife Safaris" into the parks.

1800 Spirit Dance Rd. (P.O. Box 4780), Jackson, WY 83001 (on top of the East Gros Ventre Butte). www.springcreekranch.com. ℂ **800/443-6139** or 307/ 733-8833. 126 units. $340–$500 double; $375–$2,200 condo or home. Lower rates spring and fall. AE, MC, V. **Amenities:** Restaurant; concierge; Jacuzzi; pool; room service; spa; tennis court (outdoor). *In room:* A/C, TV/VCR, kitchenette, Wi-Fi (free).

A Teton Tree House ★ 🏠 This B&B is an architectural marvel and a "quiet port in the storm" of bustling Jackson Hole, says innkeeper, builder, and longtime Jackson adventurer Denny Becker. Under construction for 40-some years on a forested hillside above Wilson, where flying squirrels glide amid the sunset canopy, the labyrinthine inn is full of books, staircases, and all sorts of funky nooks and crannies. Most every room has a private deck with a splendid view of the valley; the Downy Woodpecker room has a king bed and an outdoor swing and adjoins with the Clark's Nuthatch room, with two queens, for larger parties. Denny and his wife, Sally, eat heart-healthy breakfasts (meaning no eggs or meat) with their guests, and both have plenty of good advice.

6175 Heck of a Hill Rd. (P.O. Box 550), Wilson, WY 83014 (8 miles west of Jackson). www.atetontreehouse-jacksonhole.com. © **307/733-3233.** 6 units. $225–$285 double. 3-night minimum. Rates include complimentary full breakfast. DISC, MC, V. Closed mid-Oct to mid-May. No children 4 and under. *In room:* No phone, Wi-Fi (free).

Wildflower Inn ★★ A terrific B&B on 3 lush and secluded acres near Teton Village, the Wildflower Inn is the brainchild of jack-of-all-trades Ken Jern, a log-home builder and climbing guide, and his wife, Sherrie, a former ski instructor who now runs the inn full time. Besides being remarkable hosts, the Jerns are founts of local information. Rooms, named after local wildflowers, are comfortable and luxurious, with private decks, exposed logs, and a remarkable sense of privacy for an inn. Guests also get access to house bikes, rain gear, and trekking poles—not to mention hammocks. Breakfasts are excellent, including veggie frittatas, sour cream coffeecake, and yeast-raised waffles.

3725 Teton Village Rd. (P.O. Box 11000), Jackson, WY 83002. www.jacksonhole wildflower.com. © **307/733-4710.** Fax 307/739-0914. 5 units. $320–$350 double; $400 suite. MC, V. **Amenities:** Bikes; Jacuzzi. *In room:* TV, hair dryer, no phone, Wi-Fi (free).

IN TETON VILLAGE

You can take advantage of the attractions of Jackson, to the south, and Grand Teton, to the north, without suffering the crowds by journeying to Teton Village, which is approximately equidistant from both. Located at the foot of the ski hill, the village and surrounding area offer several fine eating and dining establishments, and activities nearby include skiing, ballooning, and hiking in Grand Teton National Park. During winter months, this is the center of activity in the valley. While lodging in the town of Jackson tends to be a little cheaper in the winter than the summer, at Teton Village the ratio is reversed—rooms by the ski hill get more expensive after the snow falls. For a wide range of basic condos and deluxe vacation homes, contact **Jackson Hole Resort Lodging** (✆ **800/443-8613** or 307/733-3990; www.jhrl.com). All establishments below are open year-round unless otherwise indicated.

The Alpenhof ★★   No other spot in the village has quite the Swiss-chalet flavor of this long-standing hostelry, which has a prize location only 150 feet from the ski-resort tram. Four stories tall, with a pitched roof and flower boxes on the balconies, it offers a little old-world atmosphere, as well as excellent comforts and service. The rooms feature brightly colored alpine fabrics, handcrafted Bavarian furnishings, and tiled bathrooms with big, soft towels. You can choose from two junior suites with wet bars and five rooms with fireplaces, and many rooms have balconies or decks. Economy rooms offer two doubles or one queen-size bed, while deluxe units are larger. The resident **Alpenrose** restaurant specializes in fondue.

3255 W. Village Dr. (P.O. Box 288), Teton Village, WY 83025. www.alpenhoflodge. com. ✆ **800/732-3244** or 307/733-3242. Fax 307/739-1516. 42 units. $189–$379 double; $479–$539 suite. Lower rates spring and fall. AE, DISC, MC, V. Closed Nov. **Amenities:** 2 restaurants; lounge; Jacuzzi; pool; sauna. *In room:* A/C, TV, hair dryer, Wi-Fi (free).

Four Seasons Resort Jackson Hole ★★★   The most deluxe lodging option in Teton Village, the ultrastylish Four Seasons sets a high bar for ski-in, ski-out luxury. From a year-round pool landscaped to resemble a mountain creek to the cowboy-hatted doorman to the rooms—stately, luxurious, and definitively Western—this is one of the top slopeside properties in the country. The range of rooms starts at the high end and goes up from there, but even the standard kings are large and plush, and most units have a balcony or a fireplace. One especially notable perk: the hotel's Base Camp, a full-service, outdoor-activity concierge who can arrange mountain biking, hiking, fishing, and ballooning excursions, and who will outfit you in style. In winter, the service transforms into a first-rate ski concierge, and s'mores and hot chocolate are served poolside. The eating and drinking facilities are also a cut above, and range from casually hip to elegant.

7680 Granite Loop (P.O. Box 544), Teton Village, WY 83025. www.fourseasons. com/jacksonhole. ✆ **307/732-5000.** Fax 307/732-5001. 156 units. $400–$750 double; $700–$4,000 condo or suite. Lower rates spring and fall. Valet parking $24 per day. AE, DISC, MC, V. **Amenities:** 2 restaurants; lounge; concierge; health club; Jacuzzis; pool; room service; sauna; spa. *In room:* A/C, TV/DVD, hair dryer, kitchen, Wi-Fi ($10/day).

The Hostel ★ 🎿 If you came to Wyoming to ski, not to lie in the lap of luxury, get yourself a room at the Hostel and hit the slopes. Open since 1967 and fortuitously spared the wrecking ball—and known as Hostel X until 2008—it's a great bargain for those who don't need the trimmings. It's not just dormitory bunks, either—private rooms (slickly renovated in 2011) with either one king bed or four twins are simple but comfortable. There's a good place to prep your skis, a library, and a common room with chessboards, a Ping-Pong table, a fireplace, Internet access, and TVs. You can also walk to the Mangy Moose and other fun spots.

3315 W. Village Dr. (P.O. Box 583), Teton Village, WY 83025. www.thehostel.us. © **307/733-3415.** 75 units. $79–$89 double; $18–$32 bunk. AE, DISC, MC, V. *In room:* No phone, Wi-Fi ($5 one-time fee).

Hotel Terra ★★ The newest—and greenest—property in Teton Village, Hotel Terra combines sustainable design and contemporary Western style, with satisfying results. The LEED-certified hotel incorporates granite stonework and understated decor into inviting and sleek spaces. The rooms, which range from studios to three-bedroom suites with full kitchens, boast organic cotton sheets and towels, rainfall shower heads, fair trade coffee, and touch-screen telephones. The hotel's facilities are excellent, including the terrific CHILL Spa and a wonderful restaurant, **Il Villaggio Osteria** (see "Where to Eat," later in this chapter).

3355 W. Village Dr. (P.O. Box 558), Teton Village, WY 83025. www.hotelterra jacksonhole.com. © **800/631-6281** or 307/739-4000. 132 units. $359–$499 double; $499–$1,700 suite. Lower rates spring and fall. Valet parking $15 per day. AE, DISC, MC, V. **Amenities:** 2 restaurants, including Il Villaggio Osteria (p. 178); lounge; concierge; Jacuzzi; pool; spa. *In room:* A/C, TV/DVD, hair dryer, kitchen, MP3 docking station, Wi-Fi (free).

Snake River Lodge and Spa ★★ Under the management of RockResorts, this is one of the slickest spots to hang your hat in Teton Village. Rooms boast exposed wooden-beam ceilings, billowy comforters, and luxurious furnishings. There are three levels of suites, from oversize rooms to three-bedroom suites with top-of-the-line kitchens. The 17,000-square-foot spa is Wyoming's largest, featuring everything from massage to hydrotherapy to free weights. Winter visitors can ski directly to a ski valet and drop their skis off for an overnight tune-up.

7710 Granite Loop Rd. (P.O. Box 348), Teton Village, WY 83025. www.snakeriver lodge.rockresorts.com. © **307/732-6000.** 130 units. $250–$499 double; $699–$2,000 suite. Lower rates spring and fall. AE, MC, V. **Amenities:** Restaurant; lounge; children's program; concierge; health club; Jacuzzi; pool; room service; spa. *In room:* TV, hair dryer, kitchenette, Wi-Fi (free).

Where to Eat

Jackson has more dining options than all the other towns in this chapter combined, running the gamut of cuisine and price. You'll find the predictable steak/seafood/pasta menus, usually injected with a few de rigueur wild-game dishes, but you'll also find more-unusual options. For a morning jump-start, head to **Shades Cafe,** 82 S. King St. (© **307/733-2015**), which serves good coffee, sandwiches, and other breakfast and lunch entrees. Another a.m. stalwart, the **Betty Rock Cafe,** 325 W. Pearl Ave. (© **307/733-0747**), serves creative breakfasts and plenty of espresso.

EXPENSIVE

The Blue Lion ★★ NEW AMERICAN   In the fast-moving, high-rent world of Jackson dining, the Blue Lion stays in the forefront by staying the same. Owned and operated by Ned Brown since 1978, the restaurant is located in a two-story blue clapboard building across from a park. Inside, in intimate rooms accented with soft lighting, or outside on a picture-perfect patio, diners enjoy slow-paced and elegant meals. The menu features rack of lamb and wild-game specialties, such as grilled elk loin in a peppercorn sauce. Fresh fish is flown in daily for dishes such as the nori-crusted ahi.

160 N. Millward St. © **307/733-3912.** www.bluelionrestaurant.com. Reservations recommended. Main courses $15–$45. AE, DC, DISC, MC, V. Summer daily 5:30–10pm; winter daily 6–9pm.

The Cadillac Grille ★ NEW AMERICAN   The nostalgic neon and hip American cuisine gives this restaurant a trendy air that attracts see-and-be-seen visitors as well as locals. The chefs work hard on presentation, but they also know how to prepare a wide-ranging variety of dishes, from fire-roasted game dishes to fresh wild salmon. A *Wine Spectator* favorite, the wine list is equally long and varied. The Grille's upscale dining room is one of three options at this address; you can also eat at the posh bar, or the '50s-themed confines of **Billy's Giant Hamburgers,** where a great burger runs about $7.

55 N. Cache St. © **307/733-3279.** Reservations recommended. Main courses $5–$18 lunch, $12–$35 dinner. AE, MC, V. Daily 11:30am–3pm and 5:30–10pm.

Il Villaggio Osteria ★★ ITALIAN   The swankiest restaurant in Teton Village, Il Villaggio Osteria features tables as well as a 12-seat wine bar and an 8-seat salami bar, where imported meats and cheeses are sliced to order. The menu includes gourmet wood-fired pizzas with such exotic toppings as figs, arugula, and hummus, as well as creative dishes with Mediterranean influences: wild mushroom risotto, braised pork with polenta, and wild boar ragu. The tantalizing dessert list includes a delectable tiramisu. The lunch menu (offered Dec–Apr) focuses on salads, pizzas, paninis, and lighter versions of the dinner entrees.

3335 W. Village Dr., Teton Village (in the Hotel Terra). ℂ **307/739-4100.** Reservations recommended. Main courses $10–$19 lunch, $15–$27 dinner. AE, DISC, MC, V. Summer daily 5:30–10pm; winter daily 11am–10pm.

Nani's Genuine Pasta House ★★★ 🍴 ITALIAN In a warmly appointed dining room with a slick wine bar, Nani's serves superb pasta favorites such as amitriciana (tomato, onion, guanciale, and freshly ground black pepper) and fresh mussels in wine broth, as well as a list of specialties from a featured region of Italy. Depending on when you visit, it might be Sicily, where Executive Chef Camille Parker's family has its roots, or Emilia-Romagna, where prosciutto, Parmesan, and balsamic vinegar are culinary staples. The only problem you might have with this restaurant is finding it—it's tucked away behind a little relic of a motel, but it's definitely worth seeking out.

242 N. Glenwood St. ℂ **307/733-3888.** www.nanis.com. Reservations recommended. Main courses $13–$34. AE, MC, V. Daily 5–10pm. Bar open most nights till 11pm.

Snake River Grill ★★★ NEW AMERICAN This is a popular drop-in spot for locals, including some of the glitterati who spend time in the valley. The front-room dining area overlooks the busy Town Square, and there's also a more private, romantic room in the back. It's an award-winning restaurant for both its wine list and its menu, which features regular fresh-fish dishes (ahi tuna is a favorite), crispy pork shank, and some game-meat entrees, such as venison chops and buffalo sirloin. The pizzas—cooked in a wood-burning oven—are topped with exotic ingredients, such as venison pepperoni or steak tartare.

84 E. Broadway (on the Town Square). ℂ **307/733-0557.** www.snakerivergrill.com. Reservations recommended. Main courses $19–$52. AE, MC, V. Summer daily 5:30–10pm; winter daily 6–10pm. Closed Nov and Apr.

Stiegler's ★ 🍴 AUSTRIAN Austrian cuisine isn't exactly lurking beyond every street corner, waiting to be summoned with a Julie Andrews yodel, but the discerning Austrian will certainly appreciate Stiegler's. Since 1983—aside from a year-long respite in 2010—Stiegler's has been confusing, astonishing, and delighting customers with such favorites as elk Försterin, bratwurst, and schnitzel, as well as less recognizable delicacies. Each plate is served with at least three veggies for a terrific presentation and variety of tastes. The desserts are more familiar: apple strudel and crepes. Peter Stiegler, the Austrian chef, invites you to "find a little Gemütlichkeit"—the feeling you get when you're surrounded by good friends, good food, and, of course, good beer. The inviting copper bar has its own menu ($10–$20, with great burgers), and there are intimate tables and booths inside and a poolside patio outside.

3535 Moose-Wilson Rd. (at the Aspens). © **307/733-1071.** Reservations recommended. Main courses $18–$44. AE, MC, V. Tues–Sun 5:30–9:30pm. Closed mid-Apr to mid-May.

MODERATE

The Kitchen ★★ NEW AMERICAN With a picture-perfect outdoor deck and plenty of creative flair, the Kitchen is the latest eatery from Gavin Fine, proprietor of **Rendezvous Bistro, Q Roadhouse,** and **Il Villaggio Osteria** (p. 181, 181, and 178, respectively). As usual, Fine doesn't disappoint: Featuring fresh seafood from its crudo bar, starters like braised pork nachos and truffle fries, and constantly changing main courses from superlative burgers (with provolone, bacon, and chipotle aioli) to cornmeal-dusted trout and seared red deer, the Kitchen showcases a wide range of culinary influences and inclinations. The restaurant also makes inspired cocktails and has a terrific wine list.

155 N. Glenwood St. © **307/734-1633.** www.thekitchenjacksonhole.com. Reservations recommended. Main courses $16–$28. AE, DISC, MC, V. Daily 5:30–10pm.

Koshu Wine Bar ★★ 🍴ASIAN FUSION Housed in the back half of the Jackson Hole Wine Company, this small, sleek dining room serves ingenious, addictive, Asian-inspired creations. The Far East is just a starting point, with offerings that meld dozens of influences into dishes such as buttermilk-battered softshell crab and pork ribs; the menu changes on a regular basis. Thanks to its location in a wine store, patrons can choose from 800 varieties of wine at retail prices (plus a nominal corking fee).

200 W. Broadway (in the Jackson Hole Wine Company). © **307/733-5283.** Reservations recommended. Main courses $15–$30. AE, MC, V. Daily 5:30–10:30pm. Bar open till 2am, depending on crowd.

Mangy Moose ☺ AMERICAN Coming off the slopes at the end of a hard day of skiing or snowboarding, you can slide right to the porch of this Teton Village institution. Good luck getting a seat inside, but if you like a lot of noise and laughter, a beer or a glass of wine, and tasty food, you'll be patient—it beats getting into your car and driving into town. The decor matches the pandemonium: It looks like an upscale junk shop, with bicycles, old signs, and, naturally, a moose head or two hanging from the walls and rafters. The food is customary Wyoming fare (steak, seafood, and pasta)—I'm a big fan of the buffalo meatloaf and the fresh Idaho trout.

There is often live music in the saloon, which serves both lunch and dinner. An affiliated cafe, the RMO Cafe, serves breakfast, lunch, and pizza in a separate room downstairs.

1 W. Village Dr., Teton Village. ✆ **307/733-4913.** www.mangymoose.net. Reservations recommended for large parties. Main courses $12–$29 dining room; $4–$13 bar and cafe. AE, MC, V. Daily 7am–10pm (cafe), 11:30am–10pm (bar), and 5:30–10pm (dining room). Saloon open later.

North Grille ★ NEW AMERICAN   The resident eatery at the Jackson Hole Golf and Tennis Club, the North Grille is located at the LEED-certified clubhouse, a slick and stylish building with incredible views of the Tetons. For sunset-watching, I recommend the outdoor patio, but the dining room, clad in dark wood and bookcases, is a cozy setting for the winter months. The menu is neatly organized into categories by price point: $14 nets you a garlic roasted chicken breast or steamed clams; $20 brings halibut medallions on biscuits with lobster gravy or a spicy pork filet; and $28 allows for rack of lamb or chargrilled king salmon.

5000 Spring Gulch Rd. ✆ **307/733-7788.** www.jhgtc.com. Reservations recommended. Main courses $8–$12 lunch; $14–$28 dinner. AE, DISC, MC, V. Sun–Tues 11:30am–2:30pm; Wed–Sat 11:30am–2:30pm and 5:30–9pm.

Q Roadhouse ★ AMERICAN   This bustling joint on the road to Teton Village offers a casual eatery on one side and a bar favored by locals on the other. There are brick walls, complimentary peanuts (toss your shells on the floor), and a laid-back vibe. The Southern-accented menu ranges from barbecued baby back ribs to veggie enchiladas to blackened catfish. Burgers and sandwiches are also available.

2550 Moose-Wilson Rd. ✆ **307/739-0700.** Reservations recommended. Main courses $10–$27. AE, DISC, MC, V. Daily 5–10pm. Bar open later.

Rendezvous Bistro ★★ AMERICAN/SEAFOOD   The Rendezvous opened in 2001 and garnered a fast local following. It's easy to see why: The food is the best upscale value in town, the atmosphere is laid-back, and the service is excellent. Climb into one of the intimate booths and order a dozen oysters on the half shell and slurp away, but save some room for a main course, ranging from steak frites to spicy chipotle trout to grilled chili-rubbed pork chops.

380 S. Broadway. ✆ **307/739-1100.** Reservations recommended. Main courses $15–$25. AE, DISC, MC, V. Daily 5:30–10pm.

Sweetwater Restaurant ★★ AMERICAN   Although this little log restaurant serves American fare, it does so in a decidedly offbeat way. The eclectic menu includes, for example, a Greek salad, a Baja chicken salad, and a cowboy-grilled roast-beef sandwich. During the summer, there's outside dining. The dinner menu is just as quirky and livened by nightly specials; try the chili–bleu cheese fondue or fried green tomatoes before diving into a blackened catfish filet topped with crab, or a delectable chipotle-tomato buffalo skirt steak with boursin cheese. Vegetarians will want to sample the spinach and feta soufflé.

85 King St. ℂ **307/733-3553.** www.sweetwaterjackson.com. Reservations recommended. Main courses $10–$13 lunch, $22–$30 dinner. AE, DISC, MC, V. Summer daily 11:30am–3pm and 5:30–10pm; winter daily 11:30am–2:30pm and 5:30–9:30pm.

Trio ★★ NEW AMERICAN   Opened in 2005 by a trio (thus the name) of owner/chefs who formerly worked at the Snake River Grill, this instant local favorite offers a winning combination of inviting atmosphere and remarkable food. Served in a dimly lit, social room with a fossil-rock bar and semiopen kitchen, the seasonal menu might include appetizers such as heirloom tomato and ricotta bruschetta and house-cured salmon and entrees like Dungeness crab pasta or a killer Idaho rainbow trout on a bed of blackened corn and avocado. The restaurant is perhaps best known for its killer fries—served with scallions, black pepper, and an addictive blue-cheese fondue.

45 S. Glenwood St. ℂ **307/734-8038.** www.bistrotrio.com. Reservations recommended. Main courses $10–$25 lunch; $15–$44 dinner. AE, MC, V. Mon–Fri 11am–2pm and 5:30–close, usually 9–10pm; Sat–Sun 5:30–close, usually 9–10pm. Closed for lunch in winter.

INEXPENSIVE

D.O.G., at Glenwood St. and Broadway (ℂ **307/733-4422**) serves coffee, burgers, and superlative breakfast burritos for breakfast and lunch and transforms into **Everest Momo Shack** Thursday through Monday evenings to plate up Nepalese cuisine.

Nora's Fish Creek Inn ★ 🎁 AMERICAN   If you like to eat among locals, and if you like to eat a lot, Nora's is the place to hang out in Wilson, 6 miles northwest of Jackson—just look for the 15-foot trout on the roof. At once rough and cozy, it's an institution, and if you come here often, you'll start to recognize the regulars, who grumble over their coffee and gossip about doings in the valley. Breakfast is especially good, when there are pancakes and *huevos rancheros* that barely fit on the huge plates. Trout and eggs is another specialty. Prices are inexpensive compared to those at any of the other restaurants in town. Dinner is burgers, barbecue, and smoked trout.

5600 W. Wyo. 22, Wilson. ℂ **307/733-8288.** Reservations accepted for dinner. Main courses $5–$13 breakfast and lunch; $10–$37 dinner. AE, DISC, MC, V.

Mon–Fri 6:30am–2pm and 5:30–9pm; Sat–Sun 6:30am–1:30pm and 5:30–9pm.
Call for winter hours.

Snake River Brewing Co. ★ 🍺 MICROBREWERY   One of
the West's best (and busiest) microbreweries, this industrial-
meets-contemporary establishment offers a menu of pasta, apple-
wood-fired pizzas and panini, and salads, plus a few entrees like
"Slash and Burn Trout," served with fennel relish. The real standouts are the beers, especially Custer's Last Ale and Zonker Stout,
regular winners at the Great American Beer Fest and other competitions. It's also a great lunch spot, with daily $7 specials like tur-
key-and-brie wraps and chipotle barbecue sandwiches.

265 S. Millward St. ℂ **307/739-2337.** www.snakeriverbrewing.com. Main courses
$8–$14. AE, DISC, MC, V. Daily 11:30am–11pm. Bar open till midnight.

Jackson After Dark

Talented musicians from well-known orchestras participate in the
Grand Teton Music Festival ★ (ℂ 307/733-3050 or 307/733-
1128 for the box office; www.gtmf.org) held in summer in the
amphitheater next to the tram lift. Tickets, typically $55 or less, are
usually available on short notice, especially for the weeknight
chamber music performances, which are often terrific.

Wyoming's only year-round professional theatrical group, the
Off Square Theatre Company, performs classic and contemporary comedies and dramas at the Center for the Arts, 265 S. Cache
St. (ℂ **307/733-3021;** www.offsquare.org). Tickets (typically
$15–$25) for all shows should be reserved.

Those less impressed with dramaturgy should head down to the
Silver Dollar Bar, at 50 N. Glenwood St. in the Wort Hotel
(ℂ **307/733-2190**), for a drink with one of the real or wannabe
cowpokes at the bar. And, yes, those 2,032 silver dollars are
authentic. At the very famous **Million Dollar Cowboy Bar** on
the Town Square, at 25 N. Cache St. (ℂ **307/733-2207;** www.
milliondollarcowboybar.com), you can dance the two-step to live
bands or just mill around and check out the unique details: knobby
pine, saddle barstools, and plenty of taxidermy. For live music and
DJs, the young, restless, and intoxicated congregate at **43° North,**
645 S. Cache St. (ℂ **307/733-0043**), near the base of Snow
King. For sports nuts, **Sidewinders Tavern,** 945 W. Broadway
(ℂ **307/734-5766**), offers a slew of flatscreen TVs and a casual
atmosphere. If you want some high-octane dancing fun led by
some talented local hoofers, head west to Wilson and the **Stagecoach Bar** (ℂ **307/733-4407**) on Wyo. 22 on a Sunday night.
It's the only night there's regularly scheduled live music in this
classic Western joint, and the place is jammed wall to wall.

CODY, WYOMING ★★

53 miles from the east entrance to Yellowstone

Almost from the moment trappers first reported the unworldly marvels of Yellowstone, would-be entrepreneurs were setting up shop. However, none could match the vision of William F. "Buffalo Bill" Cody, the famed scout and showman who, in 1887, set about building a hunting resort, an irrigation project, and a city on the eastern edge of the park. Today, Cody is one of the most beautifully situated communities in Wyoming, near the juncture of rivers that pour from the rugged Absaroka Range. The drive from the east entrance of Yellowstone to Cody cuts through the magnificent East Yellowstone (Wapiti) Valley, a drive Theodore Roosevelt once called the most scenic 50 miles in the world.

The town oozes Western charm year-round, but it's at its best during the summer: The daytime skies are cloudless, and the longest-running rodeo in the country provides nightly entertainment under the stars. Museums, a re-created Western town, and retail shops supply plenty of diversions. Cody's friendly residents preserve and promote their particular brand of Western heritage to visitors the world over. And it's not too hard of a sell: Jackson might be the state's most renowned mountain paradise, but Cody's Western charm feels much more authentic.

Essentials

For information on air service to Cody and rental-car agencies see "Getting There & Getting Around," in chapter 10.

GETTING THERE   If you're driving from Cheyenne, travel north on I-25 to Casper and then west on U.S. Hwy. 20/26 to Shoshone, where U.S. Hwy. 20 turns north to Thermopolis. From there, it's another 84 miles to Cody on Wyo. 120. From Jackson, take U.S. Hwy. 191 to the West Thumb Junction in Yellowstone, drive east along the northern boundary of Yellowstone Lake, and continue on U.S. Hwy. 14/16/20 to Cody. If you enter Wyoming from the west on I-80, drive north from Rock Springs on U.S. Hwy. 191 to Farson, Wyo. 28 to Lander, Wyo. 789 to Thermopolis, and Wyo. 120 to Cody. But the storms can get vicious in here come wintertime: Call © **888/996-7623,** or 511 (in state) or 307/772-0824 for **road and travel information.** Online, visit **www. wyoroad.info**.

VISITOR INFORMATION   For printed information on this area of Wyoming, contact **Buffalo Bill's Cody/Yellowstone Country,** 836 Sheridan Ave. (P.O. Box 2454), Cody, WY 82414 (© **800/393-2639** or 307/587-2297; www.yellowstonecountry.org), or stop by their visitor center from 8am to 6pm daily in summer, and 8am to 5pm Monday through Friday fall to spring.

Getting Outside

Because of its proximity to Yellowstone, the best place to get outdoors near Cody is the park itself, but be aware that the town's only access to Yellowstone during the winter months is by snowmobile over dizzying Sylvan Pass. Once you're outside the park, Cody doesn't have the plethora of activities that Jackson Hole does, but it's still a bustling community. **Buffalo Bill State Park,** located along the canyon and reservoir 6 miles west of Cody, is a hot spot for lovers of the outdoors, with opportunities for hiking, fishing, and a variety of watersports. Its **Buffalo Bill Reservoir** is regarded as one of the premier spots for windsurfing in the United States. The park also has facilities for camping and picnicking. In the winter, cross-country and downhill skiing, ice climbing, and snowmobiling are popular in the Cody area. Drop by **Sunlight Sports,** 1131 Sheridan Ave. (© **307/587-9517;** www.sunlightsports.com), for gear, rentals, and advice. Also worth a stop for discount gear and clothing: the **Sierra Trading Post Outlet Store,** 1402 8th St. (© **307/578-5802;** www.sierratradingpost.com).

If you'd rather not be a driver in the park's heavy summer traffic, guided Yellowstone National Park tours are available locally through **Grub Steak Expeditions,** P.O. Box 1013, Cody, WY 82414 (© **800/527-6316** or 307/527-6316; www.grubsteaktours. com). Bob Richard, Grub Steak's proprietor (and one of the most knowledgeable guides you'll find), is a third-generation Cody resident and former Yellowstone ranger. Full-day tours run about $500 for two people and $140 for additional adults, $75 for additional kids 15 and under.

Red Canyon Wild Mustang Tours (© **800/293-0148;** www.wildmustangtours.com) offers van tours of a wild mustang refuge about 20 miles outside Cody for $24 for adults and $21 for children.

BIKING If you want to explore the area on two wheels, bike rentals ($45 per day, with multiday discounts) and advice are available from **Absaroka Bikes,** 2201 17th St. (© **307/527-5566**). Although there isn't a marked network of bike paths in the Cody area, you can ride on the Forest Service trails west of town off U.S. Hwy. 14/16/20 in the Shoshone National Forest. For specific trail information, call the **U.S. Forest Service** (© **307/527-6241;** www.fs.fed.us/r2/shoshone).

CROSS-COUNTRY SKIING If you favor a groomed course for cross-country skiing, try the **North Fork Nordic Trails** in

Shoshone National Forest, near the east entrance to the park off U.S. Hwy. 14/16/20. You can circuit 25km (16 miles) of trails adjacent to the Pahaska Tepee Resort.

FISHING Yellowstone's legendary fly-fishing waters are a short drive away, though you should try the smaller but excellent angling streams west of Cody: **Clark's Fork of the Yellowstone,** the **North and South Forks of the Shoshone,** and **Sunlight Creek.** To the east, the warmer and slower **Big Horn River** and **Big Horn Lake** nurture catfish, walleye, and ling for boat fishers. For advice on the trout streams near Cody, ask at **Tim Wade's North Fork Anglers,** 1107 Sheridan Ave. (© **307/527-7274;** www.northforkanglers.com), which stocks gear and clothing and also guides day trips for $375 to $425 for two people. If you like to troll or cast from a boat, try **Buffalo Bill Reservoir,** which has produced some massive mackinaw, or lake trout, as well as rainbow, brown, and cutthroat trout.

FLOAT TRIPS In summer, one of the most popular things to do in Cody is to float along the Shoshone River, the major eastern drainage of the Yellowstone River. The mild Class I and II rapids make it an enjoyable trip for almost anyone. Contact **Wyoming River Trips,** 233 Yellowstone Ave. (© **800/586-6661** or 307/587-6661; www.wyomingrivertrips.com). Prices run from about $25 to $70, depending on the length and difficulty of the trip.

GOLF Greens fees at the 18-hole **Olive Glenn Golf and Country Club,** 802 Meadow Lane (© **307/587-5551;** www.olive glenngolf.com), are $40 for 9 holes, and $70 for 18, cart included.

SNOWMOBILING The most popular Cody snowmobiling trails originate from nearby **Pahaska Tepee Resort,** located 51 miles from Cody on U.S. Hwy. 14/16/20 (see "Where to Stay," below). Don't take the Pahaska Tepee Trail over 8,541-foot Sylvan Pass if you're afraid of heights; but if you're not, go for it: You'll connect with the Yellowstone National Park trails and the lengthy Continental Divide Snowmobile Trail, and have some breathtaking views, including some of Avalanche Peak (10,566 ft.) and Cody Peak (10,267 ft.). The **Sunlight trail system** is located 36 miles north of Cody and winds through the wilds to a stunning view of the Beartooth Mountains. Sledders start from a parking area at the junction of Wyo. 296 and U.S. Hwy. 212 and follow the Beartooth Scenic Byway east for 16 miles to a warming hut. To the east, there are 70 miles of snowmobile routes in the Bighorn Mountains. Snowmobiles can be rented in Cody from **Mountain Valley Engine Service,** 422 W. Yellowstone Ave. (© **307/587-6218;** www.mountainvalleyengine.com) for about $225 a day.

WINDSURFING The 8-mile-long, 4-mile-wide **Buffalo Bill Reservoir,** which receives wind from three mountain gorges, is one of the top windsurfing destinations in the continental United States. It's best experienced in the warmer months of June to September. There is a boat ramp near the campground on the north side of the reservoir, just off U.S. Hwy. 14/16/20. There are no places to rent a windsurf board in the vicinity.

Special Events

The Buffalo Bill Historical Center is a tremendous resource for unique events in Cody. The April festival of **Cowboy Songs and Range Ballads** features storytelling, poetry, and some fine yodeling and balladry. In mid-June, the **Plains Indian Museum Pow-wow** features traditional dance competitions, crafts shows, and Native American food. Call the **Buffalo Bill Historical Center** (© 307/587-4771; www.bbhc.org) for exact dates of these and other events and special exhibits. Every July 1 to July 4, during the **Cody Stampede** (© 800/207-0744 or 307/587-5155; www.codystampederodeo.com), the streets are filled with parades, rodeos, fireworks, street dances, barbecues, and entertainment, capped by a top-notch rodeo.

Seeing the Sights

Those with a special interest in antique firearms will also want to check out the one-of-a-kind **Cody Dug Up Gun Museum,** upstairs at 1020 12th St. (© 307/587-3344; www.codydugup gunmuseum.com), showcasing over 750 guns excavated from all over the world, including three from Custer's Last Stand and one that a tree slowly engulfed. The museum is open from 9am to 9pm daily from May to September and admission is free; donations requested.

Buffalo Bill Dam and Visitor Center The Buffalo Bill Dam drops like a slim concrete knife 325 feet into the gorge carved by the Shoshone River west of Cody, and you can walk out atop the dam and look down the steep canyon or back across the deep blue water of the **Buffalo Bill Reservoir.** Several workers died building it, and when it was completed in 1910, it was the tallest dam in the world. The lake behind it serves anglers, boaters, and windsurfers, while providing irrigation water to farmers downstream. The octagonal visitor center perched next to the dam provides exhibits on the reservoir, wildlife, and area recreation. There is a boat launch along the north lakeshore off U.S. Hwy. 14/16/20 and a clean, spacious campground that lacks much in the way of shade.

6 miles west of Cody on U.S. Hwy. 14/16/20 at the top of Shoshone Canyon. *C* **307/527-6076.** www.bbdvc.org. Free admission. Visitor Center: May and Sept Mon–Fri 8am–6pm, Sat–Sun 9am–5pm; June–Aug Mon–Fri 8am–7pm, Sat–Sun 9am–5pm. Closed Oct–Apr.

Buffalo Bill Historical Center ★★★ Nicknamed the "Smithsonian of the West," this vast museum is top-drawer, casting a scholarly eye on the relics of the West's young history while offering some flash and entertainment for the easily distracted. From its beginnings in a rustic log building, it's grown into a thoroughly impressive modern edifice that now houses five different museums in all.

The **Buffalo Bill Museum** is a monument to one of the earliest manifestations of America's celebrity culture, displaying the wares that turned a frontier scout and bison hunter into a renowned showman. Posters trumpet his world-famous Wild West shows featuring "Custer's Last Rally" and "Cossack of the Caucasus," and there are some grainy film clips of the show itself. The newly renovated **Whitney Gallery of Western Art** showcases work by the adventurous artists who carried their palettes to the frontier to record firsthand the wilderness beauty, the proud Indian cultures, and the lives of trappers and cowboys in the 19th century. Bygone Western artists, such as Frederic Remington, Charlie Russell, Albert Bierstadt, and Gutzon Borglum, share exhibition space with contemporary practitioners. The **Plains Indian Museum** is devoted to the history of Plains tribes, including the Blackfeet, Cheyenne, Crow, Gros Ventre, Shoshone, and Sioux. Interactive exhibits explain the migrations and customs of the tribes and display art and artifacts, including cradle boards, ceremonial dresses and robes, pipes, and beadwork. Situated in a rotunda populated by dozens of engaging exhibits, the **Draper Museum of Natural History** focuses on man's scientific exploration of nature over time, with specific attention on the Greater Yellowstone Ecosystem (there's a regional map composed of 27,000 tiles) and many interactive displays. The **Cody Firearms Museum** displays weaponry dating back to 16th-century Europe in its collection of more than 5,000 pieces.

The center also features rotating special exhibitions, and its research library is an unparalleled resource for all things Western. Additionally, numerous educational programs are held throughout the year. Expect to spend anywhere from 2 hours to 2 days exploring the center, depending on your level of interest.

720 Sheridan Ave. *C* **307/587-4771.** www.bbhc.org. Admission $18 adults, $16 seniors, $13 students 18 and over with valid ID, $10 children 6–17, free for children 5 and under. Admission is good for 2 consecutive days. Group tour rates available by request. Nov–Mar Thurs–Sun 10am–5pm; Apr daily 10am–5pm; May to mid-Sept daily 8am–6pm; mid-Sept to Oct daily 8am–5pm.

Cody Nite Rodeo ★★ ☺ If you want to see an authentic Wyoming rodeo, Cody (aka "The Rodeo Capital of the World") offers a sure thing: a nightly tussle between bulls, broncos, and cowboys, as well as roping, cutting, and kids' events, such as the "calf scramble"—about 100 young patrons chasing a bewildered young calf. Pay an extra $2, and you get a seat just above the chutes in the Buzzard's Roost. The 6,000-seat stadium is on an open terrace above the Shoshone River west of town—not a bad place to be on a cool Wyoming evening beneath the stars. Every year from July 1 to July 4, some of the nation's top rodeo competitors show up for the Cody Stampede (see "Special Events," above). Before the rodeo, there's a kiddie event with various activities.

Stampede Park (on U.S. Hwy. 14/16/20 west of town toward the Wapiti Valley). ✆ **800/207-0744** or 307/587-5155. www.codystampederodeo.com. Admission $18 adults, $8 children 7–12, free for children 6 and under. June–Aug nightly at 8pm; gates open at 7pm.

Cody Trolley Tours ★ An informative, witty look back at Cody's colorful past with a focus on the town's founding father himself, Buffalo Bill, this hour-long tour in a restored trolley takes visitors on a loop that includes historic homes, public art, and the Buffalo Bill Dam and Visitor Center. The owner/operators, Mike and Margie Johnson, deliver a running commentary augmented by visual aids and recorded snippets that will keep the kids interested. While the couple's narration occasionally comes off as an economic-development pitch for Cody, it also packs a dense serving of fun facts and trivia into the 60-minute drive.

1192 Sheridan Ave. (at the Irma Hotel). ✆ **307/527-7043.** www.codytrolleytours. com. Admission $24 adults, $22 seniors, $12 children 6–17, free for children 5 and under. Combination tickets for Cody Trolley Tours and the Buffalo Bill Historical Center available. Tours offered early June to late Sept daily at 11am and 3pm.

Museum of the Old West at Old Trail Town ☺ Walking the authentically creaky boardwalks here, you'll pass by gray storefronts and clapboard cabins gathered from ghost towns around the region and assembled on the original town site of Cody City, a short jog from the rodeo grounds. The curators haven't wasted any paint on these relics, which include an 1883 cabin from Kaycee, Wyoming, where Butch Cassidy and the Sundance Kid once conspired; a saloon decorated with bullet holes; and what must be the largest collection of worn-out buckboard carriages in the U.S. Also on-site: the relocated graves of a number of Western notables, including John "Liver-eatin'" Johnston, the model for Robert Redford's *Jeremiah Johnson*.

1831 DeMaris Dr. ✆ **307/587-5302.** www.museumoftheoldwest.org. Admission $8 adults, $7 seniors, $4 children 6–12, free for children 5 and under. Mid-May to Sept daily 8am–7pm.

Tecumseh's Old West Miniature Village and Museum ☺
You have to pass through a trading post of Western tourist plunder
and handcrafted beadwork to get to this finely detailed miniature
diorama of Wyoming and Montana history. Described by creator
Jerry Fick as his "lifetime work," the room-size landscape depicts
everything from fur trappers floating the rivers to Custer's last
moments at Little Big Horn. There is also a sizable collection of
Indian and pioneer artifacts and taxidermy.

142 W. Yellowstone Ave. ✆ **307/587-5362.** www.tecumsehs.com. Free admission. Mid-May to mid-Sept daily 9am–7pm; early May and late Sept daily 9am–
5pm. Call for winter hours.

Where to Stay

If you want to book lodging before you arrive, a good accommodations
resource is **Cody Lodging Company,** 1302 Beck Ave. (✆ **800/
587-6560;** www.codylodgingcompany.com), which manages numerous properties, from Victorian B&Bs to three-bedroom houses. Rates
range from about $100 to $500 a night in the summer season.

**Buffalo Bill Village Resort: Holiday Inn, Comfort Inn, and
Buffalo Bill Village Historic Cabins** ★ Consisting of three
distinct lodging options at the same convenient location, Buffalo
Bill Village Resort has something for everybody. The Holiday and
Comfort inns are similar to their chain brethren elsewhere, while
the Buffalo Bill Village Historic Cabins offers a rustic exterior and
a more Western feel, with modern conveniences inside. The former two are priced nearly identically and have similar amenities.
The one- and two-bedroom cabins at Buffalo Bill Village are simply
equipped—with a bed, phone, and TV—and surrounded by plenty
of room for the kids to roam. The cabins themselves first housed
the contractors who built the city circa 1920, and became the
centerpiece of this family-owned resort in the 1950s. The Holiday
Inn followed in the '70s, the Comfort Inn in the '90s. Also on-site:
an Old West–style boardwalk, where you can shop for curios or
sign up for tours and river trips; an outdoor heated pool; and several restaurants.

17th St. and Sheridan Ave., Cody, WY 82414. www.blairhotels.com. ✆ **800/527-
5544.** Fax 307/587-2795. Comfort Inn: 75 units. $89–$169 double. Holiday Inn:
189 units. $89–$169 double. Buffalo Bill Village Historic Cabins: 83 units. $79–$159
double. AE, DC, DISC, MC, V. Historic Cabins closed Oct–Apr. **Amenities:** Restaurant; lounge; exercise room; pool (summer only). *In room:* A/C, TV, hair dryer,
Wi-Fi (free).

The Chamberlin Inn ★★ A boardinghouse opened here in
1904, and the property evolved and devolved over the course of the
next century until Ev and Susan Diehl took it over in 2005 and

completely restored it—and then some. Centered on a serene and green courtyard, the new-and-improved Chamberlin Inn is now Cody's best lodging option, just a block from the center of town and featuring charming historic rooms and apartment units. Of special note are the Hemingway Suite—"Papa" stayed here in 1932—with an angling motif and a small Hemingway library; and the lavish Courthouse unit, the original town courthouse reimagined as a luxury apartment.

1032 12th St., Cody, WY 82414. www.chamberlininn.com. ☎ **888/587-0202** or 307/587-0202. 21 units. $165–$185 double; $235–$650 suite or apt. AE, DISC, MC, V. *In room:* A/C, TV, kitchen, Wi-Fi (free).

The Cody ★★
The Cody immediately became the top modern hotel in the town of its name when it opened in May 2008. Located on the west end of town near the rodeo grounds, the hotel has a colorful, thoroughly Western-chic design in both the common areas and the spacious guest rooms, which have one king bed or two queens, warm earth tones, and a Native American motif. Some have sleeper sofas; those on the west side have balconies with terrific views of Shoshone River Canyon. The facilities are also excellent, including the exercise room and indoor pool, and there are a number of special packages catering to anglers, rodeogoers, and Yellowstone visitors.

232 W. Yellowstone Ave., Cody, WY 82414. www.thecody.com. ☎ **307/587-5915.** 75 units. Summer $209–$249 double; off season $99–$169 double. Additional person $15. Rates include hot breakfast buffet. Pets accepted. AE, DISC, MC, V. **Amenities:** Exercise room; Jacuzzi; pool. *In room:* A/C, TV/DVD, fridge, hair dryer, MP3 docking station, Wi-Fi (free).

Cody Cowboy Village ★
This relatively new property is a couples-oriented resort in a family-oriented town. The "village," consisting of a cluster of cabin units near the rodeo grounds, is a world away from the bustling boardwalks of downtown Cody. The log cabins meld contemporary and cowboy in their decor. All have a deck in front; suites feature microwaves and fridges. Most units have one king bed, but six have two queens.

203 W. Yellowstone Ave., Cody, WY 82414. www.codycowboyvillage.com. ☎ **307/587-7555.** 50 units. $79–$159 double; $109–$199 suite. Rates include continental breakfast. AE, MC, V. Closed Nov–Mar. **Amenities:** Jacuzzi. *In room:* TV, hair dryer, Wi-Fi (free).

The Irma Hotel ★
Buffalo Bill's entrepreneurial gusto ultimately left him penniless, but it also left us this century-old hotel (named for his daughter) in the heart of town. Cody hoped to corral visitors who got off the train on their way to Yellowstone, and one of his lures was an elaborate cherrywood bar, a gift from

straight-laced Queen Victoria. You can still hoist a jar on Her Royal Majesty's slab in the Silver Saddle Saloon, or spend the night in a renovated room that might have once housed a president or prince.

Suites are named after local characters from the town's early days. The hotel's location in the middle of town and the summer schedule of reenacted gunfights out front help compensate for the lack of modern amenities. While the aura here will surely please history buffs, those acclimated to ultramodern convenience will probably want to look elsewhere.

1192 Sheridan Ave., Cody, WY 82414. www.irmahotel.com. © **800/745-4762** or 307/587-4221. Fax 307/587-1775. 73 units. $112 double; $162 suite. Lower rates fall to spring. AE, DISC, MC, V. **Amenities:** Restaurant; lounge. *In room:* A/C, TV, hair dryer, Wi-Fi (free).

The Mayor's Inn ★★ This two-story A-frame, built in 1905 for Mayor Frank Houx, found itself in the path of a wrecking ball in 1997. However, new owners moved it on a truck to its current location just a few blocks away. It's now one of Cody's best B&Bs, with rooms such as the Yellowstone, featuring a lodgepole-pine bed frame and black-and-white photos of the park's early years, and the Hart Mountain Suite, with romance and floral decor. There's also a carriage house (breakfast not included) with a well-equipped kitchen. Breakfast is a hearty treat, featuring sourdough flapjacks and buffalo sausage, and innkeepers Bill and Dale Delph also run a dinner house here Thursday through Saturday nights in the summer (see "Where to Eat," below).

1413 Rumsey Ave., Cody, WY 82414. www.mayorsinn.com. © **888/217-3001** or 307/587-0887. 5 units. $125–$160 double; $215 suite. Rates include full breakfast. AE, DISC, MC, V. **Amenities:** Restaurant. *In room:* A/C, TV, hair dryer, no phone, Wi-Fi (free).

Pahaska Tepee Resort ★ Buffalo Bill's hunting lodge, only 2 miles from the east entrance to Yellowstone, was dubbed with his Lakota name, *Pahaska* (longhair), when he opened the lodge to park visitors in 1905. Near the top of the beautiful Wapiti Valley along U.S. Hwy. 14/16/20, Pahaska is a popular stop for people visiting the Yellowstone area. The cabins are scattered on the hill behind the historic (and colorfully decorated) lodge. Accommodations have limited amenities and might best be described as "minimotels" with two to five rooms, each with a private entrance. Some bathrooms have only showers, some have tubs—it's best to ask in advance. The resort also has a gift shop, restaurant, and trail-ride stables.

183 Yellowstone Hwy., Cody, WY 82414. www.pahaska.com. © **800/628-7791** or 307/527-7701. Fax 307/527-4019. 47 units. June–Aug $115–$175 double, $575 condo, $1,095 lodge; May and late Sept to mid-Oct $70–$140 double, $450–$495

condo, $895–$995 lodge. DISC, MC, V. Closed mid-Oct to Apr. **Amenities:** Restaurant; lounge; Wi-Fi (free). *In room:* Kitchen.

Where to Eat

For its size, Cody may have more good restaurants than you'd expect. And if all you need is some fuel food or a jolt of caffeine for a busy day, Cody has a good supply of familiar fast-food joints and a few informal, inexpensive places. **Peter's Cafe Bakery,** at 1219 Sheridan Ave. (📞 **307/527-5040;** www.peters-cafe.com), across the street from the Irma, serves breakfast (freshly baked bagels, pastries, and espresso), plus subs and burgers for lunch and dinner. One of the best places day or night to get a steak or a beer and a burger (or Rocky Mountain oysters!) is the thoroughly Western **Proud Cut Saloon,** 1227 Sheridan Ave. (📞 **307/527-6905**), where lots of rodeo riders keep a running tab.

Cassie's Supper Club ★★★ WESTERN   Cassie's is the sort of classic roadhouse you might expect and look for in the West: big platters of beef, four bars serving drinks, and ornery roadhouse decor with taxidermy, antelope skulls, and assorted cowboy ephemera. This place has the routine down, having been in business since 1922. Located along the highway west of town in what was once a "house of ill fame," Cassie's is now very respectable and quite good. Besides the requisite steaks—grilled to perfection—there's seafood, pasta, and chicken, plus a full menu of specialty drinks. The near-mythical dance floor bustles to the twang of live country music every night in summer.

214 Yellowstone Ave. 📞 **307/527-5500.** www.cassies.com. Reservations recommended. Main courses $7–$25 lunch and Sun brunch, $12–$40 dinner. AE, DISC, MC, V. Daily 11am–10pm.

The Mayor's Inn Dining Room ★★ AMERICAN   The Mayor's Inn is one of very few establishments in Cody where you can get a room, a meal, and a drink. The restaurant is a great pick for a leisurely dinner: Innkeepers Dale and Bill Delph focus on just one seating an evening. The antiques-laden dining room has a nice air to it, and Bill showcases his culinary chops with steaks, seared elk medallions, buffalo meatloaf, and a regularly changing menu of flavorful preparations he dubs "regional fusion."

1413 Rumsey Ave. 📞 **307/587-0887.** Reservations recommended. Main courses $17–$25. AE, DISC, MC, V. Summer Thurs–Sat 6–9pm.

Shiki ★★ SUSHI   An anomalous standout in meat-and-potatoes Cody, Shiki is a superlative sushi bar. With spare Asian decor—consisting primarily of artfully hung cloth and an attractive water feature—and booth, table, and bar seating, the setting matches the top-notch sushi rolls and tempura, teriyaki, and curry entree. The sushi includes traditional rolls, such as spicy tuna and eel, as well as a few regional variations, like the Heart Mountain, with crab, cucumber, avocado, and crunchy tempura flakes. Don't be alarmed by the lack of an ocean nearby: Fresh fish is flown in two to three times a week from both coasts.

1420 Sheridan Ave. © **307/527-7116.** Reservations not accepted. Main courses $15-$26; sushi rolls $5-$15. AE, DISC, MC, V. Mon-Fri 11am-2pm and 4-9pm; Sat 11:30am-9pm; Sun 4-9pm.

Wyoming's Rib & Chop House ★★ STEAKS   One of an upscale regional chain with locations in Billings, Miles City, and Livingston, Montana, and Sheridan, Wyoming, this is the place to head for terrific ribs, chops, and steaks, but vegetarians will have difficulty finding a meatless main course. Desserts like "Pecan Meltaway"—a chocolate crust filled with ice cream, pecans, and more chocolate—provide decadent finales. A bar opened in 2011.

1367 Sheridan Ave. © **307/587-4917.** www.ribandchophouse.com. Main courses $6-$10 lunch, $10-$33 dinner. AE, DISC, MC, V. Daily 11am-10:30pm. Shorter hours in winter.

Cody After Dark

Cody has a lively nightlife, headed by **Cassie's** (see above), with a dance floor laden with real and wannabe cowboys and cowgirls. Downtown, the historic **Silver Dollar Bar,** at 1313 Sheridan Ave. (© 307/527-7666), has tasty burgers, live music, pool tables, and numerous TV screens. **Dan Miller's Music Revue,** 1549 Sheridan Ave. (© 307/272-7855; www.cowboymusicrevue.com), offers a cowboy-style musical variety show Monday through Saturday at 8pm May through September. Tickets are $14.

A YELLOWSTONE & GRAND TETON NATURE GUIDE

Although they are linked in many people's minds, Yellowstone and Grand Teton national parks couldn't be more different. One is an immense wilderness plateau that sits atop a caldera seething with molten lava; the other is a striking set of peaks rising from a broad river plain. One encloses some of the most remote backcountry in the lower 48 and provides crucial habitat for rare species; the other is a short drive from a chic resort town and includes an airport and grazing cattle in its mixed-use approach. What they do share is the affection of millions of visitors who come here annually to renew their ties to nature through the parks' shining mountains, alpine lakes, majestic elk, and astonishing geysers.

Unfortunately, mining, logging, and housing developments have impacted the 19 million acres known as the **Greater Yellowstone Ecosystem** that includes the parks and the surrounding area. The ecosystem is an interdependent network of watersheds, mountain ranges, wildlife habitats, and other components extending beyond the two parks into seven national forests, an Indian reservation, three national wildlife refuges, and nearly a million acres of private land. It is one of the largest intact temperate ecosystems on the planet; its 18 million acres span an area as vast as Connecticut, Rhode Island, and Delaware combined.

It's also a massive and important source of water. West of the Continental Divide, snowmelt trickles into creeks, streams, and rivers that run through Yellowstone before draining into the Snake River, traveling through Grand Teton National Park and Idaho, and running into the Columbia River, which winds its way west through Oregon and into the Pacific Ocean. Water on the eastern slopes of the divide passes through Yellowstone in the form of the Madison and Gallatin rivers, which meet the Jefferson River west of Bozeman, Montana, and merge into the Missouri, which flows into the Mississippi and, ultimately, the Gulf of Mexico.

As if that weren't enough, the headwaters of the Yellowstone River are in the remote Thorofare country south of Yellowstone Lake. After running north the length of the park, the Yellowstone meanders across Montana as the longest undammed river in America, until it converges with the Missouri in North Dakota.

9 THE PARKS TODAY

It has long been a challenge for park managers to make the parks accessible to three million annual visitors, many with different, even contradictory, expectations of a wilderness excursion. This necessitates the construction of new facilities and ongoing road maintenance and repair. At the same time, the parks are wild preserves, and the National Park Service must cope with the impact of six million feet on the forests, meadows, and thermal areas, as well as on the day-to-day lives of the millions of animals that inhabit the area.

It's a tough balancing act. Some of the pivotal issues in the parks today include the impact of snowmobiles; the reintroduced gray wolves and the resulting livestock losses of ranchers in and around the parks; the inadequacy of the park's infrastructure to cope with three million human visitors each year; invasive nonnative species, such as lake trout and zebra mussels; and the reduction of habitat surrounding the parks, coupled with a growing population of elk and bison seeking forage beyond park boundaries and possibly infecting domestic animals with a disease called brucellosis that, when transmitted to cattle, causes cows to abort fetuses. And that's just the short list.

Possible solutions are often "too little, too late," layering complex management strategies on an ecosystem that might do better if it were allowed to work things out naturally. The problem is that Grand Teton and Yellowstone have already been altered significantly by humans, so "natural" becomes a relative concept.

A good example is the reintroduction of a natural predator of the overpopulated elk: gray wolves, which were eliminated in the 1920s. These days, ranchland surrounds the parks, so the Defenders of Wildlife set up a trust to pay anyone who loses a calf to a wolf—and ranchers do because the wolves haven't read the management plan. And wolves from Yellowstone have migrated south into Grand Teton and beyond; besides the packs that den in and around the Gros Ventre area, a lone wolf was spotted at the Wyoming-Colorado border, and two others turned up dead in Colorado in 2004 and 2009.

Yellowstone's artificial boundaries also cause problems for bison. The state of Montana now allows hunters to shoot bison when they stray outside the park. Because ranchers fear brucellosis, over 1,600 animals were killed when they left the park for low country in Montana in the winter of 2007–2008 alone, and over 250 have been killed since then—although so far there are almost no documented cases of bison or elk infecting livestock.

As for snowmobiles and cars, most people agree that changes must be made as park visitation continues to grow. Currently, snowmobilers flock to the park as soon as the snow starts falling and remain until late February. While the popularity of the sport has had a positive effect on the tourism industry in the gateways of West Yellowstone, Jackson, and Gardiner, park officials are concerned about the long-term environmental impact of the machines: They are noisy, and engine emissions create air pollution, which some say presents a health hazard. While technology has reined in the noise and smog to a large degree, snowmobiles still share narrow trails with wildlife during months when the animals' energy levels are depleted by bad weather and a lack of food. A 3-year phase-out of snowmobiles was agreed upon in 2000 but was overturned before park policy could be changed. The compromise resulted in a quota system that limits the number of snowmobiles in the park to 318 per day.

Then there's the traffic issue. Park roads are narrow and twisty, so the intrusion of 30-foot-long motor homes and pickup trucks towing trailers creates congestion, especially during the peak summer months. There have been studies of transportation alternatives to unclog park roadways, even a costly monorail that would wind through Yellowstone, but no decisive action has been taken.

Recently, park scientists have battled to protect the native cutthroat trout in Yellowstone Lake from the impact of lake trout introduced by man. They have also recognized the enormous value of the microbes evolving in Yellowstone's superhot thermal areas, and scientists are using them in new technologies ranging from nanocircuitry to industrial bleaching products. As the world awakens to the accelerating loss of vital species in shrinking wild habitats, it becomes ever more imperative to find ways in which to preserve the relatively unspoiled ecosystems, like that of Greater Yellowstone.

LANDSCAPE & GEOLOGY

The Yellowstone and Grand Teton region is one of the most dynamic seismic areas in the world—wracked by earthquakes, cracked by water boiling to the surface, and littered with the detritus of previous volcanic eruptions. Today, the bowels of the Yellowstone caldera are again filling with magma. Geologic studies show that, for the past 2 million years, the plateau has blown its top every 600,000 years or so—and the last explosion was about 600,000 years ago. That means that a titanic blow—bigger than anything seen in recorded history—could happen, well, any century now, give or take thousands of years. The geological time frame is a long one, by human standards, but this didn't stop people from getting excited when an unprecedented "swarm" of minor earthquakes rattled the park in early 2009. The good news is that the big one is not imminent; geologists say things need to heat up considerably first.

As you'll learn when you visit the exhibits on the park's geology at Moose, Mammoth, and the various geothermal areas, what you see on the surface—great layers of ash and the core of volcanic vents, such as Mount Washburn and Bunsen Peak—is only a fraction of the story of Yellowstone and Grand Teton.

Situated on 2.2 million acres, Yellowstone is significantly larger than its sister to the south. Encompassing 3,472 square miles, Yellowstone boasts 310 miles of paved roads and 1,000 miles of backcountry trails, and it is home to more geysers and hot springs than the combined total in the rest of the world.

Although it can't match Yellowstone's size, Grand Teton National Park is nothing to sneeze at. It has towering mountain spires, which have been compared to cathedral towers, reaching almost 14,000 feet skyward; picturesque glacial lakes; and a great deal of interesting topography. The roughly 500 square miles of Grand Teton contain about 160 miles of paved roads and over 250 miles of hiking trails.

The Faces of Yellowstone National Park

By the end of the 1872 Hayden expedition, explorers had identified several distinct areas in the park, each with its own physical characteristics. Less spectacular than the craggy mountain scenery of Grand Teton, and less imposing than the vast expanses of the Grand Canyon in Arizona, Yellowstone's beauty is subtle, reflecting the changes it has undergone during its explosive past.

Although Yellowstone has its share of mountains, much of the park is a high mountain plateau. The environment changes dramatically as you ascend the mountain slopes from the foothill zones in the valleys—the elevation at the entrance at West Yellowstone is 6,666 feet, for example, compared to 5,314 feet at the Gardiner entrance. Because the park lies about halfway between the equator and the North Pole, its summers consist of long, warm days that stimulate plant growth at the lower elevations.

As you walk the park trails, you'll find that plant distribution changes with the elevation. At the lowest elevations, down around 5,300 feet above sea level, you'll find **grassy flats** and sagebrush growing on dry, porous soils, with creeks and rivers cutting through to form wildlife-rich **riparian zones.** Next up: the **foothills,** sloping upward toward peaks, sometimes dotted by deposits of glacial moraine. Douglas fir, pine, and other conifers, as well as stands of aspen, clad these slopes, and there are marshes and ponds fed by the spring snowmelt. Shrubs and flowers, such as huckleberry and columbine, favor these wet, shady spots.

Then comes the **mountain zone** (6,000–7,600 ft.), thickening forests dominated by lodgepole pine, broken by meadows where deer, elk, and moose often graze. The transition area between the highest forest and the bare surface above timberline is known as the **subalpine zone** (7,600–11,300 ft.). Finally, we come to the bare rock at the very top of the continental shelf, where small, hardy plants, such as glacier lilies and sky pilot, bloom briefly after the annual thaw.

Although the park is most famous for its geysers, visitors can choose among very different environments, reflections of the long-term effects of geologic activity and weather.

The limestone terraces at **Mammoth Hot Springs** give testimony to the region's subsurface volcanic activity. The park sits atop a rare geologic hot spot where molten rock rises to within 2 miles of the Earth's surface, heating the water in a plumbing system that still mystifies scientists.

The **northern section of the park,** between Mammoth Hot Springs and the Tower-Roosevelt region, is a high-plains area that is primarily defined by mountains, forests, and broad expanses of river valleys that were created by ice movements.

The road between the Tower-Roosevelt junction and the northeast entrance winds through the **Lamar Valley,** an area that has been covered by glaciers three times, most recently during an ice age that began 25,000 years ago and continued for 10,000 years—in geologic terms, just yesterday. Because this area was a favorite of Theodore Roosevelt, it is often referred to as "Roosevelt Country." The beautiful valley where elk, bison, and wolves interact is dotted with glacial ponds and strewn with boulders deposited by moving ice.

Farther south are **Pelican** and **Hayden valleys,** the two largest ancient lake beds in the park. They feature large, open meadows with abundant plant life that provides food for a population of bison and elk.

In the warm months, you'll enjoy the contrast between the lush green valleys and **Canyon Country,** in the center of the park. Canyon Country is defined by the Grand Canyon of Yellowstone, a colorful, 1,000-foot-deep, 24-mile-long gorge—in many opinions, just as dramatic as its cousin in Arizona. The Yellowstone River cuts through the valley, in some places moving 64,000 cubic feet of water per second, and creating two waterfalls, one of which is more than twice the height of Niagara Falls.

When you arrive at the **southern geyser basins,** you might feel that you've been transported through a geologic time warp. Here you will find the largest collections of thermal areas in the world—there are perhaps 600 geysers and 10,000 geothermal features in the park—and the largest geysers in Yellowstone. The result: boiling water that is catapulted skyward and barren patches of sterile dirt; hot, bubbling pools that are unimaginably colorful; and, of course, the star of this show, the geyser **Old Faithful.** Plan on spending at least 80 minutes here, as that's the typical period between the eruptions that send thousands of gallons of boiling water through the sky at a speed exceeding 100 mph.

You'll see the park's volcanic activity on a 17-mile journey east to the **lake area,** the scene of three volcanic eruptions that took place more than 600,000 years ago. When the final eruption blasted more than 1,000 square miles of the Rocky Mountains into the stratosphere, it created the Yellowstone caldera, a massive

A NATURE GUIDE | Landscape & Geology

depression measuring 28 by 47 miles, and Yellowstone Lake basin, some 20 miles long and 14 miles wide, reaching depths of 390 feet. The landscape here consists of flat plateaus of lava that are hundreds of feet thick.

The Spires of Grand Teton National Park

Your first sight of the towering spires of the **Cathedral Group**—the *trois tetons* (three breasts), as lonesome French trappers called them—will create an indelible impression. A bit of history makes them even more interesting.

Their formation began more than 2.5 billion years ago when sand and volcanic debris settled in an ancient ocean that covered this entire area. Scientists estimate that roughly 40 million to 80 million years ago, a compression of the Earth's surface caused an uplift of the entire Rocky Mountains from Mexico to Canada. This was just the first step in an ongoing series of events that included several periods during which a miles-thick crust of ice covered the area. Then, 6 million to 9 million years ago, the shifting of the Earth's tectonic plates caused movement along the north-south Teton fault that produced a tremendous uplift. The valley floor also dropped precipitously. These simultaneous forces pushed the rock that is now the **Teton Range** to its present site, from a position 20,000 to 30,000 feet *below* what is today the floor of Jackson Hole. The west block of rock tipped upward to create the Teton Range, and the eastern block swung downward to form the valley that is now called **Jackson Hole**—kind of like a pair of horizontal swinging doors that moved the Earth 5 miles.

After this upheaval, and after eons of erosion and glacier activity, **Grand Teton,** the centerpiece of this 40-mile-long fault area, towered 13,770 feet above sea level—more than a mile above the visitor center at Moose Junction. There are eleven other peaks over 12,000 feet high in the park today, with conditions that support mountain glaciers. As you gaze upward at this magnificent range, you will notice that many of the cliffs are more than half a mile in height.

During geologic explorations of **Mount Moran** (elevation 12,605 ft.), which gets less attention than it deserves, it was discovered that erosion had removed some 3,000 feet of material from its summit, meaning that it once must have been more than 15,000 feet high. Equally remarkable is the fact that the thin layer of Flathead sandstone on top of this peak is also found buried at least 24,000 feet below the valley's surface—further evidence of the skyward thrust of the mountains.

Although this is the youngest range in the Rockies—yet another geologic anomaly—the rocks here are some of the oldest in North America, consisting of granitic gneisses and schists, which are the hardest and least-porous rocks known to geologists.

The Teton area experienced a cooling trend about 150,000 years ago, during which glaciers more than 2,000 feet thick flowed from higher elevations, and an ice sheet covered Jackson Hole. When it melted for the final time, some 60,000 to 80,000 years ago, it gouged out the 386-foot-deep, 16-mile-long depression now known as **Jackson Lake.**

The receding layers of ice also left other calling cards. Several beautiful **glacial lakes** were created, including Phelps, Taggart, Bradley, Jenny, String, and Leigh. The sides of **Cascade Canyon** were polished by receding ice. Glacial lakes, called **cirque lakes,** were carved at the heads of canyons, and the peaks of the mountains were honed to their present jagged edges. Five glaciers have survived on Mount Moran. The best trail for glacial views is the Cascade Trail, which leads to the Schoolroom Glacier. But you shouldn't walk on the Mount Moran glaciers unless you are experienced and have the proper gear; the terrain is icy and can be unstable.

PLANT LIFE IN THE PARKS

When it comes to the variety of plants in the two parks, the only limiting factor is the high altitude—otherwise, the diversity of terrain, weather, and soils permits a fairly wide range of vegetation. Estimates vary, but in the ecosystem known as Greater Yellowstone, there are more than 1,500 native plant varieties. In an area larger than many of our states on the eastern seaboard—more than 3,900 square miles in the two parks combined—there's plenty of room for plants to stretch their roots and branches. Because of the diverse terrain, some species are found living on the dry valley beds in hostile soil, close to other species that predominate in lush meadows and riverbeds. Some thrive in thermal areas, while others do well in alpine areas, near mountain lakes, and in cirques near glaciers.

The history of the parks' plant life makes for interesting reading. Examination of plant fossils indicates that life began during the Eocene epoch, approximately 55 million years ago, and continued for 17 million years. The inspection of petrified tree stumps in

Yellowstone's Lamar Valley led to the identification of 27 distinct layers of forests, one atop the other.

Climatic conditions during the Eocene period were similar to those in the southeastern and south-central United States. Difficult as it might be to imagine, the area was once a warm, temperate zone in which rainfall might have averaged 50 to 60 inches per year at what was then an elevation of 3,000 feet above sea level.

These days, the elevation ranges from 5,000 to 13,000 feet, the average low temperature is approximately 30°F (–1°C), and hundreds of inches of snow fall each year. Plants have adapted to a growing season that is a mere 60 days in duration. As a consequence, forests once populated with hardwoods, such as maple, magnolia, and sycamore, are now filled with conifers, the most common of which are pine, spruce, and fir. A smattering of cottonwood and aspen also thrive in the cool park temperatures.

Some experts speculate that during the glacial periods, the tallest mountains in the Lamar Valley of Yellowstone were islands amid a sea of ice, providing refuge for some species of plant life.

The parks have several growing zones. Above 10,000 feet in the alpine zone, plants adapt to wind, snow, and lack of soil by growing close to the ground, flowering soon after the snows melt. You'll find such flora on trails near Dunraven Pass in Yellowstone and in Cascade Canyon in Grand Teton.

In Yellowstone, the canyon and subalpine regions, at 7,000 to 10,000 feet, are known for **conifer forests** and open meadows of **wildflowers.** As elevation increases, wildflowers are abundant and healthy, while trees are stunted and shrublike.

In the valley in Grand Teton, at 6,400 to 7,000 feet, the porous soil supports plants that tolerate hot and dry summertime conditions. **Sagebrush, wildflowers,** and **grasses** thrive and predominate. Plants bloom in a pageant of colors from early June to early July.

Identifying the plants described below does not require a degree in botany, but Richard J. Shaw's book *Plants of Yellowstone and Grand Teton National Park* (Wheelwright Press, 1981) will help.

Trees

Coniferous trees are most common in the parks because of the high altitude and short growing season, but there are some hardy deciduous trees as well, such as cottonwood and aspen. The most common cone-bearing trees in the parks are lodgepole pines, which cover as much as 80% of Yellowstone, and Douglas fir,

Lodgepole Pine

Douglas Fir

subalpine fir, Engelmann spruce, blue spruce, and whitebark pine. The key to identification is the trees' basic shape, the shape of their needles, and various characteristics of their cones.

Lodgepole Pine This familiar tree grows tall and slender, with bare trunk at the bottom and needles near the top resulting in dense stands that look like the spears of a closely ranked army. The needles of the lodgepole are clustered in pairs, typically around 3 inches long. You'll see logs from this tree supporting tepees and forming the walls of cabins.

Douglas Fir "Doug fir" is actually a member of the pine family, with prickly cones and dark, deeply etched bark. This tree has flat, flexible, single needles that grow around the branch, giving the tree the appearance of fullness. Another giveaway is that its cones hang downward and do not disintegrate aloft, but litter the forest floor. These trees like the north-facing side of the mountain.

Subalpine Fir You can distinguish firs by their needles, which sprout individually from branches instead of in clusters, like a pine; and by their cones, which grow upright on the branch until they dry up and blow away. Look for the slender, conical crown of this tree. When heavy snows weigh down the lower branches, they often become rooted, forming a circle of smaller trees called a snow mat. You'll find subalpine fir at high elevations near the timberline.

Subalpine Fir

Engelmann Spruce This tree also likes the higher elevations, growing in shaded ravines and in the canyons of the Teton Range above 6,800 feet and sometimes much higher. Look for it near

Kepler Cascades, Spring Creek, and the south entrance of Yellowstone National Park. It is distinguished by single needles that are square and sharp to the touch, and by cones with papery scales that are approximately 1½ inches long.

Blue Spruce The Engelmann spruce's cousin, this tree is most commonly found along the Snake River near Jackson. True to its name, it is characterized by its bluish appearance; rather stiff, sharp needles; and cones that are twice the size of the Engelmann's.

Engelmann Spruce

Other Plants

Here's a brief listing of some of the most common and interesting plants found in the ecosystem.

Glacier Lily A member of the lily family with a nodding bloom on a 6- to 12-inch stem, this bright yellow spring flower is found in abundance in both parks at elevations of more than 7,500 feet. Also known as the fawn lily, trout lily, and adder's-tongue, it is especially common near Sylvan Pass and on Dunraven Pass.

Indian Paintbrush This is the Wyoming state flower. It has a distinctive narrow, bright scarlet bloom that is most commonly found from mid-June to early September in the Snake River bottomland. Other species are white, yellow, orange, and pink.

Plains Prickly Pear This member of the cactus family is only one of two such species found in the park, usually in the

Blue Spruce

Glacier Lily

Indian Paintbrush

Plains Prickly Pear

Fringed Gentian

Silky Phacelia

Mammoth area and near the Snake River. It is distinguished by thick, flat green stems armed with spines and, during midsummer, a conspicuous yellow flower with numerous petals. American Indians, who recognized prickly pear's medicinal qualities, treated warts by lacerating them and then applying juice from the plant.

Fringed Gentian This member of the gentian family is the official flower of Yellowstone Park, where it is common and blooms throughout the summer. Its purple petals are fused into a 2-inch-long corolla and sit atop 1- to 3-foot-tall stems. It is also found below Jackson Lake Dam in Grand Teton.

Silky Phacelia This is one of the most photogenic and easily recognized species in the parks. Growing in purple clumps alongside the road at Dunraven Pass, the flower derives its name from the silvery pubescence that covers its stems and leaves. It's best photographed in July and August.

Shooting Star The shooting star is characterized by pinkish ½- to 1-inch-long flowers that dangle

Photo Tip

To successfully record your discovery of the parks' flora, consider adding a microlens to your arsenal of camera gear that will allow you to focus within 6 inches of blossoms. Film speeds of 200 ISO or faster will add to the chances of proper exposure, even on cloudy days.

earthward like meteorites from a 12-inch stem; they bloom in June. It is commonly found near thermal areas, streambeds, and Yellowstone Lake.

Yellow Monkey Flower This flower exhibits a bright yellow petal that, together with orange spots, attracts insect pollinators near streambeds at elevations of 7,000 to 9,000 feet all summer. It is also found near thermal areas and Yellowstone Lake.

Fairyslipper (also known as the Calypso Orchid) Finding this beautiful orchid might require some serious detective work, but the payoff is worth the effort. It is one of 15 orchid species found in the parks and is considered by many to be the most beautiful and striking. Seen during May and June, it usually has one small, green leaf and a red-pink flower that resembles a small lady's slipper, hence the name. It is found in cool, deep-shaded areas and is becoming rare because its habitat is disappearing.

Bitterroot The state flower of Montana, the bitterroot makes its first appearance in early June in dry, open, sometimes-stony soil and in grassy meadows. Its fleshy rose and white petals extend up to 1 inch in length. It was a source of food for Indians, who introduced it to Captain Meriwether Lewis of Lewis and Clark fame, hence its botanical name (*Lewisia rediviva*).

Shooting Star

Yellow Monkey Flower

Fairyslipper (aka Calypso Orchid)

Bitterroot

Columbia Monkshood This purple flower has a hood-shape structure with two sepals at its side and two below (all of which make up the calyx, the leafy parts surrounding the flower). Its stem varies in height from 2 to 5 feet. You'll find these flowers in wet meadows and on stream banks from June to August, often near thermal areas, streambeds, and Yellowstone Lake.

Columbia Monkshood

WILDLIFE IN THE PARKS

For many, the primary reason for a visit to these parks is the wildlife: bears, bighorn sheep, bison, elk, bald eagles, river otters, and moose all wandering free, often within roadside view of travelers. Yellowstone and Grand Teton are home to the largest concentration of free-roaming wildlife in the lower 48. This includes one of the largest herds of elk in North America, the largest free-roaming herd of bison in the United States, and the only significant population of grizzly bears south of Canada.

But it doesn't stop there. Also in the parks are pronghorns, mountain goats, and two species of deer (totaling eight species of ungulates, or hoofed mammals); black bears; three species of wildcats; coyotes; wolverines; pine martens; about 60 smaller species of mammals; and 322 species of birds. Add to that the gray wolves reintroduced in 1995—they now number about 375 in the entire ecosystem—and you have a rich array of wildlife. Most of these creatures steer clear of humans. But humans, never shy, want to get ever closer to the animals, and that can cause problems. Unlike the critters that inhabit petting zoos, the animals in the Greater Yellowstone Ecosystem are wild and pose an unpredictable threat to the safety of visitors.

 Photo Tip

Photographers need a telephoto lens, preferably a zoom, to get good shots of wildlife. Even the biggest animals in the park present minimal risks to humans, unless you move in for a close-up. Invest in a 300-millimeter lens, or 100- to 300-millimeter zoom, and you should get some good shots without disturbing the wildlife or putting yourself at risk.

Death is a day-to-day affair in the parks. In the spring, you'll see carcasses of elk and bison that died during the long winter, attracting bears and other carnivores looking for a free lunch. That's part of the picture when you vow to interfere as little as possible with nature's way.

Park naturalists generally agree that every major vertebrate wildlife species that was present during the most recent ice age (over 10,000 years ago) is a resident of the parks today, as are several rare or endangered species, the most notable being the grizzly bear and the bald eagle.

Mammals

Bear (Black & Grizzly)   In recent years, grizzly bears have enjoyed a comeback, in part because of the reintroduction of gray wolves, which create plenty of carcasses for bears to scavenge. But unless you have the patience to spend weeks outdoors in bear country, such as the Lamar and Hayden valleys, your chances of seeing a grizzly in Yellowstone or Grand Teton aren't all that good—you might have to go to the zoo in West Yellowstone.

Estimates vary, but there are probably 600 grizzly bears in the Greater Yellowstone Ecosystem today, and an equal or greater number of black bears. Rangers say you're more likely to spot the black bears, especially during the spring months after they emerge with new cubs from their winter dens. However, the black bears are probably more visible because they are more likely to venture near human development than are grizzlies, meaning that an encounter with a grizzly is most likely to occur in the backcountry. Neither type of bear sits along park roads, the way both once did, begging for food or wrestling over park-lodge garbage while tourists sat watching on bleachers. Bears that get a taste for human food, or get too comfortable around human campsites, are relocated to the depths of the wilderness. Black bears are most commonly sighted in the Canyon-Tower and Madison–Old Faithful areas, where they feed on green grass, herbs, berries, ants, and carrion.

Black Bear

black **BEAR OR GRIZZLY BEAR?**

Because a black bear can be black, brown, or cinnamon, here are some identifiers. The grizzly is the larger of the two: typically 3½ feet at the shoulder with a dish-face profile and a pronounced hump between the shoulders. The black bear's ears are rounder, just like those you see on stuffed animals. The grizzly's color is typically yellowish brown, but the coat is sometimes recognized by its cinnamon color, often highlighted by silver tips. In terms of tracks, the black bear's toes follow an arc around the foot pad while the grizzly's toes are arranged in a nearly straight line. The grizzly's claws are also considerably longer.

Caution: Park rangers attempt to keep track of grizzlies to prevent human/bear encounters. However, it is best to assume that they are always around; make noise when traveling in isolated spots.

Grizzly bears are most commonly seen in the northeast area of the park, in the meadows on the hillsides of the Lamar Valley, or wandering the Hayden Valley north of Yellowstone Lake. They also feed on trout spawning in Yellowstone Lake tributaries during the late spring (campgrounds by these streams are closed during spawning). They are most active in spring, when they emerge from hibernation hungry, and in the fall, when they busy themselves fattening up for winter.

Grizzly bears can do you the most damage, particularly when their cubs are around or when they think you're after their food.

Bighorn Sheep　If there's a hint of a foothold, a bighorn sheep will find it. Its hooves are hard and durable on the outside but soft and clamplike underneath—perfect for steep, rocky terrain. You'll often hear them clattering before you spot their stocky, gray-brown

Grizzly Bear

Bighorn Sheep

bodies and white rumps. Six feet long, the males weigh up to 300 pounds. Their horns are coiled; the females' are straight. The Greater Yellowstone Ecosystem probably contains the largest concentration of bighorns in the United States. Look for them on Mount Washburn, along Specimen Ridge, and in the Gallatin Range in Yellowstone; they are also seen occasionally in the Heart Mountain area in southern Yellowstone. In Grand Teton, smaller herds are found in the Gros Ventre Valley, as well as the western slopes of the Teton Range. In the winter, a large herd of bighorn sheep congregates south of the town of Dubois in Whiskey Basin, in the Wind River Range east of the Teton Range.

Bison   Bison (commonly, but incorrectly, called buffalo) appear indifferent to humans as they wander the roads and go about their grazing, but don't think for a minute that they're docile. Their prodigious size, cute calves (which look like cattle calves), and fearless nature ensure that bison are very visible symbols of Yellowstone. On ballerina-thin ankles, these burly brown animals carry as much as 2,000 pounds, concentrated in thick shoulders and massive chests. Those big heads help them clear snow for winter browsing, but during harsh winters they instinctively migrate to lower elevations (some biologists insist that both grizzlies and bison were

Bison

WOLF **OR COYOTE?**

Wolves and coyotes both bear a striking resemblance to large dogs. Here are some ways to distinguish them.

- Coyotes grow to a height of 20 inches; wolves often grow to 34 inches and are far more massive.
- Coyotes have long, pointed ears; wolf ears are rounded and relatively short.
- Coyotes have thin, delicate legs, similar to those of a fox; wolves' legs are thick and long.

driven up on the plateau from their natural home on the prairie). Bison are very easy to spot in the summer; you'll see them munching grass and wallowing in dust pits in Hayden Valley, Pelican Valley, the Madison River area, and the geyser areas near the Firehole River. In the winter, snowmobilers often have to make way for the shaggy beasts because bison take advantage of the snow-packed roads to travel around.

Coyote   The wily coyote is the predator most often spotted by park visitors. Looking something like small, lanky shepherd dogs with grizzled, gray-brown coats, the coyotes number around 450, living in about 60 packs that make their homes in burrows and caves. Numbers have dropped some since the gray wolf reintroduction, but coyotes are very adaptable. Active hunters year-round, they feast on small animals, such as squirrels and rabbits, as well as the carcasses of animals that died naturally or were killed by larger carnivores, such as bears and wolves. They are seen near most park roads, in the meadows, and in the sagebrush. Coyote pups are considered a delicacy by great horned owls, eagles, mountain lions, and bears.

Gray Wolf   In a controversial move, gray wolves were reintroduced to Yellowstone in 1995 for the first time since the 1920s,

Coyote

Gray Wolf

when they were eliminated by hunters operating under a federal predator control program designed to protect cattle herds. The population of Canadian gray wolves is thriving in its new environment, though numbers are still down after a bout with deadly distemper virus in 2008 (the population was estimated at 100 in 2011). They are high-profile occupants of the Lamar Valley, under constant observation by visitors with binoculars or spotting scopes who travel the area.

Elk   It is estimated that the Yellowstone herd has 8,000 to 10,000 elk (also called wapiti) in summer, down from its mid-1990s high of 19,000, and other herds spend time in the park as well. The most common large animal in both parks, elk are rather sociable and travel in small groups. Males are easily identifiable by a massive set of antlers. Although they shed

Elk

them every spring, by early summer, bulls are beginning to display prodigious racks that, by year's end, are the envy of their cousins in the deer family. The elk's grayish brown body, which typically weighs as much as 900 pounds, is accented by a chestnut brown head and neck, a shaggy mane, a short tail, and a distinctive tan patch on the rump.

One herd can often be located in the vicinity of Mammoth Hot Springs, often on the lawn of the main square. Others are found throughout each park. During winter months, the northern Yellowstone herd heads to a winter grazing area near Gardiner, while their cousins in Grand Teton head for the National Elk Refuge, just north of Jackson, where the Forest Service supplements their diet with bales of alfalfa.

Moose   Perhaps because of their size, their homely appearance, or their broad antler racks that can grow to 6 feet across, moose elicit unequaled excitement from park visitors. The largest member of the deer family, a typical adult male moose weighs 1,000 pounds and is most easily recognizable by a pendulous muzzle and fleshy dewlap that hangs beneath its neck like a bell.

Moose

> *The most remarkable animal of these regions is the moose, and the most unearthly, hideous-looking monster that roams the mountains on four legs . . . the most uncomely animal in the West.*
> —Edwin Stanley, from *Rambles in Wonderland*, 1878

Sightings are most frequent on the edges of ponds and in damp, lush valley bottoms, where moose feed on willows and water plants, especially along the Moose-Wilson Road and near the Jackson Lake Lodge in Grand Teton.

The plodding, nibbling moose in a meadow is not to be approached—and is not likely to budge if you move closer. Although it appears ungainly, a moose is capable of traveling at 30 mph. Cows will charge any perceived threat to a calf, and bulls become particularly ornery in the fall, so give both a wide berth.

Mountain Lion After their near-eradication in the early 1900s, today there are approximately 20 mountain lions (also

Mountain Lion

known as cougars, panthers, or pumas) in Yellowstone, and a smaller number in Grand Teton. Adults weigh 100 to 150 pounds, making them the largest feline in the parks and the Rocky Mountains. Largely opportunistic predators, the parks' mountain lions hunt deer, elk, and porcupine. They are seldom seen in Yellowstone but more often heard: Listeners often mistake their high-pitched wails for a human.

Mule Deer

Mule Deer Not to be outnumbered by their larger cousins, an estimated 2,500 mule deer live within park borders. They are most often spotted near forest boundaries or in areas covered with grass and sagebrush. Their most distinguishing characteristics are their huge ears and a black tip on their tail that contrasts with their white rump. When they run, they bounce, with all four legs in the air. Fawns are typically born in late spring, often in pairs.

Most of the larger, four-legged animals roaming the parks have lavish headpieces that are either horns or antlers. But what's the difference? Antlers are shed every year; horns last a lifetime. Male deer, elk, and moose shed their antlers every spring, so they're as bald as cue balls when the parks open. By early June, though, new velvet-covered protuberances are making their appearance. In comparison, both sexes of bison and pronghorn grow only one set of horns during their lifetimes.

Pronghorn The often-sighted pronghorns graze near the north entrance to Yellowstone and on the valley floors of Grand Teton, but they are shy and difficult to approach or photograph because of their excellent vision and speed. Often mistakenly referred to as antelope—they're actually unrelated to true African antelope— the pronghorn is identified by its short, black horns, tan-and-white

Pronghorn

body, and black accent stripes. They can run 45 mph, but they can't clear fences. In the past decade, Yellowstone's pronghorn population has dwindled from 600 to about 300, due to development, wolves, and harsh weather.

BIRDS IN THE PARKS

The skies above the parks are filled with predators on the wing, including eagles and 27 species of hawks, not to mention ospreys, falcons, and owls.

Bald Eagle The bald eagle holds a position in the pecking order that parallels that of the grizzly. Of all the birds in the park, visitors are most interested in spotting this photogenic species, once almost wiped out by the pesticide DDT. The Yellowstone

Bald Eagle

and Grand Teton national parks are now home to one of largest populations of eagles in the continental United States; there are more than 200 of these magnificent birds in the parks. Bald eagles are most recognizable by a striking white head, tail feathers, and wingspans up to 7 feet. They typically live within 2 miles of water, so the Yellowstone Plateau, Snake River, Yellowstone Lake, and headwaters of the Madison River are prime spotting areas for this spectacular bird.

Golden Eagle

Golden Eagle   The bald eagle's cousin, the golden eagle, is similar in appearance, although it is smaller and does not have a white cowl. The golden eagle goes after small mammals, such as jack rabbits and prairie dogs. They work out in the open country; sometimes you'll find one feeding on roadkill.

Osprey

Osprey   The osprey, nicknamed the "fish eagle" on account of its diet, is the eagle's smaller relative, growing from 21 to 24 inches and with a white underbody and a brown topside. It is recognizable by a whistling sound it makes while hunting. Ospreys tend to create large nests made of twigs and branches on the tops of trees and power poles. Look for this handsome, interesting bird in the Snake River area and the Grand Canyon of the Yellowstone River, a popular nesting area.

   Birding Spot

Take a picnic lunch, or plan a relaxing break, at the **Oxbow Bend** overlook in Grand Teton. Weather permitting, you can soak up some sunshine and observe the great blue herons, ospreys, pelicans, cormorants, and just maybe a bald eagle. Although it's a popular spot, there's always room for one more vehicle.

Trumpeter Swan

American Kestrel

Raven Sporting a 50- to 60-inch wingspan, the raven is jet black and markedly larger than the crow. The most intelligent bird in the parks, the raven plays an interesting role in the Greater Yellowstone Ecosystem: Biologists have observed ravens communicating with wolves, leading them to carcasses, and even playing with pups. Ravens benefit from wolf kills because they are scavengers, so this relationship is symbiotic. They can be seen just about everywhere in both parks.

Trumpeter Swan The trumpeter swan, one of the largest birds on the continent, has made the Greater Yellowstone Ecosystem a sanctuary. Easily recognizable by its long, curved neck, snowy white body, and black bill, it is found in marshes and on lakes and rivers, namely the Madison River in Yellowstone and Christian Pond, Swan Lake, and Cygnet Pond in Grand Teton.

Other Raptors **American kestrels, prairie falcons,** and **red-tailed hawks** are seen on Antelope Flats–Kelly Road in Grand Teton, where they search for small rodents.

Prairie Falcon

Red-Tailed Hawk

Great Blue Heron

Other Aquatic Birds The **great blue heron,** a skinny, long-legged wading bird, is found in wetlands and rocky outcrops, especially near the end of Jackson Lake. Yellowstone Lake is a prime viewing area for the best fishers in the park, the **American white pelicans** that capture fish in their long, yellow-pouched bill. The **American dipper,** the only aquatic songbird in North America, revels in cold, fast-flowing mountain streams. The **slate-gray dipper** is tiny, only 7 to 8 inches tall, and is recognized by its long bill and stubby tail.

PLANNING YOUR TRIP TO YELLOWSTONE & GRAND TETON NATIONAL PARKS

It's no one's idea of a fun vacation to end up inhaling exhaust behind a long line of cars waiting for a break in construction at Yellowstone's east entrance, or wearing a T-shirt in a Montana snowstorm. Few things can do more to ruin a much-anticipated vacation than poor planning. So look over some of the crucial information in this chapter before you hit the road—it might make the difference between a trip you'll never forget and one you'd rather not remember. For additional help in planning your trip and for further on-the-ground resources in Yellowstone and Grand Teton, see "Fast Facts," later in this chapter.

GETTING THERE & GETTING AROUND

The automobile is the main method of transport within the parks. You won't find any trains or buses with regular schedules in the parks, although many tour operators utilize buses. Bikes are a common sight on park roads, but both riders and drivers should exercise extreme caution here: They're twisty and rife with wildlife, pulled-over vehicles, and jaw-dropping scenery.

By Plane

The closest airport to Yellowstone is Montana's **West Yellowstone Regional Airport** (℃ 406/646-7631; www.yellowstoneairport. org), just 1 mile north of the town of West Yellowstone (and 2 miles north of the west entrance to the park) on U.S. Hwy. 191. The airport has commercial air service seasonally, June through the end of September only, on **Delta Connection/SkyWest,** connecting through Salt Lake City.

American Airlines, Delta/SkyWest, Frontier, and **United** all have flights to and from **Jackson Hole Airport** (℃ 307/733-7682; www.jacksonholeairport.com), which is right in Grand Teton National Park in **Jackson,** Wyoming, and only 56 miles of scenic driving from the southern entrance of Yellowstone.

To the north, **Gallatin Field Airport** (℃ 406/388-8321; www. gallatinfield.com) in **Bozeman,** Montana, provides daily service via **Alaska, Allegiant, Delta, US Airways,** and **United** as well as **Horizon** and **Frontier.** From Bozeman, you can drive 87 miles on U.S. Hwy. 191 to the west Yellowstone entrance, or you can drive 20 miles east on I-90 to Livingston and then 53 miles south on U.S. Hwy. 89 to the Gardiner entrance.

Also to the north, **Logan International Airport** (℃ 406/247-8609; www.flybillings.com), Montana's busiest airport, is only 2 miles north of downtown **Billings,** Montana. Daily service is provided by **Allegiant, Delta, Frontier, Horizon,** and **United.** From Billings, it's a 65-mile drive south on U.S. Hwy. 212 to Red Lodge, and then 30 miles on the Beartooth Highway to the northeast Yellowstone entrance in Cooke City.

Yellowstone Regional Airport (℃ 307/587-5096; www.flyyra. com) in **Cody,** Wyoming, serves the Bighorn Basin as well as the east and northeast entrances of Yellowstone with year-round commercial flights via **Delta/SkyWest** and **United.** From Cody, it's a gorgeous 53-mile drive west along U.S. Hwy. 14/16/20 to the east entrance of Yellowstone.

Airfares to the small airports surrounding the parks can be pricey, so if you like to drive, consider flying into **Salt Lake City,** Utah, and driving about 300 miles to Grand Teton National Park, a route that has some nice scenic stretches. Even **Denver,** a drive of roughly 500 miles, is an alternative, although the route is not nearly as scenic.

By Car

If interstate highways and international airports are the measure of accessibility, then Yellowstone is as remote as Alaska's Denali

Salt Lake City	390 miles
Denver	563 miles
Las Vegas	809 miles
Seattle	827 miles
Portland	869 miles
Omaha	946 miles
Washington, D.C.	2,081 miles

The difference in distance to Grand Teton is about 70 miles, depending on your route.

National Park. But three million people make it here every year, on tour buses, in family vans, on bicycles, and astride snowmobiles—even from the other side of the world. Car is the most common method of travel in and around the parks, and the most convenient. Public transportation is sparse in these parts, and the lack of trains make it nearly impossible to get anywhere near the parks without some sort of vehicle.

Grand Teton's gateways are from the north, south, and east. Drivers naturally enter from whichever side they approach the parks. From the west, U.S. 20 or U.S. 191 takes you to West Yellowstone, Montana. From the south, U.S. 191 runs through Jackson and the length of Jackson Hole before entering Yellowstone. From the east, U.S. 20 bisects Cody, Wyoming, and continues west 53 miles to the east entrance of Yellowstone. The northeast entrance of Yellowstone is accessible from U.S. 212 via Cooke City, Montana. Finally, the north entrance is just outside Gardiner, Montana, on U.S. 89.

Most of the major auto-rental agencies have operations in the gateway cities. **Hertz** (② 800/654-3131; www.hertz.com) has operations in **Billings, Bozeman, Cody,** and **Jackson. Thrifty** (② 800/847-4389; www.thrifty.com) is in **Billings, Bozeman, Cody,** and **Jackson. Alamo** (② 800/462-5266; www.alamo.com) and **National** (② 800/227-7368; www.nationalcar.com) have locations in **Bozeman, Billings,** and **Jackson. Avis** (② 800/230-4898; www.avis.com) has locations in **Billings, Bozeman, West Yellowstone,** and **Jackson. Budget** (② 800/527-0700; www.budget.com) serves **Billings, Bozeman, Cody,** and **West Yellowstone.** Additionally, **Dollar** (② 800/800-5252 www.dollar.com) operates in **Bozeman** and **Jackson,** and **Enterprise** (② 800/736-8222; www.enterprise.com) serves **Billings** and **Bozeman. Big Sky**

Car Rentals (© 800/426-7669; www.yellowstonevacations.com/car-rentals) also operates out of **West Yellowstone.**

Taxes are already included in the printed price. One U.S. gallon equals 3.8 liters or .85 imperial gallons. Gasoline is sold in the gateway cities, but at only a select few locations in the park; fill up well before empty. International visitors should note that insurance and taxes are almost never included in quoted rental car rates in the U.S. Be sure to ask your rental agency about additional fees for these. They can add a significant cost to your car rental.

By Bus

Greyhound (© 800/231-2222; www.greyhound.com) is the sole nationwide bus line. International visitors should inquire about the **Greyhound North American Discovery Pass.** The pass, which offers unlimited travel and stopovers in the U.S. and Canada, can be obtained from foreign travel agents or through www.discoverypass.com.

Tips for RVers

You love 'em, or you hate 'em—the large, lumbering vehicles that serve some travelers as both transport and home. There are some retirees, self-named "full-timers," who sell their homes and most of their possessions and spend the rest of their lives chasing comfortable weather down the highway. Others might see it as a cost-saving way to vacation in the West—by renting a rolling room for the whole family at perhaps $1,000 per week plus gas. Is that a better deal than an economy car and inexpensive motels? You do the math.

You don't have to carry your bags, or even unpack them, and you'll sleep in campgrounds instead of motels, hear the sounds of the night outside, and have great flexibility in planning your itinerary. The trade-off will be making your own beds, horrid gas mileage, and preparing your own breakfast most of the time.

A few years back, Yellowstone officials considered closing the RV campground at Fishing Bridge, on the north end of Yellowstone Lake. The outcry was enormous, testimony to the immense popularity of RV travel, so the Fishing Bridge facility remains open today. You can drive most of the major roads in both parks with an RV or a trailer; but there will be some areas where large vehicles are prohibited, and most of the camping areas don't provide hookups—Colter Bay, Flagg Ranch, and Fishing Bridge are the exceptions.

TIPS ON ACCOMMODATIONS

In the parks, your options for lodging are fairly limited; the finite number of rooms and seemingly limitless number of peak-season visitors makes for high occupancy and rates. And the fact that many of the parks' hostelries have historic designations might mean they don't fit some visitors' modern tastes. In the gateway cities, there is more variety, from dorm-style hostels to luxury ski resorts. House swapping is a possibility in Jackson and Cody, but less likely in the smaller gateways. In Yellowstone, information regarding lodging is available from **Xanterra Parks & Resorts,** P.O. Box 165, Yellowstone National Park, WY 82190 (*C* **866/439-7375** or 307/344-7311; www.yellowstonenationalparklodges.com). In Grand Teton, lodging information is available from park concessionaires: **Grand Teton Lodge Company,** P.O. Box 250, Moran, WY 83013 (*C* **800/628-9988** or 307/543-2811; www.gtlc.com), and **Signal Mountain Lodge Co.,** P.O. Box 50, Moran, WY 83013 (*C* **307/ 543-2831;** www.signalmountainlodge.com); just north of the park is **Flagg Ranch,** P.O. Box 187, Moran, WY 83013 (*C* **800/443-2311** or 307/543 2861; www.flaggranch.com). For more information about where to stay, see chapters 7 and 8.

SPECIAL PERMITS
Backcountry Permits

If you want to sleep in the Yellowstone or Grand Teton backcountry, you have to get a permit, follow limits for length of stay and campfires, and stay in a designated area. The permit is free if you pick it up at the park during the final 48 hours before you begin your trip or on the day of your trip. Alternatively, you can reserve a site by paying a $25 fee to Grand Teton or $20 to Yellowstone. If you wish to make a reservation, you must do so in writing, and you still need to pick up your permit in person upon your arrival in the park. Yellowstone reservations can be made for the current year starting on April 1. In Grand Teton, you can reserve a permit from January 1 to May 15; thereafter all permits are first-come, first-served. If you're going during the parks' busy season, you'd be wise to make a reservation.

In Yellowstone, permits can be obtained at any ranger station (most of which are open 8am–7pm during the summer), no more than 2 days before embarking on a trip. To make a reservation by mail (for a $20 fee), write the **Backcountry Office,** P.O. Box 168,

Yellowstone National Park, WY 82190. Phone reservations are not accepted, but if you want information about the system, call ✆ **307/344-2160.**

In **Grand Teton,** permits are issued at the Craig Thomas (Moose) and Colter Bay visitor centers and the Jenny Lake Ranger Station. For a $25 fee, you can make reservations from January to mid-May by writing the **Permits Office,** Grand Teton National Park, P.O. Drawer 170, Moose, WY 83012. Phone reservations are not accepted, but information is available by calling ✆ **307/739-3602.** Reservations can also be made online at **www.nps.gov/grte** or by fax at 307/739-3443.

Boating Permits

For motorized craft in Yellowstone, the cost is $20 for annual permits and $10 for 7-day permits. Fees for nonmotorized boats are $10 for annual permits and $5 for 7-day permits. Boating permits are required for all vessels. Motorized boating is restricted to designated areas. Boating is prohibited on all of Yellowstone's rivers and streams except for the Lewis River Channel, where hand-propelled vessels are permitted. In Grand Teton, the fees are $40 for annual permits and $20 for 7-day permits. Fees for nonmotorized boats are $10 for annual permits and $5 for 7-day permits. Powerboaters are permitted on Jenny, Jackson, and Phelps lakes; nonmotorized boats are allowed on most park lakes and the Snake River. Sailboats, windsurfers, and jet skis are allowed only on Jackson Lake. U.S. Coast Guard–approved personal flotation devices are required for each person boating.

Fishing Permits

In **Yellowstone,** park permits are required for anglers ages 16 and over; the permit costs $15 for 3 days, $20 for 7 days, and $35 for the season. Children 15 and under don't need a permit if they are fishing with an adult, but they need to pick up a free permit if they're fishing without supervision. Permits are available at any ranger station, any visitor center, Yellowstone Park General Store, and most fishing shops in the gateways. The season usually begins on the Saturday of Memorial Day weekend and continues through the first Sunday in November. Exceptions to this rule are Yellowstone Lake, its tributaries, and sections of the Yellowstone River, which have shorter seasons.

In **Grand Teton,** state of Wyoming fishing licenses are required for everyone ages 14 years and over. An adult nonresident license costs $14 per day and $92 for the season. Youth fees (ages 14–18) are $3 per day and $15 for the season. A $13 Conservation Stamp is also required for all licenses except the 1-day variety. The river season generally opens April 1 and ends on October 31; Jackson Lake is closed all of October.

PLANNING A BACKCOUNTRY TRIP

While I've given the particulars for both Yellowstone and Grand Teton national parks in their respective chapters (see chapters 3 and 5), the following tips are useful when planning a backcountry trip.

Regulations

The theme in the backcountry is "leave no trace," and that means packing out any garbage you take in, not taking pets, and avoiding leaving scars on the landscape by staying on designated trails and reusing existing campsites. Fires are allowed only in established fire rings, and only dead and downed material may be used for firewood; fires are prohibited in some areas, but backpacking stoves are allowed throughout the parks. You must have a park permit for overnight stays in the backcountry. There's a complete list of do's and don'ts in the **Backcountry Trip Planner,** available at most visitor centers. For more information on "leave no trace" ethics, see **www.lnt.org**.

Backpacking for Beginners

Be sure to wear comfortable, sturdy hiking shoes that will resist water if you're planning an early-season hike; cotton socks are not a good idea because the material holds moisture, whereas wool and synthetics, such as fleece, "wick" it away from your body. Your sleeping bag should be rated for the low temperatures found at high elevations; if you bring a down bag, keep it dry or suffer the consequences. Most campers are happy to have a sleeping pad. An argument continues to rage about the merits of old-fashioned, external-frame packs versus the newer, internal-frame models. In the long run, the newer versions are more stable and comfortable, but a big-frame pack can shoulder bigger loads. Good padding, a lumbar support pad, and a wide hip belt are pluses. Be sure that you've tried out the pack—wear it around the house!—before you take it on a long trip with heavy loads, so that your body and the pack frame have a chance to adjust to each other.

Personal Safety Issues

It's best not to backpack alone, but if you must, be sure that you have told park rangers and friends where you'll be and how long you'll be gone. Don't leave the parking lot without the following gear: a compass, topographical maps, a first-aid kit, bug repellent, toilet paper and a trowel of some sort, a flashlight, matches, a knife, food supplies, a rope to hang food supplies from a tree, and a bell or other noisemaker to alert any bears in the neighborhood to your presence, as well as a tent, a stove, and a sleeping bag. At this altitude, sunscreen and sunglasses with UV protection are also wise. A recently developed bear repellent generically referred to as "pepper spray," available in most sporting goods stores, has proven successful in countering bear attacks. You'll also need iodine pills or a good water filter because that seemingly clear stream is filled with parasites that are likely to cause intestinal disorders. If you don't have iodine or a filter, boil water for at least 5 minutes before you drink it.

RECOMMENDED READING

The following books are interesting, informative, and easy to find: *Yellowstone: A Visitor's Companion,* by George Wuerthner, (Stackpole Books, 1992); *The Yellowstone Story* (two volumes), by Aubrey Haines (Colorado Associated University Press, 1977); *Searching for Yellowstone,* by Paul Schullery (Montana Historical Society Press, 2004); *Yellowstone Trails: A Hiking Guide,* by Mark C. Marschall (Yellowstone Association, Yellowstone National Park); *Top Trails Yellowstone & Grand Teton,* by Andrew Dean Nystrom (Wilderness Press, Berkeley, California); *Death in Yellowstone,* by Lee H. Whittlesey (Roberts Rinehart Publishers, Boulder, Colorado); *Grand Teton National Park* (available from the Grand Teton Natural History Association); *A Guide to Exploring Grand Teton National Park,* by Linda L. Olson and Tim Bywater (RNM Press, Salt Lake City, Utah); *Crucible for Conservation,* by Robert Righter (Grand Teton Natural History Association, Moose, Wyoming); and *Teton Trails: A Guide to the Trails of Grand Teton National Park,* by Katy Duffy and Darwin Wile (Grand Teton Natural History Association, 1995). **Falcon Press** (Helena, Montana) also publishes a long list of hiking, fishing, climbing, and other guides to the Yellowstone/Grand Teton region.

If you cannot find these publications in your local bookstore, many can be ordered from either the **Yellowstone Association** (© 406/848-2400; www.yellowstoneassociation.org) or the **Grand Teton Association** (© 307/739-3403; www.grandtetonpark.org).

[FastFACTS] YELLOW-STONE & GRAND TETON NATIONAL PARKS

Area Codes   **Yellowstone** is almost entirely in Wyoming, with the area code **307.** The park also extends slightly into Montana (area code **406**) and Idaho (area code **208**). **Grand Teton** is entirely in Wyoming, and its area code is also **307.**

Car Rental   See "Getting There & Getting Around," earlier in this chapter.

Cellphones   See "Mobile Phones," later in this section.

Crime   See "Safety," later in this section.

Customs   Every visitor to the U.S. 21 years of age or over may bring in, free of duty, the following: (1) 1 liter of wine or hard liquor; (2) 200 cigarettes, 100 cigars (but not from Cuba), or 3 pounds of smoking tobacco; and (3) $100 worth of gifts. These exemptions are offered to travelers who spend at least 72 hours in the U.S. and who have not claimed them within the preceding 6 months. It is forbidden to bring into the country almost any meat product (including canned, fresh, and dried meat products, such as bullion, soup mixes, and so on). Generally, condiments including vinegars, oils, spices, coffee, tea, and some cheeses and baked goods are permitted. Avoid rice products, as rice can often harbor insects. Bringing fruits and vegetables is not advised, though not prohibited. Customs will allow produce depending on where you got it and where you're going after you arrive in the U.S. International visitors may carry in or out up to $10,000 in U.S. or foreign currency with no formalities; larger sums must be declared to U.S. Customs on entering or leaving, which includes filing form CM 4790. For details regarding U.S. Customs and Border Protection, consult your nearest U.S. embassy or consulate, or **U.S. Customs** (www.customs.gov).

Disabled Travelers   Both parks are becoming increasingly user-friendly for travelers with disabilities. Those who are blind or have permanent disabilities can obtain a free **Interagency Access Pass,** which allows lifetime access to all national parks and federal fee areas. The pass must be obtained in person and is available at any entrance point to Yellowstone or Grand Teton.

YELLOWSTONE   **Wheelchair-accessible accommodations** are available in the Dunraven and Cascade lodges and Western cabins at Canyon Village, Grant Village, Old Faithful Inn, Old Faithful Snow Lodge and Cabins, and Lake Yellowstone Hotel. For a free *Visitors Guide to Accessible Features in Yellowstone National Park,* write to the **Park Accessibility Coordinator,** P.O. Box 168, Yellowstone National Park, WY 82190 (℘ **307/344-2314;** www.nps.gov/yell), or pick up the guide at the gates or visitor centers. There are **wheelchair-accessible camp-sites** at Fishing Bridge, Bridge Bay, Madison, Canyon, and Grant campgrounds, which you can reserve by calling ℘ **307/344-7311.**

Wheelchair-accessible restrooms with sinks and flush toilets are located at all developed areas except West Thumb and Norris. Accessible vault toilets are located at West Thumb and Norris, and in most scenic areas and picnic areas.

Many of Yellowstone's **roadside attractions,** including the south rim of the Grand Canyon of the Yellowstone, West Thumb Geyser Basin, much of the Norris and Upper Geyser basins, and parts of the Mud Volcano and Fountain Paint Pot areas, are negotiable by wheelchair. **Visitor centers** at Old Faithful, Grant Village, and Canyon are wheelchair accessible, as are the Norris Museum and the Fishing Bridge Visitor Center. The Albright Visitor Center at Mammoth is also accessible via a rear entrance.

Wheelchair-accessible parking is available at Old Faithful, Fishing Bridge, Canyon, Norris, and Grant Village; at some locations, it is near a Yellowstone General Store.

GRAND TETON Campsites at Colter Bay, Jenny Lake, and Gros Ventre campgrounds are on relatively level terrain; Lizard Creek and Signal Mountain are hilly and less accessible.

Wheelchair-accessible dining facilities are located at Flagg Ranch, Leeks Marina, Jackson Lake Lodge, and Jenny Lake Lodge.

Visitor centers at Moose, Colter Bay, Jenny Lake, and Flagg Ranch provide interpretive programs, displays, and visitor information in several forms, including visual, audible, and tactile. Large-print scripts, Braille brochures, and narrative audiotapes are available at Moose and Colter Bay.

Wheelchair-accessible parking spaces are located close to all visitor center entrances; curb cuts are provided, as are **accessible restroom facilities.**

More information is available from **Grand Teton National Park,** P.O. Drawer 170, Moose, WY 83012 (℘ **307/739-3600;** www.nps. gov/grte).

Doctors In Yellowstone, the **clinic at Mammoth Hot Springs** (℘ **307/344-7965**) is open daily in summer and weekdays year-round. In Grand Teton, the **clinic at Jackson Lake Lodge** (℘ **307/ 733-3636**) is open daily from May to October. In Jackson, Wyoming, **St. John's Medical Center,** 625 E. Broadway (℘ **307/733-3636**) has a 24-hour emergency room. The nearest hospital is in Jackson.

PLANNING YOUR TRIP : Disabled Travelers

Drinking Laws   The legal age for the purchase and consumption of alcoholic beverages is 21; proof of age is required and often requested at bars, nightclubs, and restaurants, so it's always a good idea to bring ID when you go out. Do not carry open containers of alcohol in your car or any public area that isn't zoned for alcohol consumption. The police can fine you on the spot. Don't even think about driving while intoxicated. Alcohol is widely available at stores in both parks and in the gateway cities. Bars in both Montana and Wyoming close at 2am.

Driving Rules   See "Getting There & Getting Around," earlier in this chapter.

Electricity   Like Canada, the U.S. uses 110 to 120 volts AC (60 cycles), compared to 220 to 240 volts AC (50 cycles) in most of Europe, Australia, and New Zealand. Downward converters that change 220–240 volts to 110-120 volts are difficult to find in the U.S., so bring one with you.

Embassies & Consulates   All embassies are in the nation's capital, Washington, D.C. Some consulates are in major U.S. cities, and most nations have a mission to the United Nations in New York City. If your country isn't listed below, call for directory information in Washington, D.C. (© **202/555-1212**) or check **www.embassy.org/embassies**.

The embassy of **Australia** is at 1601 Massachusetts Ave. NW, Washington, DC 20036 (© **202/797-3000;** www.usa.embassy.gov.au). Consulates are in New York, Honolulu, Houston, Los Angeles, and San Francisco.

The embassy of **Canada** is at 501 Pennsylvania Ave. NW, Washington, DC 20001 (© **202/682-1740;** www.canadainternational.gc.ca/washington). Canadian consulates are in Buffalo (New York), Detroit, Los Angeles, New York, and Seattle.

The embassy of **Ireland** is at 2234 Massachusetts Ave. NW, Washington, DC 20008 (© **202/462-3939;** www.embassyofireland.org). Irish consulates are in Boston, Chicago, New York, San Francisco, and other cities. See the embassy's website for a complete list.

The embassy of **New Zealand** is at 37 Observatory Circle NW, Washington, DC 20008 (© **202/328-4800;** www.nzembassy.com). New Zealand consulates are in Los Angeles, Salt Lake City, San Francisco, and Seattle.

The embassy of the **United Kingdom** is at 3100 Massachusetts Ave. NW, Washington, DC 20008 (© **202/588-6500;** http://ukinusa.fco.gov.uk). British consulates are in Atlanta, Boston, Chicago, Cleveland, Houston, Los Angeles, New York, San Francisco, and Seattle.

Emergencies   Call © **911.** In Yellowstone, you can also call the park's main information number (© **307/344-7381**), which is staffed

24 hours a day. In Grand Teton, dial ℂ **307/739-3301** and ask for park dispatch.

Family Travel   The best general advice I've discovered is in Lisa Gollin Evans's book *An Outdoor Family Guide to Yellowstone and Grand Teton National Parks* (Mountaineers Books, 2006). Older children can learn about nature by enrolling in the **Yellowstone Junior Ranger Program** (p. 84). The **Young Naturalist** program at **Grand Teton** provides children with a similar opportunity to explore the natural world of the park and costs $1 (p. 114).

To locate accommodations, restaurants, and attractions that are particularly kid-friendly, look for the "Kids" icon throughout this guide.

Gasoline   See "Getting There & Getting Around," earlier in this chapter.

Health   Health hazards range from mild headaches to run-ins with wild animals, but the latter happens less frequently than car accidents in the parks. To be safe, you might want to keep a first-aid kit in your car or luggage, and have it handy when hiking. It should include at least butterfly bandages, sterile gauze pads, adhesive tape, an antibiotic ointment, pain relievers for children and for adults, alcohol pads, a pocket knife with scissors, and tweezers. Healthcare is available at clinics in both parks; hospitals with 24-hour emergency rooms are located in Jackson and Cody, Wyoming, as well as in Bozeman, Montana.

Altitude Sickness   Because most of us live at or near sea level, the most common health hazard in the parks is discomfort caused by altitude sickness. Adjusting to the parks' high elevations is a process that can take a day or more. Symptoms of alcohol sickness include headache, fatigue, nausea, loss of appetite, muscle pain, and lightheadedness. Doctors recommend that, until acclimated, travelers should avoid heavy exertion, consume light meals, and drink lots of liquids but little caffeine or alcohol.

Bugs, Bites & Other Wildlife Concerns   Wildlife are to be treated with utmost respect in both parks. Keep your distance—at least 300 feet if possible—from any wild animal in either park. Mosquitoes, spiders, and ticks are the most bothersome biters, aside from the occasional rattlesnake you might see around Gardiner, Montana.

Waterborne Illnesses   See "Water," below.

For information on traveler's insurance, trip cancellation insurance, and medical insurance while traveling, visit www.frommers.com/planning.

Internet & Wi-Fi   When it comes to modern telecommunications, Yellowstone and Grand Teton national parks have extremely limited infrastructure: Lack of connectivity is the rule, not the exception. These are not the best destinations for those who need to check e-mail every minute—or even every day. The lodgings in the park typically lack Internet connections. Wi-Fi is prohibited at Lake Yellowstone Hotel, Roosevelt Lodge, Old Faithful Inn, Old Faithful Lodge, Lake Lodge, and Mammoth Hot Springs Hotel; the concessionaires are permitted to offer it at other lodgings and general stores, but as of this writing, it was not available. In Grand Teton National Park, Wi-Fi is available in public areas at Jenny Lake Lodge, Jackson Lake Lodge, Signal Mountain, and Colter Bay Village. Internet access is widely available in all of the gateways, but can be notably slow in Gardiner and West Yellowstone.

Legal Aid   While driving, if you are pulled over for a minor infraction (such as speeding), never attempt to pay the fine directly to a police officer; this could be construed as attempted bribery, a much more serious crime. Pay fines by mail, or directly into the hands of the clerk of the court. If accused of a more serious offense, say and do nothing before consulting a lawyer. In the U.S., the burden is on the state to prove a person's guilt beyond a reasonable doubt, and everyone has the right to remain silent, whether he or she is suspected of a crime or actually arrested. Once arrested, a person can make one telephone call to a party of his or her choice. The international visitor should call his or her embassy or consulate.

LGBT Travelers   While Wyoming and Montana have earned reputations as intolerant destinations in the past, Yellowstone and Grand Teton national parks are generally gay-friendly. However, gay culture and nightlife are very limited in Jackson and nearly nonexistent in other gateways.

Mail   At press time, domestic postage rates were 29¢ for a postcard and 45¢ for a letter. For international mail, a first-class letter of up to 1 ounce costs 98¢ (80¢ to Canada or Mexico); a first-class postcard costs the same as a letter. For more information visit www.usps.com.

If you aren't sure what your address will be in the U.S., mail can be sent to you, in your name, c/o General Delivery at the main post office of the city or region where you expect to be. (Call ✆ **800/275-8777** for information on the nearest post office.) The addressee must pick up mail in person and must produce proof of identity (a driver's license or passport, for example). Most post offices will hold mail for up to 1 month and are open Monday to Friday from 8am to 6pm and Saturday from 9am to 3pm.

Always include a zip code when mailing items in the U.S. If you don't know the zip code, visit www.usps.com/zip4.

Medical Requirements   Unless you're arriving from an area known to be suffering from an epidemic (particularly cholera or yellow fever), inoculations or vaccinations are not required for entry into the U.S. See "Health," above.

Mobile Phones The parks have several cell towers in developed areas. Cell service is widely available on the floor of Jackson Hole throughout Grand Teton National Park; in Yellowstone, it is available in Canyon, Grant, Mammoth Hot Springs, and Old Faithful villages but largely unavailable on the roads and in wilderness areas. Cell service is available in all of the gateway cities. International travelers may want to buy a pay-as-you-go phone for the trip.

Money & Costs Throughout this guide, Frommer's lists prices in the local currency. See the table below for currency conversions. These conversions were accurate at press time. Rates fluctuate, however, so before departing consult a currency exchange website such as www.oanda.com/currency/converter to check up-to-the-minute rates.

THE VALUE OF THE U.S. DOLLAR VS. OTHER POPULAR CURRENCIES

US$	A$	C$	Euro €	NZ$	UK£
1	A$0.97	C$1.02	€0.78	NZ$1.26	£0.65

ATMs are widely available in the gateway cities and developed areas in both parks. Beware of hidden credit card fees while traveling. If you are visiting from outside the U.S., check with your credit or debit card issuer to see what fees, if any, will be charged for overseas transactions. Recent reform legislation in the U.S., for example, has

WHAT THINGS COST IN YELLOWSTONE & GRAND TETON	US$
Admission to both parks for a week	25.00
Double motel room in or around the parks, peak season	89.00–229.00
Double motel room, winter season	59.00–199.00
Cabin with bed and bathroom	79.00–299.00
Dinner main course in a full-service hotel restaurant	15.00–50.00
Horseback riding for 1 hour	40.00–70.00
1-hour lake cruise	9.00–15.00
Bus sightseeing tour (Yellowstone)	26.00–85.00
Round-trip snowcoach to Old Faithful	110.00–140.00
1 gallon/1 liter of premium gas	2.95/1.90

curbed some exploitative lending practices. But many banks have responded by increasing fees in other areas, including fees for customers who use credit and debit cards while out of the country—even if those charges were made in U.S. dollars. Fees can amount to 3% or more of the purchase price. Check with your bank before departing to avoid any surprise charges on your statement.

For help with currency conversions, tip calculations, and more, download Frommer's convenient Travel Tools app for your mobile device. Go to www.frommers.com/go/mobile and click on the Travel Tools icon.

Newspapers & Magazines   The primary papers in the region are the *Billings Gazette* and the *Cody Enterprise*. In **Yellowstone,** the best source of park information is the free *Yellowstone Today,* the free park newspaper available at all entrances and visitor centers. In **Grand Teton,** the free *Teewinot* is full of park information. In **Jackson,** the newspaper is the *Jackson Hole News & Guide*

Packing   Nothing will ruin a trip to the parks faster than sore or wet feet. Bring comfortable walking shoes, even if you plan to keep walking to a minimum. **Bring shoes that are broken in,** and if you plan to do some more serious hiking, get sturdy boots that support your ankles and wick away water. Early in the season, trails might be wet or muddy; late in the fall, you can get snowed on. The more popular trails are sometimes also used by horses, which can make stream crossings a mucky mess.

Wear your clothing in layers, and bring a small, empty backpack or fanny pack so that you have somewhere to put the clothes as you take those layers off and on as temperature, altitude, and your level of physical exertion change. Cotton is a no-no in the backcountry; synthetic fabrics are recommended because they dry much faster. Gloves or mittens are useful before the park heats up, or in the evening when it cools down again, *even in summer.*

The atmosphere is thin at higher altitudes, so protect your skin. Bring a strong sunblock, a hat with a brim, and sunglasses. I also recommend bringing insect repellent, water bottles, and a first-aid kit.

Take into account that elevations at the parks are between 5,000 and 11,000 feet; in campgrounds and on hiking trails, you'll want clothing appropriate to the temperatures—in summer, 40°F (4°C) in the evening, 75°F (24°C) during the day.

For more helpful information on packing for your trip, download our convenient Travel Tools app for your mobile device. Go to www.frommers.com/go/mobile and click on the Travel Tools icon.

Passports   Virtually every air traveler entering the U.S. is required to show a passport. All persons, including U.S. citizens, traveling by air between the U.S. and Canada, Mexico, Central and South America, the Caribbean, and Bermuda are required to present a valid passport.

Note: U.S. and Canadian citizens entering the U.S. at land and sea ports of entry from within the Western Hemisphere must now also present a passport or other documents compliant with the Western Hemisphere Travel Initiative (WHTI; see www.getyouhome.gov for details). Children 15 and under may continue entering with only a U.S. birth certificate, or other proof of U.S. citizenship.

To obtain a passport, contact a passport office in your home country:

Australia   Australian Passport Information Service (📞 **131-232,** or visit www.passports.gov.au).

Canada   Passport Office, Department of Foreign Affairs and International Trade, Ottawa, ON K1A 0G3 (📞 **800/567-6868;** www.ppt.gc.ca).

Ireland   Passport Office, Setanta Centre, Molesworth Street, Dublin 2 (📞 **01/671-1633;** www.foreignaffairs.gov.ie).

New Zealand   Passports Office, Department of Internal Affairs, 47 Boulcott St., Wellington, 6011 (📞 **0800/225-050** in New Zealand or 04/474-8100; www.passports.govt.nz).

United Kingdom   Visit your nearest passport office, major post office, or travel agency or contact the **Identity and Passport Service (IPS),** 89 Eccleston Sq., London, SW1V 1PN (📞 **0300/222-0000;** www.ips.gov.uk).

United States   To find your regional passport office, check the U.S. Department of State website (http://travel.state.gov/passport) or call the **National Passport Information Center** (📞 **877/487-2778**) for automated information.

Petrol   Please see "Getting There & Getting Around," earlier in this chapter.

Police   Call 📞 **911.**

Safety   The roads are the most dangerous places in Yellowstone, so be especially cautious while driving. Lightning and falls are also killers, but wildlife is the most unique peril in the parks. The most dangerous animal in either park might well be the grizzly bear, but all wildlife has the potential to injure a human. Keep a safe distance from buffalo, deer, moose, and other animals—at least 300 feet. Most people have a healthy respect for bears and are content to view them from a distance. But because a close encounter can happen unexpectedly, you need to know what to do in this situation. First, be aware that what matters most to a bear are food and cubs. If you get between a sow and her cubs, you could be in trouble. If a bear thinks that the food in your backpack is his, you also have a problem.

Unless bears have already developed a taste for human food, though, they won't come looking for you. Make a lot of noise on the trail through bear habitat, and *Ursus arctos horribilis* will give you a wide berth. Don't camp anywhere near the carcass of a dead animal; grizzlies sometimes partially bury carrion and return to it. Hang your food bag high in a tree, keep your cooking area distant from your campsite, and don't keep any food or utensils in your tent—or even clothes worn while cooking. Soaps and other perfumed items can also be attractants.

Avoid hiking at night or in the meadows of mountain areas if visibility is poor. Bears have an extremely good sense of smell but poor eyesight.

If you encounter a bear, here are some things you should and should not do:

o **Do not run.** Anything that flees looks like prey to a bear, and it might attack. Bears can run at more than 30 mph. The bear might bluff charge, but you're best off holding your ground.

o Avoid direct eye contact.

o If the bear is unaware of you, **stay downwind** (so that it doesn't catch your scent) and **detour away from it slowly.**

o If the bear is aware of you but has not acted aggressively, **slowly back away.**

o **Do not climb a tree.** Although black bears have more suitable claws for climbing, grizzly bears can climb trees, too.

o Make noise and act intimidating if the bear does not retreat.

o If you're attacked, drop to the ground face down, clasp your hands over the back of your neck, tuck your knees to your chest, and **play dead.** Keep your backpack on—it can help protect your body. Only as a last resort should you attempt to resist an attack and fight off a bear.

o If you carry **pepper spray,** be sure that it's handy when you're in possible bear habitat, not buried in a backpack. If you use it, aim for the bear's face and eyes. After you use it, leave the area: Bears have been seen returning to sniff about an area where spray has been used.

Smoking Montana has a statewide smoking ban; Wyoming does not, but smoking is banned in most public places in the park and Jackson Hole.

Taxes Lodging and sales tax in Yellowstone and its gateways varies from 4% to 8%. Tax is 6% in Grand Teton Park and 6% to 8% in Jackson Hole. The U.S. has no value-added tax (VAT) or other indirect tax at the national level. Every state, county, and city may levy its own local tax on all purchases, including hotel and restaurant bills and airline tickets. These taxes do not appear on price tags.

Telephones Many convenience stores and packaging services sell **prepaid calling cards** in denominations up to $50. Many public pay phones at airports accept American Express, MasterCard, and Visa.

Local calls made from most pay phones cost either 25¢ or 35¢. Most long-distance and international calls can be dialed directly from any phone. **To make calls within the U.S. and to Canada,** dial 1 followed by the area code and the seven-digit number. **For other international calls,** dial 011 followed by the country code, city code, and the number you are calling.

Calls to area codes **800, 888, 877,** and **866** are toll free. Calls to area codes **700** and **900** (chat lines, bulletin boards, "dating" services, and so on) can be expensive, with charges of 95¢ to $3 or more per minute. Some numbers have minimum charges that can run $15 or more.

For **reversed-charge or collect calls,** and for person-to-person calls, dial the number 0 then the area code and number; an operator will come on the line, and you should specify whether you are calling collect, person-to-person, or both. If your operator-assisted call is international, ask for the overseas operator.

For **directory assistance** ("Information"), dial 411 for local numbers and national numbers in the U.S. and Canada. For dedicated long-distance information, dial 1, then the appropriate area code plus 555-1212.

Time   Both parks are in the **Mountain Standard Time** zone. **Daylight saving time (summer time)** is in effect from 1am on the second Sunday in March to 1am on the first Sunday in November. Daylight saving time moves the clock 1 hour ahead of standard time.

For help with time translations and more, download our Travel Tools app. Go to www.frommers.com/go/mobile and click on the Travel Tools icon.

Tipping   In hotels, tip **bellhops** at least $1 per bag ($2–$3 if you have a lot of luggage) and tip the **chamber staff** $1 to $2 per day (more if you've left a big mess for him or her to clean up). Tip the **doorman** or **concierge** only if he or she has provided you with some specific service (for example, calling a cab for you or obtaining difficult-to-get theater tickets). Tip the **valet-parking attendant** $1 every time you get your car.

In restaurants, bars, and nightclubs, tip **service staff** and **bartenders** 15% to 20% of the check, tip **checkroom attendants** $1 per garment, and tip **valet-parking attendants** $1 per vehicle.

Tip **cab drivers** 15% of the fare; tip **skycaps** at airports at least $1 per bag ($2–$3 if you have a lot of luggage); and tip **hairdressers** and **barbers** 15% to 20%.

For help with tip calculations, currency conversions, and more, download our convenient Travel Tools app for your mobile device. Go to www.frommers.com/go/mobile and click on the Travel Tools icon.

Toilets   You won't find public toilets or "restrooms" on the streets in most U.S. cities but they can be found in hotel lobbies, bars, restaurants, museums, department stores, railway and bus stations, and service stations. Large hotels and fast-food restaurants are often the best bet for clean facilities. Restaurants and bars in resorts or heavily visited areas may reserve their restrooms for patrons. Both Yellowstone and Grand Teton have vault (flushless) toilets at numerous pullouts along the roads, and there are toilets at some trail heads, though not all.

VAT   See "Taxes," above.

Visas   The U.S. Department of State has a **Visa Waiver Program (VWP)** allowing citizens of the following countries to enter the U.S. without a visa for stays of up to 90 days: Andorra, Australia, Austria, Belgium, Brunei, Czech Republic, Denmark, Estonia, Finland, France, Germany, Greece, Hungary, Iceland, Ireland, Italy, Japan, Latvia, Liechtenstein, Lithuania, Luxembourg, Malta, Monaco, Netherlands, New Zealand, Norway, Portugal, San Marino, Singapore, Slovakia, Slovenia, South Korea, Spain, Sweden, Switzerland, and the United Kingdom. (**Note:** This list was accurate at press time; for the most up-to-date list of countries in the VWP, consult http://travel.state.gov/visa.) Even though a visa isn't necessary, in an effort to help U.S. officials check travelers against terror watch lists before they arrive at U.S. borders, visitors from VWP countries must register online through the Electronic System for Travel Authorization (ESTA) before boarding a plane or a boat to the U.S. Travelers must complete an electronic application, providing basic personal and travel eligibility information. The Department of Homeland Security recommends filling out the form at least 3 days before traveling. Authorizations will be valid for up to 2 years or until the traveler's passport expires, whichever comes first. Currently, there is a $14 fee for the online application. Existing ESTA registrations remain valid through their expiration dates. **Note:** Any passport issued on or after October 26, 2006, by a VWP country must be an **e-Passport** for VWP travelers to be eligible to enter the U.S. without a visa. Citizens of these nations also need to present a round-trip air or cruise ticket upon arrival. E-Passports contain computer chips capable of storing biometric information, such as the required digital photograph of the holder. If your passport doesn't have this feature, you can still travel without a visa if the valid passport was issued before October 26, 2005, and includes a machine-readable zone; or if the valid passport was issued between October 26, 2005, and October 25, 2006, and includes a digital photograph. For more information, go to **http://travel.state.gov/visa**. Canadian citizens may enter the U.S. without visas, but will need to show passports and proof of residence.

Citizens of all other countries must have (1) a valid passport that expires at least 6 months later than the scheduled end of their visit to the U.S.; and (2) a tourist visa.

For information about U.S. visas, go to **http://travel.state.gov/visa**, or visit one of the following websites:

Australian citizens can obtain up-to-date visa information from the **U.S. Embassy Canberra,** Moonah Place, Yarralumla, ACT 2600 (© **02/6214-5600**) or by checking the U.S. Diplomatic Mission's website at http://canberra.usembassy.gov/visas.html.

British subjects can obtain up-to-date visa information by calling the **U.S. Embassy Visa Information Line** (© **09042-450-100** from within the U.K. at £1.20 per minute; or © **866/382-3589** from within the U.S. at a flat rate of $16 and is payable by credit card only) or by visiting http://london.usembassy.gov/visas.html.

Irish citizens can obtain up-to-date visa information through the **U.S. Embassy Dublin,** 42 Elgin Rd., Ballsbridge, Dublin 4 (© **1580-47-VISA** [8472] from within the Republic of Ireland at €2.40 per minute; http://dublin.usembassy.gov).

Citizens of **New Zealand** can obtain up-to-date visa information by contacting the **U.S. Embassy New Zealand,** 29 Fitzherbert Terrace, Thorndon, Wellington (© **644/462-6000;** http://newzealand.usembassy.gov).

Visitor Information   The primary entries to Yellowstone and Grand Teton are through Montana and Wyoming, so if you want information about the surrounding areas, contact these states' travel services: **Montana Office of Tourism,** 301 S. Park Ave. (P.O. Box 200533), Helena, MT 59601 (© **800/847-4868;** www.visitmt.com); and **Wyoming Travel & Tourism,** 1520 Etchepare Circle, Cheyenne, WY 82007 (© **800/225-5996** or 307/777-7777; www.wyomingtourism.org).

To receive maps and information before your arrival, contact Visitor Services Office, P.O. Box 168, **Yellowstone National Park,** WY 82190 (© **307/344-7381;** www.nps.gov/yell) and **Grand Teton National Park,** P.O. Drawer 170, Moose, WY 83012 (© **307/739-3300;** www.nps.gov/grte). For information about educational programs at the Yellowstone Association Institute and other resources, contact the **Yellowstone Association,** P.O. Box 117, Yellowstone National Park, WY 82190 (© **406/848-2400;** www.yellowstoneassociation.org). The **Grand Teton Association** is a not-for-profit organization that provides information about the park through retail book sales at park visitor centers; you can also buy books about the park from the organization by mail. Contact the association at P.O. Box 170, Moose, WY 83012 (© **307/739-3403;** www.grandtetonpark.org).

National forests and other public lands surround the parks. For information about national forests and wilderness areas in Montana, as well as **Bridger-Teton National Forest** in Wyoming, contact the **U.S. Forest Service Intermountain Region Office,** 324 25th St., Ogden, UT 84401 (✆ **801/625-5306;** www.fs.fed.us/r4). The rest of Wyoming's forests, including the **Shoshone National Forest** east of the Tetons over Togwotee Pass, are covered by the **Rocky Mountain Region Office,** 740 Simms St., Golden, CO 80401 (✆ **303/275-5350;** www.fs.fed.us/r2).

The federal **Bureau of Land Management** also manages millions of acres of recreational lands and can be reached at its Wyoming state office, 5353 Yellowstone Rd. (P.O. Box 1828), Cheyenne, WY 82009 (✆ **307/775-6256;** www.blm.gov/wy); or its Montana state office, 5001 Southgate Dr., Billings, MT 59101 (✆ **406/896-5000;** www.blm. gov/mt).

Other sources of information include Montana's **Yellowstone Country,** P.O. Box 3048, Bozeman, MT 59772 (✆ 800/736-5276; www.yellowstonecountry.net); **Gardiner Chamber of Commerce,** 222 Park St. (P.O. Box 81), Gardiner, MT 59030 (✆ 406/848-7971; www. gardinerchamber.com); **Cooke City/Colter Pass/Silver Gate Chamber of Commerce,** 206 W. Main St. (P.O. Box 1071), Cooke City, MT 59020 (✆ 406/838-2495; www.cookecitychamber.org); **West Yellowstone Chamber of Commerce,** 30 Yellowstone Ave. (P.O. Box 458), West Yellowstone, MT 59758 (✆ 406/646-7701; www.west yellowstonechamber.com); **Jackson Hole Chamber of Commerce,** 112 Center St. (P.O. Box 550), Jackson, WY 83001 (✆ 307/733-3316, www.jacksonholechamber.com); **Jackson Hole Central Reservations** (✆ 888/838-6606; www.jacksonholewy.com); **Cody Country Chamber of Commerce,** 836 Sheridan Ave., Cody, WY 82414 (✆ 307/587-2777; www.codychamber.org); and **Buffalo Bill's Cody/Yellowstone Country,** 836 Sheridan Ave., (P.O. Box 2454), Cody, WY 82414 (✆ 800/393-2639 or 307/587-2297; www.yellowstonecountry.org).

Water Two waterborne hazards are *Giardia* and *Campylobacter,* with symptoms that wreak havoc on the human digestive system. If you pick up these pesky bugs, they might accompany you on your trip home. Untreated water from the parks' lakes and streams should be boiled for at least 5 minutes before consumption or pumped through a fine-mesh water filter specifically designed to remove bacteria.

Wi-Fi See "Internet & Wi-Fi," earlier in this section.

Index

See also Accommodations and
Restaurant indexes, below.

General Index

A

Academic trips, 26–27
Access/entry points
 Grand Teton, 91, 94
 Yellowstone, 30
Accommodations, 223. *See also*
 Accommodations Index
 best, 10, 11
 Cody, 190–193
 Gardiner, 158–159
 Grand Teton, 141–145
 Jackson/Jackson Hole area, 171–177
 Teton Village, 175–177
 West Yellowstone, 153–155
 Yellowstone, 127–133
AdventureBus, 27, 65
Adventure Sports, 120, 121, 163
Adventure trips and guided tours, 27–28
Aerial touring, Jackson area, 167–168
Air travel, 220
Alaska Basin, 120
Albright Visitor Center (Yellowstone),
 30, 38, 44–45
Altitude sickness, 230
Amphitheater Lake Trail
 (Yellowstone), 114
Anemone Geyser (Yellowstone), 60
Angel Terrace (Yellowstone), 45
Antelope Flats Road (Mormon Row),
 106, 120
Apres Vous Mountain (Grand Teton), 167
Area codes, 227
Art galleries, 171
Artist Paint Pot Trail (Yellowstone),
 40, 69
Artist Point (Yellowstone), 6, 51–52
ATMs (automated-teller machines), 232
Attractions outside the parks, best, 11
Austin-Lehman Adventures, 27
Australia
 embassy of, 229
 passports, 234
 visas, 238
Avoiding the crowds, 24

B

Back Basin Loop (Yellowstone), 41, 69
Backcountry
 best trails, 8
 Grand Teton, 117–120
 permits, 223–224
 planning a trip, 225
 Yellowstone National Park, 77–83

Backpacking for beginners, 225
Backroads, 27–28
Bakers Hole (Grand Teton), 135
Bald eagles, 215–216
Ballooning, 168
Bannocks, 17–18
Bannock Trail (Yellowstone), 18
Bears, 14, 15, 209–210
 safety concerns, 234–235
Beartooth Highway, 19
Beaver Lake Picnic area (Yellowstone), 42
Beaver Ponds Loop Trail (Yellowstone),
 45, 70
Bechler Meadows Trail (Yellowstone), 81
Bechler region (Yellowstone), 81
Bechler River Trail (Yellowstone), 81
Big Wild Adventures (Yellowstone), 80
Biking
 Cody, 185
 Grand Teton, 120
 Yellowstone, 34, 83–84
Birds and bird-watching, 215–218
Biscuit Basin (Yellowstone), 59, 62
Bison, 14–15
Black Dragon's Caldron (Yellowstone), 53
Black Sand Basin (Yellowstone), 59, 62
Blacktail Plateau Drive (Yellowstone), 46
Blacktail Ponds Overlook (Grand
 Teton), 106
Boardroom (Jackson), 163
Boating
 Grand Teton, 121
 permits, 224
 Yellowstone, 84
Boiling River (Yellowstone), 43
Books, recommended, 226
Bradley Lake (Grand Teton), 117
Bridge Bay Campground
 (Yellowstone), 135
Bridge Bay Marina (Yellowstone), 55, 84
Bridger–Teton National Forest, 83, 107,
 119, 125, 164, 165
Brink of the Upper Falls (Yellowstone),
 6, 51
Bud Lilly's Trout Shop (West
 Yellowstone), 86
Buffalo Bill Dam and Visitor Center
 (Cody), 187–188
Buffalo Bill Historical Center (Cody),
 11, 187, 188
Buffalo Bill Museum (Cody), 188
Buffalo Bill Reservoir (Cody), 185–187
Buffalo Bill's Cody/Yellowstone
 Country, 239
Buffalo Bill State Park (near Cody), 185
Bumpus Butte (Yellowstone), 48
Bunsen Peak Road Trail (Yellowstone), 84
Bunsen Peak Trail (Yellowstone), 70
Bureau of Land Management, 239
Bus travel, 222

C

Calcite Springs Overlook
(Yellowstone), 48
Campgrounds
best, 8–9
Grand Teton, 145–147
Jackson area, 165
wheelchair-accessible, 228
Yellowstone, 34
Yellowstone and environs, 133–136
Camping fees
Grand Teton, 95
Yellowstone, 34
Canada
embassy of, 229
passports, 234
Canary Spring (Yellowstone), 44
Canyon Campground (Grand Teton), 135
Canyon Country (Grand Teton), 200
Canyon Village area (Yellowstone),
36, 49–52
accommodations, 120
restaurants, 138
Canyon Visitor Education Center
(Yellowstone), 31, 50
Carbonfund.org, 25
Car travel and rentals, 220–222
Cascade Canyon (Grand Teton), 202
Cascade Canyon Loop (Grand Teton),
8, 119
Cascade Canyon Trail (Grand Teton),
8, 115, 119
Cassie's (Cody), 194
Castle Geyser (Yellowstone), 61
Cathedral Group (Grand Teton), 6–7,
96, 201
Cathedral Group Turnout (Grand
Teton), 97
Cayuse Western Americana
(Jackson), 171
Cellphones, 232
Chapel of the Transfiguration (Grand
Teton), 97, 104
Chief Joseph Scenic Highway (Wyo.
296), 12, 19, 47–48
Children, families with, 230. See also
Junior Ranger program
Christian Pond Trail (Grand Teton),
112, 114
Circle of Fire (Yellowstone), 65
Clear Lake and Ribbon Lake Loop Trail
(Yellowstone), 72
Clematis Gulch (Yellowstone), 45
Cleopatra and Minerva terraces
(Yellowstone), 44
Climate, 22–23
Climbers' Ranch (Grand Teton), 103–104
Climbing
Grand Teton, 118–119, 122
Yellowstone, 34

Cody, 48, 184–194
accommodations, 190–193
getting there, 184
nightlife, 194
outdoor activities, 185–187
restaurants, 193–194
sights and attractions, 187–190
special events, 187
visitor information, 184
Cody Country Chamber of
Commerce, 239
Cody Dug Up Gun Museum, 187
Cody Firearms Museum, 188
Cody Nite Rodeo, 11, 189
Cody Stampede, 187
Cody Trolley Tours, 189
Colter, John, 18
Colter Bay (Grand Teton), 96, 100
hiking, 110–111
restaurants, 148
Colter Bay Campground and Trailer
Village, 146
Colter Bay Village area (Grand Teton), 97
accommodations, 142–143
Colter Bay Visitor Center (Grand Teton),
94, 97, 100, 102
Continental Divide (Yellowstone), 56
Continental Divide Trail (Yellowstone), 68
Cooke City, 19, 47, 160–161
Cooke City/Colter Pass/Silver Gate
Chamber of Commerce, 239
Cowboy Songs and Range Ballads
(Cody), 187
Coyotes, 212
Craig Pass (Yellowstone), 58
Craig Thomas Discovery and Visitor
Center (Grand Teton), 94, 98, 104
Cross-country skiing
Cody, 185–186
Grand Teton, 124–125
Jackson area, 165
Yellowstone, 87–88
Cunningham Cabin (Grand Teton), 107
Customs regulations, 227
Cygnet Lake (Grand Teton), 110

D

Dan Miller's Music Revue (Cody), 194
Dave Hansen Whitewater (Jackson), 165
Day hikes
best, 7
Grand Teton, 109–117
Yellowstone, 68–76
Deadman's Bar (Grand Teton), 106
Death Canyon Shelf (Grand Teton), 120
Defacing park features, 34
DeLacy Creek Trail (Yellowstone),
75, 80, 81
Disabled travelers, 227–228
Doctors, 228

Dog sledding, Jackson, 166
Dornan's (Grand Teton), 104
Doublet Pool (Yellowstone), 61
Downhill skiing, Jackson area, 166–167
Dragon's Mouth Spring (Yellowstone), 52–53
Draper Museum of Natural History (Cody), 188
Drinking laws, 229
Dunraven Pass (Yellowstone), 49

E

East entrance (Yellowstone), 30
Echinus Geyser (Yellowstone), 41, 69
Electric Divide (Yellowstone), 83
Electricity, 229
Elephant Back Loop Trail (Yellowstone), 53–54, 74
Elk (Grand Teton), 7
Elk Park (Yellowstone), 40
Embassies and consulates, 229
Emerald Pool (Yellowstone), 62
Emergencies, 229–230
Emma Matilda Lake (Grand Teton), 102
Emma Matilda Lake Trail (Grand Teton), 113
Entry points
    Grand Teton, 91, 94
    Yellowstone, 30
Environmentally Friendly Hotels, 25
Escape Adventures, 28, 65
Excelsior Geyser (Yellowstone), 62

F

Fairy Falls (Yellowstone), 64
Fairy Falls Trail (Yellowstone), 75, 88
Fall, 23
Families with children, 230. See also Junior Ranger program
Fees and permits
    backcountry, 78, 118, 223–224
    boating, 224
    fishing, 224–225
    Grand Teton, 95
    Yellowstone, 31, 34, 86
Fern Cascades Trail (Yellowstone), 87–88
Firearms, 34–35
Firehole Canyon Drive (Yellowstone), 64
Firehole Falls (Yellowstone), 64
Firehole Lake Drive (Yellowstone), 63
Firehole River (Yellowstone), 64, 76, 85
Fires, Yellowstone, 16
Fishing
    Cody, 186
    Grand Teton, 122–123
    Jackson, 163–164
    permits, 224–225
    Yellowstone, 85
Fishing Bridge (Yellowstone), 53
Fishing Bridge Junction (Yellowstone), 48

Fishing Bridge RV Park (Yellowstone), 34, 53, 135
Fishing Bridge Visitor Center (Yellowstone), 31, 53
Fishing Cone (Yellowstone), 56
Flagg Ranch (Grand Teton), 34, 94–95
Flagg Ranch Village area (Grand Teton), accommodations, 141–142
Float trips
    Cody, 186
    Grand Teton, 123
Flowers, 205–208
Forces of the Northern Range Trail (Yellowstone), 46, 70
Fort Yellowstone, 44
43° North (Jackson), 183
Fountain Flat (Yellowstone), 64
Fountain Flat Drive (Yellowstone), 64
Fountain Paint Pots (Yellowstone), 59, 63–64
Fountain Paint Pot Trail (Yellowstone), 75
Free Heel and Wheel (West Yellowstone), 84

G

GaperGuide, 65
Gardiner, 157–160
Gardiner Chamber of Commerce, 239
Gays and lesbians, 231
Geology, 198–202
Geyser Hill Loop (Yellowstone), 75–76
Geysers, 200. See also specific geysers
    Norris Geyser Basin (Yellowstone), 36
Giantess Geyser (Yellowstone), 61
Gibbon Falls (Yellowstone), 40
Gibbon River (Yellowstone), 40, 85
Glacier View Turnout (Grand Teton), 99, 106
Golden Gate (Yellowstone), 43
Golf
    Cody, 186
    Jackson, 164
Grand Canyon of the Yellowstone River, 6, 36, 48–49
Grand Geyser (Yellowstone), 61
Grand Loop (Yellowstone), 37
Grand Loop Road (Yellowstone), 38–39
Grand Prismatic Spring (Yellowstone), 62
Grand Targhee Resort (Jackson), 166, 167
Grand Teton Association, 109, 118, 238
Grand Teton Lodge Company, 26, 107, 121, 123, 145
Grand Teton mountain, 96, 201
Grand Teton Music Festival, 183
Grand Teton National Park
    access/entry points, 91, 94
    accommodations, 141–145
    activities (other than hiking), 120–125
    camping, 145–147

current conditions, 196–198
exploring
  backcountry, 117–120
  in 1 day, 97–99
  extended tour, 99–107
  highlights, 95–97
  organized tours and ranger
    programs, 107–108
fees, 95
geology of, 201–202
hikes, 109–120
  backcountry, 117–120
  day hikes, 109–117
overview of, 15–16
restaurants, 147–150
visitor centers and information, 94
Grand View (Yellowstone), 50
Granite Canyon (Grand Teton), 119
Grant Village/West Thumb areas
  (Yellowstone), 37
  accommodations, 131
Grant Visitor Center (Yellowstone), 31, 57
Grassy Lake Road (Grand Teton), 120
Greater Yellowstone Ecosystem, 195
Greater Yellowstone Flyfishers, 87
Greater Yellowstone Visitor Center, 117
Great Fountain Geyser (Yellowstone), 63
Green Hotels Association, 25
Green travel, 25–26
Grizzly and Wolf Discovery Center
  (Grand Teton), 152–153
Grizzly bears, 14, 15, 209–210
  safety concerns, 234–235
Grizzly RV Campground (Grand
  Teton), 136
Gros Ventre (Grand Teton), 146
Gros Ventre River Road (Grand
  Teton), 107
Gros Ventre Slide area (Grand Teton), 117
Grub Steak Expeditions (Cody), 185

H

Harlequin Lake Trail (Yellowstone),
  39–40, 69
Hayden Valley (Yellowstone), 52, 200
Health concerns, 230
Heart Lake Loop (Yellowstone), 82
Heart Lake Trail (Yellowstone), 82
Hebgen Basin Campgrounds (Grand
  Teton), 135
Hermitage Point Loop (Grand Teton),
  110, 111
Hermitage Point Trailhead (Grand
  Teton), 110
Heron Pond (Grand Teton), 125
Heron Pond Trail (Grand Teton), 111
Hidden Falls (Grand Teton), 98
Hidden Falls Trail (Grand Teton), 115–116
High Country Flies (Jackson), 163

High Country Snowmobile Tours
  (Jackson Hole), 167
Hiking. *See also* **Backcountry; Day hikes**
  Grand Teton National Park, 109–120
    backcountry, 117–120
    day hikes, 109–117
  Jackson area, 164
  Yellowstone National Park. *See*
    Yellowstone National Park,
    exploring
History
  Grand Teton National Park, 20–21
  Yellowstone National Park, 17–20
Hoback Sports (Jackson), 84, 163
Hole Hiking Experience (Jackson
  Hole), 164
Holidays, 24
Hoodoos, 43
Horseback riding
  Grand Teton, 123–124
  Jackson area, 164–165
  Yellowstone, 86, 87
Hotels. *See* **Accommodations**
House swapping, 223
Howard Eaton Trail (Yellowstone),
  68, 72
Hurricane Pass (Grand Teton), 119

I

Ice skating, Yellowstone, 88
IMAX Theater, Yellowstone, 153
Imperial Meadows Trailhead, 64
Indian Arts Museum (Grand Teton),
  96, 102
Inspiration Point, 6
Inspiration Point (Yellowstone), 50
Inspiration Point Trail (Grand Teton),
  114–116
Interagency Access Pass, 34, 95, 227
Interagency Annual Pass, 31, 34, 95
Internet and Wi-Fi, 230–231
Ireland
  embassy of, 229
  passports, 234
  visas, 238
Isa Lake (Yellowstone), 58

J

Jackson, William Henry, 20
Jackson and Jackson Hole area,
  161–183, 201
  accommodations, 171–177
  getting around, 162–163
  getting there, 162
  nightlife, 183
  outdoor activities, 163–168
  restaurants, 178–183
  visitor information, 162

Jackson Hole Aerial Tram, 12, 170
Jackson Hole Central Reservations, 239
Jackson Hole Chamber of
    Commerce, 239
Jackson Hole Galleries Association, 171
Jackson Hole Golf and Tennis Club, 164
Jackson Hole Historical Society
    Museum, 170
Jackson Hole Iditarod, 166
Jackson Hole Mountain Resort, 166
Jackson Hole Nordic Center, 166
Jackson Hole Snowmobile Tours, 167
Jackson Lake, 96, 99–100, 202
Jackson Lake Junction, 102
    restaurants, 148–150
Jackson Lake Lodge (Grand Teton),
    clinic at, 228
Jackson Lake Lodge area, hiking, 112–114
Jackson Point Overlook (Grand Teton),
    102–103
Jedediah Smith Wilderness, 119
Jenny Lake (Grand Teton), 96–97, 103
Jenny Lake area (Grand Teton)
    accommodations, 144
    hiking, 114–117
    restaurant, 150
Jenny Lake Boating Company (Grand
    Teton), 103, 121
Jenny Lake Campground (Grand
    Teton), 9, 146
Jenny Lake Loop Trail (Grand Teton), 116
Jenny Lake Ranger Station (Grand
    Teton), 122
Jenny Lake Trail (Grand Teton), 124
Jenny Lake Visitor Center (Grand
    Teton), 94
John D. Rockefeller, Jr. Memorial
    Parkway (Grand Teton), 91, 99
Junior Ranger program
    Grand Teton, 108, 114
    Yellowstone, 84
Junior Ranger Station (Yellowstone), 31

K

Kayaking, Jackson area, 165
Kelly, 107
Kepler Cascades (Yellowstone), 58
Kids, 230. *See also* Junior
    Ranger program

L

Lakes, 202
Lakeshore Trail (Grand Teton), 97–98, 110
Lake Solitude (Grand Teton), 119
Lake Village area (Yellowstone),
    36–37, 54
    accommodations, 130–131
Lamar River (Yellowstone), 85
Lamar Valley (Yellowstone), 6, 38, 47, 200

Landscape and geology, 198–202
Laurance S. Rockefeller Preserve Center
    (Grand Teton), 94
Lava Creek (Yellowstone), 84
Leather Pool (Yellowstone), 64
Leave No Trace, 26
Leeks Marina (Grand Teton), 100
Legal aid, 231
Le Hardy Rapids (Yellowstone), 53
Leigh Lake (Grand Teton), 103
Leigh Lake Trail (Grand Teton), 116
Leisure Sports (Jackson), 90, 167
Lewis Lake (Yellowstone), 58
Lewis River Channel (Yellowstone), 85
LGBT travelers, 231
Liberty Cap (Yellowstone), 44
Lily Pad Lake (Yellowstone), 52
Lion Geyser (Yellowstone), 61
Lion Group (Yellowstone), 61
Littering, 35
Little Firehole Meadows Trail
    (Yellowstone), 76
Lizard Creek Campground (Grand
    Teton), 146
Lonesomehurst Campground
    (Yellowstone), 135
Lonestar Geyser Trail (Yellowstone),
    8, 58, 76, 84, 87
Lonestar Geyser Trailhead
    (Yellowstone), 81
Lookout Point (Yellowstone), 50
Lower Geyser Basin (Yellowstone), 60
Lower loop (Yellowstone), 36–38
Lower Terrace Interpretive Trail
    (Yellowstone), 44, 70

M

Madison Arm Resort (Hebgen Lake),
    RV and tent sites, 136
Madison Campground (Yellowstone),
    40, 135
Madison Information Station
    (Yellowstone), 31
Madison Junction (Yellowstone), 39, 40
Madison River (Yellowstone), 37, 85
Mad River Boat Trips (Jackson), 165
Mae West Curve (Yellowstone), 48
Mail, 231
Mammoth Hot Springs (Yellowstone),
    35, 37, 38, 42–46, 67, 199–200
    clinic at, 228
Mammoth Hot Springs area (Yellowstone)
    accommodations, 127–129
    ice rink, 88
    restaurants, 137–138
Mammoth Hot Springs Terraces
    (Yellowstone), 7, 35, 38, 67
Maps
    Grand Teton, 118
    Yellowstone, 79–80

Mary Bay (Yellowstone), 48
Medical requirements for entry, 231
Menor/Noble Historic District (Grand
    Teton), 97
Menor's Ferry (Grand Teton), 104
Middle Teton (Grand Teton), 96
Midway Geyser Basin (Yellowstone),
    59, 62
Million Dollar Cowboy Bar (Jackson), 183
Minerva Terrace (Yellowstone), 44
Mobile phones, 232
Money and costs, 232–233
Montana Office of Tourism, 238
Moose (animal), 213–214
Moose (town), 97, 104
    accommodations, 144–145
    restaurant, 150
Moosely Seconds (Jackson), 163
Moose Ponds (Grand Teton), 115
Moose-Wilson Road (Grand Teton),
    124–125
Moran, Thomas, 20
Morning Glory Pool (Yellowstone), 62
Motorcycles, 35
Mount Moran (Grand Teton), 96, 110,
    112, 201–202
Mount Owen (Grand Teton), 96
Mount Washburn (Yellowstone), 48
Mount Washburn Trail (Yellowstone),
    7, 49, 72–73, 84
Mud Volcano (Yellowstone), 52, 53
Museum of the National Park Ranger
    (Yellowstone), 31, 41
Museum of the Old West at Old Trail
    Town (Cody), 189
Mystic Falls Trail (Yellowstone), 76

N

The Narrows (Yellowstone), 48
National Elk Refuge (Jackson), 168, 170
National Geographic Maps, 80
National Museum of Wildlife Art
    (Jackson), 12, 170–171
The National Parks: America's Best Idea
    (film), 17
National Passport Information Center, 234
National Smokejumper Center (West
    Yellowstone), 152
Native Americans, 17
Natural Bridge (Yellowstone), 55–56
Nature guide, 195–226
New Blue Spring (Yellowstone), 44
New Highland Terrace (Yellowstone), 45
Newspapers and magazines, 233
New Zealand
    embassy of, 229
    passports, 234
    visas, 238
Nightlife
    Cody, 194
    Jackson/Jackson Hole area, 183

Norris Campground (Yellowstone),
    9, 42, 135
Norris Geyser Basin (Yellowstone),
    36, 37, 40–42, 67
Norris Geyser Basin Museum
    (Yellowstone), 41
Norris Geyser Basin Museum and
    Information Station (Yellowstone), 31
Northeast entrance (Yellowstone), 30
North Rim Drive (Yellowstone), 50
North Rim Trail (Yellowstone), 50, 73
North Shoshone Trail (Yellowstone), 81

O

Observation Point Trail (Yellowstone), 60
Observation Point Trail-Solitary Geyser
    (Yellowstone), 76
Obsidian Cliff (Yellowstone), 42
Obsidian Creek (Yellowstone), 42
Off Square Theatre Company
    (Jackson), 183
Old Faithful area (Yellowstone),
    36, 59, 67
    accommodations, 132–133
    restaurants, 140–141
Old Faithful geyser (Yellowstone),
    7, 60, 200
Old Faithful Inn (Yellowstone), 59
Old Faithful Visitor Center
    (Yellowstone), 38
Old Faithful Visitor Education Center
    (Yellowstone), 31, 59
Olive Glenn Golf and Country Club
    (Cody), 186
Osprey Falls Trail (Yellowstone),
    70–71, 84
Oxbow Bend (Grand Teton), 99, 100, 216

P

Packing tips, 233
Paintbrush Canyon Trail (Grand
    Teton), 119
Palette Spring (Yellowstone), 44
Park Accessibility Coordinator
    (Yellowstone), 228
Parking, wheelchair-accessible, 228
Parks' Fly Shop (Gardiner), 86
Passports, 233–234
Pelican Valley (Yellowstone), 200
Pelican Valley Trail (Yellowstone), 74
Pepper spray, 235
Permits and fees
    backcountry, 78, 118, 223–224
    boating, 224
    fishing, 224–225
    Grand Teton, 95
    Yellowstone, 31, 34, 86
Petrified Tree (Yellowstone), 46
Pets, 35

Pillar of Hercules (Yellowstone), 43
Pink Cone Geyser (Yellowstone), 63
Pitchstone Plateau (Yellowstone), 58
Plains Indian Museum (Cody), 188
Plains Indian Museum Powwow (Cody), 187
Planning your trip, 227–239
    customs regulations, 227
    disabled travelers, 227–228
    drinking laws, 229
    electricity, 229
    embassies and consulates, 229–230
    families with children, 230
    gays and lesbians, 231
    health concerns, 230
    Internet and Wi-Fi, 230–231
    legal aid, 231
    mail, 231
    mobile phones, 232
    money and costs, 232–233
    newspapers and magazines, 233
    packing tips, 233
    passports, 233–234
    safety, 234–235
    smoking, 235
    taxes, 235
    telephones, 235–236
    time zone, 236
    tipping, 236
    toilets, 237
    visas, 237–238
    visitor information, 238–239
Plant life, 202–208
Point Sublime (Yellowstone), 52
Poison Spring (Yellowstone), 44
Police, 234
Porcelain Basin Trail (Yellowstone), 41, 69–70
Pumice Point (Yellowstone), 56
Purple Mountain Trail (Yellowstone), 40

R
Rafting, Snake River, 165
Rainbow Point (Grand Teton), 135
Ranger programs. See also Junior Ranger program
    Yellowstone, 66–67
Red Canyon Wild Mustang Tours (Cody), 185
Red Spouter (Yellowstone), 64
Regulations and warnings
    backcountry, 225
    campgrounds, 134
    Yellowstone, 34
Rendezvous Mountain (Grand Teton), 119, 166–167
Rendezvous River Sports (Jackson), 165
Responsible travel, 25–26
Restaurants. See also Restaurant Index
    best, 9–11
    Cody, 193–194

    Gardiner, 159–160
    Grand Teton, 147–150
    Jackson/Jackson Hole area, 178–183
    West Yellowstone, 155–157
    Yellowstone, 136–141
Restrooms, wheelchair-accessible, 228
River Road (Grand Teton), 120
Riverside Geyser (Yellowstone), 62
Road openings and closings, 19
Roaring Mountain (Yellowstone), 42
Rockin' HK Outfitters (Yellowstone), 86–87
Rocky Mountain Region Office (Golden, CO), 239
Rocky Mountain Snowmobile Tours (Grand Teton), 167
Rodeos, Cody, 187, 189
Roosevelt Lodge (Yellowstone), 46–47, 66
Roosevelt Rendezvous (Yellowstone), 66
RV travel and campgrounds, 34, 222. See also Campgrounds

S
Safety, 234–235
    backcountry trips, 226
Sailing, Jackson area, 165
St. John's Medical Center (Jackson), 228
Sapphire Pool (Yellowstone), 62
Scenic drives, best, 12
Scenicruises (Yellowstone), 66
Scenic Safaris (Grand Teton), 108
Schoolroom Glacier (Grand Teton), 119
Schwabacher Landing (Grand Teton), 106
Seasons, 21–22
    Grand Teton, 118
    Yellowstone, 78
Sepulcher Mountain Trail (Yellowstone), 71–72, 83
Seven-Mile Hole (Yellowstone), 85
Seven-Mile Hole Trail (Yellowstone), 74
Shadow Mountain Road (Grand Teton), 120
Sheepeater Cliffs (Yellowstone), 42–43
Shoshone Geyser Basin Trail (Yellowstone), 80
Shoshone Lake (Yellowstone), 80–81
Shoshone Lake Loop (Yellowstone), 8
Shoshone Lake Trail (Yellowstone), 81, 82
Shoshone National Forest, 164, 239
Sidewinders Tavern (Jackson), 183
Sierra Trading Post Outlet Store (Cody), 185
Signal Mountain (Grand Teton), 12, 96, 98, 102, 125
Signal Mountain area (Grand Teton), 96
    accommodations, 143
Signal Mountain Campground (Grand Teton), 96, 146
Signal Mountain Lodge (Grand Teton), 96

Signal Mountain Summit Trail (Grand Teton), 8, 112
Silver Dollar Bar
    Cody, 194
    Jackson, 183
Skiing. *See* Cross-country skiing; Downhill skiing
Skinny Skis (Jackson), 163
Slough Creek Campground (Grand Teton), 134
Slough Creek Campground (Yellowstone), 9
Slough Creek Trail (Yellowstone), 83
Smoking, 35, 235
Snake River (Grand Teton), 97
    boating, 165
    fishing, 163
Snake River Kayak and Canoe School (Jackson), 165
Snake River Land Company, 21
Snake River Overlook (Grand Teton), 99, 100
Snake River Park KOA, 147
Snowcoach tours, Yellowstone, 66, 89
Snow King Resort, 167
Snowmobiles, 16–17
Snowmobiling, 197
    Cody, 186
    Grand Teton, 125
    Jackson area, 167
    Yellowstone, 35, 89–90
Snow Pass Trail (Yellowstone), 71–72
Snowshoeing, Grand Teton, 108
Solitary Geyser (Yellowstone), 60, 76
South entrance (Yellowstone), 30
South Jenny Lake (Grand Teton), 98
    parking lot at, 103
South Rim Road (Yellowstone), 51
South Rim Trail (Yellowstone), 52, 74
South Teton, 96
Spalding Bay (Grand Teton), 103
Specimen Ridge (Yellowstone), 47
Sporting goods and equipment rentals
    Cody, 185
    Grand Teton, 124
    Jackson, 163
Sportsman Lake Trail (Yellowstone), 83
Spring, 22–23
Stagecoach Bar (Jackson), 183
Steamboat Geyser (Yellowstone), 41, 69
Storm Point Trail (Yellowstone), 75
String Lake (Grand Teton), 103
String Lake Trail (Grand Teton), 116
Sulphur Caldron (Yellowstone), 52
Summer, 23
Sunlight Basin Road (Chief Joseph Highway), 19, 47–48
Sunlight Sports (Cody), 185
Sustainable tourism, 25–26
Sustainable Travel International, 25

Swan Lake (Yellowstone), 43
Swan Lake Trail (Grand Teton), 111
Swimming, Yellowstone, 35
Sylvan Pass (Yellowstone), 48

T

Taggart and Bradley Lakes Trail (Grand Teton), 117
Taggart Lake-Beaver Creek Loop (Grand Teton), 124
Taxes, 235
Tayloe Piggott Gallery (Jackson), 171
Tecumseh's Old West Miniature Village and Museum (Cody), 190
Teewinot (Grand Teton), 96
Telephones, 235–236
Temperatures, average, 23, 24
Teton Aviation, 167–168
Teton Crest Trail (Grand Teton), 119
Teton Glacier Turnout (Grand Teton), 104
Teton Mountaineering, 163
Teton Park Road (Grand Teton), 98
Teton Pines Cross Country Skiing Center (Grand Teton), 166
Teton Pines Resort (Grand Teton), 164
Teton Range (Grand Teton), 112, 201
Teton Science Schools (Grand Teton), 27, 107–108
Teton Village accommodations (Grand Teton), 175–177
Thermal attractions. *See also* Geysers
    best, 7
    Yellowstone, 37
Thermal features, Yellowstone, 2–3
Thorofare area (Yellowstone), 82–83
Thorofare Trail (Yellowstone), 8, 82
Time zone, 236
Tim Wade's North Fork Anglers (Cody), 186
Tipping, 236
Togwotee Pass (Grand Teton), 94, 96
Toilets, 237
Tours, 26–28
Tower Fall (Yellowstone), 36, 48
Tower Fall Campground (Yellowstone), 134
Tower-Roosevelt area (Yellowstone), 36, 46–47
    accommodations, 129–130
    restaurant, 138
Tower Soldier Station (Yellowstone), 46
Traffic issue, 197
Traveling to the parks, 219–222
Tread Lightly, 25
Trees, 203–205
Trout Lake Trail (Yellowstone), 72
Two Ocean Lake Road (Grand Teton), 120
Two Ocean Lake Trail (Grand Teton), 113–114
Two Ribbons Trail (Yellowstone), 39, 69

U

Uncle Tom's Trail, 6
Uncle Tom's Trail (Yellowstone), 51, 74
Union Geyser (Yellowstone), 80–81
United Kingdom
    embassy of, 229
    passports, 234
    visas, 238
Upper and Lower terraces, Mammoth Hot Springs (Yellowstone), 43–44
Upper Falls View (Yellowstone), 51
Upper Geyser Basin (Yellowstone), 59, 60
Upper Geyser Basin Loop (Yellowstone), 60
Upper loop (Yellowstone), 35–37
Upper Terrace Loop Drive (Yellowstone), 45

V

Views, best, 6–7
Visas, 237–238
Visitor centers, wheelchair-accessible, 228
Visitor information, 238–239

W

Warming huts, Yellowstone, 89
Washburn Hot Springs Overlook (Yellowstone), 49
Washburn Range (Yellowstone), 48
Water, drinking, 239
West entrance (Yellowstone), 30
West Thumb (Yellowstone), 7
West Thumb area (Yellowstone), 56
West Thumb Geyser Basin (Yellowstone), 37, 56
West Thumb Information Station (Yellowstone), 31, 56
West Yellowstone, 88, 151–157
    campgrounds, 135
West Yellowstone Chamber of Commerce, 152, 239
West Yellowstone Visitor Information Center (Yellowstone), 31
Wheelchair accessibility, 227–228
White Dome Geyser (Yellowstone), 63
Whitney Gallery of Western Art (Cody), 188
Wilcox Gallery (Jackson), 171
Wildlife, 208–215
    health concerns, 230
    Jackson area, 168
    safety concerns, 234–235
    Yellowstone, 35
Wildlife Expeditions, 27
Willow Flats (Grand Teton), 110
Willow Flats Trail (Grand Teton), 111
Windsurfing, Cody, 187
Winter, 23

Winter road conditions
    Grand Teton, 124
    Yellowstone, 88
Winter sports and activities
    Grand Teton, 124–125
    Jackson area, 165–167
    Yellowstone, 87–90
Wolves, 14–16, 212–213
World Outdoors, 28
Wyoming Adventures, 90, 167
Wyoming Balloon Company, 168
Wyoming River Trips, 186
Wyoming Travel & Tourism, 238

X

Xanterra Parks & Resorts, 25, 27
    campgrounds, 134
    horseback riding, 86
    tours, 65–66

Y

Yellowstone Adventures, 89–90
Yellowstone Alpen Guides, 65
Yellowstone Arctic/Yamaha, 89
Yellowstone Association, 238
Yellowstone Association Institute, 26–27, 66, 79
    headquarters (Gardiner), 157
    winter courses, 87
Yellowstone Backcountry Office, 78, 134
Yellowstone Country (Bozeman, MT), 239
Yellowstone Heritage and Research Center, 31
Yellowstone Historic Center, 153
Yellowstone Historic Center (West Yellowstone), 12
Yellowstone IMAX Theater, 153
Yellowstone Lake, 6, 12, 54, 84, 85
Yellowstone Lake area, 54–56
Yellowstone National Park, 29–90
    access/entry points, 30
    accommodations, 127–133
    activities (other than hiking), 83–90
    current conditions, 196–198
    exploring, 29–67
        backcountry, 77–83
        extended tour, 38–64
        highlights, 35–37
        in one or two days, 37–38
        organized tours, 65–66
        ranger programs, 66–67
        self-guided driving tours, 65
    landscape and geology, 198–201
    overview of, 2–4
    restaurants, 136–141
    road openings and closings, 19
    visitor centers, 30
    wildlife, 14–15
    winter sports and activities, 87–90

Yellowstone National Park Lodges, 127
Yellowstone Park General Stores, 137
Yellowstone Raft Company, 157
Yellowstone River, 85
Yellowstone Safari Co., 80
Yellowstone's Nature, 84

Accommodations

Absaroka Lodge (Gardiner), 11, 158
The Alpenhof (Teton Village), 176
Alpine House (Jackson), 172
Alpine Motel (Cooke City), 161
Amangani (near Jackson), 174
Anvil Motel (Jackson), 172
A Teton Tree House (near Jackson), 175
Bar N Ranch (West Yellowstone), 11, 154
Best Western (West Yellowstone), 154
Best Western by Mammoth Hot Springs
   (Gardiner), 158
Buckrail Lodge (Jackson), 172
Buffalo Bill Village Resort: Holiday Inn,
   Comfort Inn, and Buffalo Bill Village
   Historic Cabins (Cody), 190
Canyon Lodge and Cabins
   (Yellowstone), 129
The Chamberlin Inn (Cody), 11, 190–191
The Cody, 11, 191
Cody Cowboy Village, 191
Colter Bay Village (Grand Teton), 10, 142
Comfort Inn (Gardiner), 158–159
Comfort Inn (West Yellowstone), 153
Cowboy Lodge & Grille (Gardiner), 159
Days Inn (Jackson), 171
Days Inn (West Yellowstone), 153
Four Seasons Resort Jackson Hole, 176
Grant Village (Yellowstone), 131–132
Headwaters Lodge and Cabins at Flagg
   Ranch (Grand Teton), 142
Holiday Inn West Yellowstone, 154–155
The Hostel (Teton Village), 177
Hotel Terra (Teton Village), 177
Inn on the Creek (Jackson), 172
The Irma Hotel (Cody), 191–192
Jackson Lake Lodge (Grand Teton), 143
Jenny Lake Lodge (Grand Teton), 10, 144
Jim Bridger Motor Court (Gardiner), 158
Lake Lodge Cabins (Yellowstone),
   130–131
Lake Yellowstone Hotel and Cabins
   (Yellowstone), 10, 131
Lexington at Jackson Hole, 171
Madison Hotel (West Yellowstone), 154
Mammoth Hot Springs Hotel and
   Cabins (Yellowstone), 128–129
The Mayor's Inn (Cody), 192
Moose Creek Cabins (West
   Yellowstone), 11, 155

Motel 6 (Jackson), 171
Moulton Ranch Cabins (Grand Teton), 144
Old Faithful Inn (Yellowstone), 10, 132
Old Faithful Lodge Cabins
   (Yellowstone), 132–133
Old Faithful Snow Lodge and Cabins
   (Yellowstone), 133
One Horse Motel (West Yellowstone), 154
Pahaska Tepee Resort (Cody), 192–193
Parade Rest Guest Ranch (West
   Yellowstone), 154
Roosevelt Lodge Cabins
   (Yellowstone), 130
Rustic Inn (Jackson), 172–173
Rusty Parrot Lodge and Spa
   (Jackson), 173
Signal Mountain Lodge (Grand Teton), 143
Snake River Lodge and Spa (Teton
   Village), 177
Soda Butte Lodge (Cooke City), 161
Spring Creek Ranch (near Jackson), 174
Spur Ranch Cabins (Grand Teton),
   144–145
Super 8 (Cooke City), 161
Super 8 (Gardiner), 158
Super 8 (Jackson), 171
A Teton Tree House (Wilson), 11
Three Bear Lodge (West
   Yellowstone), 155
Wildflower Inn (near Jackson), 175
Woods Hotel (Jackson), 173
Wort Hotel (Jackson), 11, 173–174
Yellowstone Park Travelodge
   (Gardiner), 158
Yellowstone River Motel (Gardiner), 158
Yellowstone Suites Bed and Breakfast
   (Gardiner), 159

Restaurants

Beartooth Barbecue (West
   Yellowstone), 156
Beartooth Cafe (Cooke City), 161
Betty Rock Cafe (Teton Village), 178
Blue Heron, 148
The Blue Lion (Teton Village), 178
Book Peddler (West Yellowstone), 155
Buns 'N' Beds (Cooke City), 161
The Cadillac Grille (Teton Village), 178
Canyon Glacier Pit Snack Bar
   (Yellowstone), 138
Canyon Lodge Cafeteria
   (Yellowstone), 138
Canyon Lodge Dining Room
   (Yellowstone), 138
The Canyon Street Grill (West
   Yellowstone), 156
Cassie's Supper Club (Cody), 10, 193
The Chico Dining Room (Gardiner),
   159–160

RESTAURANT INDEX

The Corral Drive-In (Gardiner), 160
D.O.G. (Teton Village), 182–183
Dornan's (Grand Teton), 150
Eino's Tavern (West Yellowstone), 156
Grand Teton Colter Bay Village, 148
Grant Village Dining Room (Yellowstone), 140
Il Villaggio Osteria (Teton Village), 178–179
Jenny Lake Lodge Dining Room (Grand Teton), 9, 150
John Colter Café Court (Grand Teton), 148
The Kitchen (Teton Village), 180
Koshu Wine Bar (Teton Village), 180
Lake House (Yellowstone), 57, 139
Lake Yellowstone Hotel, 9
Leeks Marina (Grand Teton), 148
Log Cabin Café and B&B (Cooke City), 161
Mammoth Hotel Dining Room (Yellowstone), 137–138
Mangy Moose (Teton Village), 180–181
The Mayor's Inn Dining Room (Cody), 193
Morning Glory Coffee & Tea (West Yellowstone), 155
The Mural Room (Grand Teton), 148–149
Nani's Genuine Pasta House (Teton Village), 179
Nora's Fish Creek Inn (Wilson), 10, 182–183
North Grille (Teton Village), 181
Obsidian Dining Room (Yellowstone), 140

Old Faithful Inn Dining Room (Yellowstone), 9, 140–141
The Outpost Restaurant (West Yellowstone), 156–157
Peter's Cafe Bakery (Cody), 193
Pioneer Grill (Grand Teton), 149
Proud Cut Saloon (Cody), 193
Q Roadhouse (Teton Village), 181
Ranch House (Grand Teton), 148
Rendezvous Bistro (Jackson), 10
Rendezvous Bistro (Teton Village), 181
Roosevelt Lodge Dining Room (Yellowstone), 138
Sawtooth Deli (Gardiner), 160
Shades Cafe (Teton Village), 178
Shiki (Cody), 193–194
Signal Mountain Lodge (Grand Teton), 9, 149–150
Snake River Brewing Co. (Teton Village), 183
Snake River Grill (Teton Village), 179
The Steak-house (Grand Teton), 148
Stiegler's (Teton Village), 179–180
Sweetwater Restaurant (Teton Village), 181–182
Sydney's Mountain Bistro (West Yellowstone), 11, 157
Terrace Grill (Yellowstone), 137
Trio (Teton Village), 182
Wyoming's Rib & Chop House (Cody), 194